The Invisible Hand
of Planning

GUY ALCHON

The Invisible Hand of Planning

Capitalism, Social Science, and the State in the 1920s

PRINCETON UNIVERSITY PRESS
PRINCETON, NEW JERSEY

330.124
A35 i

Library of Congress Cataloging in Publication Data
will be found on the last printed page of this book

ISBN 0-691-04723-5

Publication of this book has been aided by a grant from
the Louis A. Robb Fund of Princeton University Press

This book has been composed in Linotron Baskerville
Clothbound editions of Princeton University Press books
are printed on acid-free paper, and binding materials are
chosen for strength and durability

Printed in the United States of America
by Princeton University Press
Princeton, New Jersey

To the memory of my brother

CONTENTS

ACKNOWLEDGMENTS

Many people have contributed to this book, and I am happy to be able to thank some of them. Ellis W. Hawley devoted his time and careful attention to its several incarnations, and I am especially grateful for his generosity and counsel. No student could hope for a better teacher. Also at the University of Iowa, Hermann Rebel helped me to think through the subject; along with Scott Hall and Maureen Roach, he made significant contributions.

Samuel P. Hays offered particularly valuable comments on a draft of the study. Other scholars also read the manuscript, and for their thoughtful criticism I especially want to thank Mansel Blackford, Robert Collins, Robert Cuff, Solomon Fabricant, Louis Galambos, Barry D. Karl, Linda K. Kerber, Christopher Lasch, and Dorothy Ross. Thanks as well to Gail Filion Ullman of the Princeton University Press for her advice and encouragement, and to Alida Becker for her careful editing.

Others who helped me to uncover my subject include Robert Wood, Thomas Thalken, Dwight Miller, Dale Mayer, and Betty Gallagher of the Herbert Hoover Presidential Library; Eleanor M. Lewis of the Sophia Smith Collection, Smith College; Edmond Dwyer of the Russell Sage Foundation; Florence Anderson at the Carnegie Corporation of New York; Adorjan I. de Galffy of the Hoover Institution; and Reginald H. Fitz of the Commonwealth Fund. And for their kindness during my stay in Van Hornesville, I am grateful to Josephine Young and Everett Needham Case.

Thanks also to Christine Atkinson of the University of California, Santa Barbara; Eunice Prosser of the University of Iowa; and Elsbeth Connaughton, Connie Dantuono, and their staffs at the Ohio State University, who provided essential assistance in typing the manuscript under deadlines.

My work has been supported by research grants and fellowships from the University of Iowa, the Herbert Hoover

ACKNOWLEDGMENTS

Presidential Library Association, and the Rockefeller Archives Center. Even earlier, I found support in the teaching and friendship of Vernon Hein, Louis Silverstein, Mirron Alexandroff, and Michael Hoffman.

For the earliest and most lasting contribution, however, and for their constancy, I owe the most to my parents, Marion and Bernard. And finally, this book is for Fred.

Newark, Delaware
August 1984

The Invisible Hand
of Planning

INTRODUCTION

This is a study of a neglected chapter in the intertwined histories of business and government planning, the social sciences, and modern managerial society. It is, in particular, a study of mutually supportive collaboration between social science and managerial institutions in the attempt to create America's first peace-time system of macroeconomic management, a collaboration that appeared to be moving toward success in the 1920s but was incapable of preventing the Great Depression.

Under the leadership of such individuals as Herbert Hoover, Wesley C. Mitchell, Mary Van Kleeck, Henry S. Dennison, and Beardsley Ruml, there developed between 1921 and 1933 a three-legged apparatus resting, in different ways, on philanthropic foundations, the National Bureau of Economic Research, and the U.S. Commerce Department. This apparatus sought through its influence on the microeconomic decisions of individual business managers to enhance the stability of the economy as a whole. As envisioned and advertised, such "planning," with its expanded arenas for the public exercise of private yet "scientized" managerial authority, would provide a "middle way" between statist collectivism and laissez-faire individualism. And in the construction of this mechanism, business managers and social scientists would assist each other to assume new social and political roles.

Efforts to build a continuously productive capitalism evolved in three stages. Initially, the base was constructed in the two decades before World War I, primarily through the emergence of professional economics, philanthropy, social work, and management as modern technocratic institutions. In this era, against a backdrop of market chaos and mass unemployment, social scientists generated visions of a society reorganized and harmonized around technical elites. During the second stage, from 1917 to 1921, America's war mobilization was built, to a significant extent, on this foundation, and left in its wake a variety of attempts to adapt the war experience to the resolution of a postwar productivity crisis and a resurgent class conflict. While most of these faded quickly, one group gradually coalesced around the new commerce secretary, Herbert Hoover, thus ushering in the third stage, from 1921 to 1933. During these years, Hoover helped to build an apparatus in which funding from the major foundations, national income and countercyclical investigations by the National Bureau of Economic Research, and a cooperative conference and committee system developed by the Department of Commerce came together and sought to function as a nonstatist system of countercyclical planning.[1]

This New Era planning reflected both the antistatism of American political culture and the modern search for national managerial capabilities. Committed to voluntarism, it embraced the kind of "individualism" that concentrated private power at the level of the business firm and refused to challenge managerial prerogatives. But it also fixed responsibility for the economy's overall performance at the level of the firm, and sought to organize and educate individual businessmen to respond to the countercyclical prescriptions of social scientists. Such planning was, in effect, a microeconomic approach to macroeconomic coordination, one based on the assumption that if enough managers stabilized their operations along the lines recommended, then the sum of individual decisions, much like the invisible hand of the classical market, would add up to increased productivity, moderation of distributive conflict, and, thus, the collective good.

That this system has long been ignored is testimony to both its fragility and its failure. Clearly it could claim little credit for the expansion of the 1920s. In fact, its inability to fathom the boom's weaknesses or to manage well the ensuing contraction made plain its inadequacies and demoralized its proponents. Nevertheless, in its operations and claims to legitimacy, the New Era apparatus was an important passage in the modern development of joint public and private managerial systems. The chapters to follow uncover and emphasize several aspects of this story.

First, they reveal that antistatism and the desire for countercyclical management were reconciled during the 1920s within a system of public and private linkages in which government (specifically the Commerce Department) encouraged private business and social science institutions to assume public planning functions. Developing here was a kind of techno-corporatist state, one in which national management was to be achieved not by an enlarged government but by one contained and redirected toward the creation of public roles for technically informed private authorities.

Second, the chapters to follow make plain that this techno-corporatism also involved a legitimating process, both for capitalist institutions and for America's rising social sciences. Mass unemployment can expose both the existence of class privileges and the market's pretensions to be free of power, thus subjecting business institutions to a crisis of legitimacy. As the social sciences emerged, one source of this legitimacy for political and business elites came with the findings of a scientific rationality, allegedly transcending class interests, that unemployment and other capitalist ills were curable through better organization and management—that they were, in other words, vulnerable to the prescriptions of social scientists. By providing such a rationale, the new engineers, economists, and social workers not only legitimated their own activities but also helped to advance the technocratic identity and claims to public authority of American social science. By this means they became the tools of modern progress, deserving of a respected professional status and important positions in an expanding managerial culture.[2]

Third, it is now clear that underlying and shaping this process was a lag between technocratic vision and competence, for throughout this period visions of a society reorganized around enlightened elites ran ahead of the information available to social scientists. Thus inadequate data competence not only frustrated the construction of a rationalized capitalism, it also

5

illuminated the internal crisis of scientific legitimacy within social science. Because it lacked a significant body of data, social science remained ignorant of causal connections and was therefore unable properly to test its hypotheses. For this reason, the movement toward the apparatus of the 1920s was punctuated by economic and social surveys, the establishment of research institutes, and other exercises in data production. And in the elaboration of these efforts, philanthropy assumed its modern role as financial sponsor, organizer, and protector of technocratic institutions.

Fourth, it is evident that efforts to expand data competence resulted in a remarkably uniform process of science- and profession-building within economics, management, and social work. During the immediate prewar years these disciplines independently generated categories of empirical description and analysis that would cohere by 1917 in a multidisciplinary critique of mismanagement and malproduction. This technocratic critique insisted that managerial, or microeconomic, decisions were the critical factors determining macroeconomic performance; this critique would also subsequently inform both wartime planning and data-gathering operations, as well as the elaboration of New Era planning.

Fifth, as the focus of the postwar period turned increasingly to fashioning peacetime substitutes for the war mobilization's novel managerial mechanisms, the quest for a new authority with which to meet the urgent demands for economic coordination came together with concerns about data competence and scientific legitimacy. From this came the institutionalization of what I have termed a "technocratic bargain" between social science and managerial institutions, one that underwrote the construction of New Era techno-corporatism. Most clearly revealed in professional economics and in the origins and operations of the National Bureau of Economic Research after 1919, this bargain promised the expansion of data competence necessary to achieve both macroeconomic coordination and scientific legitimacy. And throughout the period from 1924 to 1929, perceptions that it had done so would contribute to the

spread of a managerial ideology, one that hailed the emergence of a "new capitalism" led by a new kind of business
leader whose claims to an expanded social authority seemed
an appropriate result of the merger of social science and business planning.

What follows, finally, addresses the larger history of modern
American authority, business-government relations, and economic planning. Most accounts of the latter, in particular, tend
toward an exclusive focus on the statist experiments of the
two world wars, the 1930s, and the Nixon presidency. These
interpretations emphasize the planning activities of public
managers, a perspective that has obscured the links between
the public sector and private planning institutions and the ways
in which the latter have acted often in a public capacity. By
recasting a portion of this history, the study also addresses the
late-twentieth-century planning debate that is only now emerging. In this debate, legitimacy and the uses of technical authority will be important issues, but they cannot hope for a
fair hearing, nor can the debate be fully informed, so long as
our understanding is hampered by an inadequate history.

CHAPTER 1

Technocratic Progressivism

The last decades of the nineteenth century saw the emergence of the large corporation and the beginnings of modern bureaucratic society. With this emergence, the authority once exercised by traditional, locally centered institutions would be challenged and weakened by a new world of mammoth organizations, powerful hierarchies, and an industrial working class. This new world brought with it, among other things, mass unemployment and industrial violence so severe that by the early twentieth century the words "capitalist" and "proletariat" could be used and understood in America. Thus neither its frontier nor its political institutions could apparently protect the United States from the hardening of class feeling.[1]

Believing these changes to be not only dangerous but possibly permanent, many reformers in the two decades before World War I would speak less of fighting an emerging order than of finding ways to make a going concern more efficient and less brutal. In other words, more and more people who were actively working to improve the lot of the poor and the worker came to identify progress not with a radical agenda but with the streamlining of a system that was considered to be here to stay. To them, poverty, disease, unemployment, and social discontent were not the result of an inexorably unjust social order. Rather, they were the effects of an unstable, ill-managed, but improvable corporate capitalism.[2]

Unfortunately, social improvement was frustrated, according to a variety of industrial inquiries and investigating commissions, by a vacuum of authority. As they saw it, there was a need for new institutions that could claim convincingly to stand above class conflict and exercise authority in the social interest. Also needed, they believed, were bodies capable of finding objective information about the formation of capital and the distribution of income. Such information, they argued, would help break the impasse between capital and labor, lay the foundation for "fair" settlements, bring forth more efficient production and more orderly marketing, and halt the increasing fragmentation of society.[3]

Meeting such needs was also a dream increasingly embraced by the newer technical disciplines of economics, social work, and scientific management. The introduction of statistical analysis and institutionalism in economics, the merger of engineering and administration in the new scientific management, and the wedding of the new social work to philanthropy were all indications of this growing technocratic sensibility. Lagging far behind, however, was the development of new bodies of information with which to build the authority necessary to resolve conflicting claims about the nation's income and its economic performance.[4]

This lag stood out sharply in the frustrating record of the commission approach to industrial warfare. In fact, both President McKinley's and President Wilson's commissions on industrial relations helped to focus national attention on the necessity for industrial reform. But their inability to provide basic facts about the nation's capital and income structure was seen as a hindrance to the achievement of consensus, thus failing to allay class suspicions. The pre-World War I development of the technocratic social sciences was therefore punctuated by economic and social surveys, by the organization of research institutes, and by other exercises in data production that were designed to meet the need for greater enlightenment and better social management. These activities reflected a technocratic progressivism that focused on organizational solutions to economic and social problems, one that was part of a larger impulse toward organizational and associational activity. It was within this kind of progressivism, which was especially concerned with the social evils of unemployment, that technocratic social scientists would devise and promote microeconomic strategies for macroeconomic management.[5]

II

It was not until World War I provided a massive subsidization of macroeconomic research that the lag between technocratic vision and competence would be substantially altered. Nevertheless, some progress toward such competence was made in the prewar years, and nowhere as much as in the evolving relationship between philanthropy and social work. In this sphere, funding from the major foundations enabled social workers to organize and carry out comprehensive surveys of America's cities, surveys that were the first systematic attempts to assess the social costs of industrialization. Thus knowledge about working conditions, unemployment, and urban family life was greatly enhanced. And as other foundation programs were established—programs aimed at developing libraries, health sciences, research facilities, and new institutions of higher learning—the role that could be played by philanthropic giving underwent a major redefinition. No longer would the mere treatment of the symptoms of social illness suffice. Now it was imperative that attention also be turned to the systematic alleviation of its causes.[6]

This reorientation encouraged and was in part the product of a general movement toward the professional administration of philanthropy, one in which the Rockefeller organizations pioneered. Beginning in the 1890s, Frederick T. Gates, a former Baptist minister, had taken the lead in imposing upon John D. Rockefeller's scattered "retail" giving a pattern of "scientific" wholesale giving. Under his scheme, a large principal sum, always to remain intact, was controlled by a group of self-perpetuating trustees, who administered corporations empowered to use the income to accomplish rather flexible general aims. Thus the General Education Board, the Institute for Medical Research, and the Rockefeller Sanitary Commission became the earliest instances of what would later be the standard model of twentieth-century philanthropic organization.[7]

This widely hailed movement toward professional administration was a reflection in the philanthropic sphere of the tendency of large organizations to come under the direction of professional managers. And it signaled, in particular, a tendency to turn management and program formulation over to the rising technocratic professionals, with their claims to systematic expertise and broad social understanding. This process is most clearly revealed in two areas, the inauguration of modern social work and the establishment of the Russell Sage Foundation.[8]

Social work had undergone a reorganization in the 1890s. In most large American cities, so-called "charity organization societies," modeled on those in England, has assumed control of relief and charitable activities and were attempting to make more systematic and efficient use of private relief funds. Settlement houses had also been established, and both kinds of institutions were helping to develop professional training for social workers.[9]

Increasingly, moreover, the extent and severity of urban industrial misery had prompted scholars and reformers to reconsider traditional theories of poverty. In particular, the empirical studies of men like Charles Booth and Seebohm Rowntree, whose clandestine investigations of the English underclass had earned them the sobriquet of "social explorers," led analysts in the United States to begin to see the vices of the "undeserving" poor as the results rather than the sources of poverty.[10]

As attitudes changed, the economist Simon Nelson Patten was also preaching a new economics of abundance, arguing that the enormous increase in the productive powers of Western society had now called into question the entire range of assumptions that had been made under earlier conditions of scarcity. Patten's influence on the establishment of modern social work was considerable. At the University of Pennsylvania, he taught the first courses on modern poverty, and one of his doctoral students, Edward T. Devine, would later become one of the country's leading philanthropic executives. As general secretary of the New York Charity Organization

Society, as professor of social economy at Columbia University, and as editor of *Charities and The Commons*, Devine was at the very center of a new technocratic profession; and in 1907 he was among those who hailed the "thrilling" possibilities opened up by the creation of a powerful new institution for the "improvement of working and living conditions" in the United States, the Russell Sage Foundation.[11]

The new organization owed its inspiration and endowment to the charitable sympathies of Olivia Sage, but in the definition of its mission and strategy it reflected the thinking of men who were closely identified with the "scientific" movement then underway in philanthropic circles. As friends and counselors of Mrs. Sage, such men as Daniel Coit Gilman, Jeffrey Brackett, John M. Glenn, and Robert and Henry de Forest saw the Sage fortune as an instrument that could be used to push organized charity beyond relief to develop systematic research into the causes, consequences, and cures of poverty itself. Indeed, they argued that such a foundation could act for the nation just as the charity organization societies acted for the larger cities, functioning as an overarching administrative and research center.[12]

It was to the establishment of a research apparatus that the new foundation first turned. To this end, modest appropriations were quickly made to support investigations into the standard of living in New York state. But of greater consequence was the support given to the Charities Publications Committee's Pittsburgh Survey, the first major effort to do for an American city what Charles Booth had done for London.

Having arranged such support, moreover, Sage trustees Gilman, Glenn, and de Forest (who were also members of the Charities Publications Committee) saw to it that the survey's results were published under the foundation's auspices, thus offering the first comprehensive view of industrial accidents among working-class families, of the effects of the twelve-hour day and the seven-day week, and of the harshness of working conditions in the steel industry.[13]

At the same time, in January 1908, the trustees took the

initial steps that would lead to the creation of a Department of Industrial Studies. These involved a grant to a young social worker, Mary Van Kleeck, "for investigations into trades for women and women's lodgings." Since 1905, one year after her graduation from Smith College, Van Kleeck had been studying the overtime required of young women in New York factories. Subsequently, she would begin a study of child labor in the city of New York, supported by Sage Foundation grants to the Alliance Employment Bureau, a local philanthropic agency. In 1910 this work would be incorporated into the foundation's new Committee on Women's Work, with Van Kleeck as director.[14]

In this capacity Van Kleeck emerged as an embodiment of the prewar marriage between social science and philanthropy, as well as an expression of the rising scientism of social work and of such leaders as Edward Devine and Mary Richmond. Not only was Van Kleeck responsible for the establishment and direction of a significant research apparatus, but her work shaped the modern redefinition and attack on unemployment as well. From 1910 to 1917, her investigations led both to reform legislation and to new judicial decisions concerning working conditions and employee rights in New York industries. But of even greater importance, at least from the standpoint of our story, was the way her work pointed to microeconomic stabilization as a strategy for maintaining full employment.[15]

During these years her initial concern for the plight of women workers in the sweatshops carried over into a series of studies of New York City industries that were heavily dependent on female labor. In such industries, it was generally recognized that wages were low, hours long, employment irregular, and health and safety provisions inadequate. But about the specifics of the situation little was known, and without authoritative data reform efforts were stymied.[16]

Van Kleeck's studies encompassed the millinery, artificial flower, and bookbinding trades. In these and other investigations, she emphasized her concern with tying science to re-

13

form and thereby fashioning a technocratic foundation for organizing and managing social change. In this endeavor, she urged the disinterested pursuit and reporting of facts, the unearthing of causes rather than superficial manifestations, and the enunciation of principles and methods for broad social action.[17]

Bookbinding commended itself for study for several reasons, the most important being a 1907 New York state appeals court decision invalidating a law that prohibited night work for women. In a test case concerning a woman on a night shift in a bindery, the court seemed unaware that bookbinding was one of the major trades for women in New York City, that it offered employment not only to artists and craftsmen but to machine tenders and errand girls, and that its extreme irregularity of operations compelled women to accept all work that was available, when it was available. In other words, they had little choice but to agree to overtime and night work during peak periods, particularly in view of the weakness of union organization. Yet the court in rendering its decision treated them as free individuals voluntarily accepting such conditions.[18]

The full report, *Women in the Bookbinding Trade*, did not appear until 1913, but following a preliminary report in 1910 the New York state legislature created the Factory Investigating Commission and subsequently passed a law prohibiting the employment of women between the hours of 10 p.m. and 6 a.m. In 1915 this law was upheld by the same court that had struck down the earlier one, and in the new opinion the court noted the fresh data that had become available on the evils of night work for women. Much of it, as submitted in a brief by Louis Brandeis and Josephine Goldmark, consisted of quotations from *Women in the Bookbinding Trade*.[19]

A similar process of research followed by reform legislation attended Van Kleeck's investigations of the millinery and artificial flower industries. However, in these cases, as with bookbinding, the reform measures did not offer correctives for what Van Kleeck had identified as the most critical problem,

14

namely the irregularity of employment. Thus the problem's solution, she concluded, must come through improved business management as well as government intervention.[20]

In effect, Van Kleeck's investigations pushed forward the redefinition of poverty that was already underway. They found seasonal unemployment rather than personal vices to be a major source of that poverty, a source that could be eliminated partly through statist actions that would raise the costs of irregularity but mostly through the actions of responsible managers making enlightened decisions in their individual firms. The latter was an emphasis congenial to American institutions and traditions, and, as we shall see, one whose existence antedated its discovery by social workers.[21]

III

Scientific management, or Taylorism, grew up within the systematic management movement of the late nineteenth century. The concerns of this larger movement had been with securing better managerial control over materials, labor, and the productive process. Taylorism, named after the engineer Frederick Winslow Taylor, had offered one way of doing so. It envisioned engineering studies of the wastes to be found in work processes and managerial procedures, the development of scientific plans for eliminating these wastes, and the imposition of such plans through administrative hierarchies. At its core it involved the substitution of technocratic direction for the traditional authority of skilled craftsmen, foremen, and rule-of-thumb supervisors, allegedly in the interests of greater efficiency, more output, and expanded income.[22]

Even if unemployment had never been explicitly addressed, Taylorism's influence on the worker-manager relationship would still have been significant. But its real importance for our story lies in its application by Taylorite revisionists to the analysis of social problems and especially to the problem of unemployment and the wastes that it involved. This was a development that became more pronounced after World War

15

I, but there were foreshadowings of it in the immediate prewar years.[23]

One center of this revisionist movement was the Taylor Society, founded in 1910 by a small group of Taylor's followers, who soon became involved in efforts to break through the narrow bounds of the master's thought, preoccupied as it had been with the factory process. Instead, they concerned themselves with the "human factor," eventually absorbing into Taylorism an interest in personnel management, employee betterment, and industrial psychology. They also began to define unemployment as a species of industrial waste, an underlying source of larger inefficiencies, and, therefore, as something amenable to the microeconomic ministrations of scientific managers. This became the concern, in particular, of such Taylorites as Morris Cooke, Harlow Person, and Henry Dennison, all of whom had earlier shifted their focus from factory processes to human relations and the wastes to be associated with labor turnover, absenteeism, and workers who were ill suited to their jobs.[24]

In 1914 this concern led to the first and second National Conferences on Unemployment, the former held in Philadelphia in February, the latter in New York City in December. The sponsor was an organization of economists, social reformers, political scientists, and social workers known as the American Association for Labor Legislation, which since its founding in 1906 had stood in the forefront of the campaign against unemployment and in support of workmen's compensation and other labor reforms. It had attracted people interested in these issues and, as a result, had become an early technocratic vehicle, bringing social workers like Van Kleeck together with economists like John Commons and Edwin F. Gay, as well as Taylorite revisionists like Henry Dennison.

Dennison, a key organizer of both conferences and a major organizational thinker and innovator, was a paper products manufacturer, a student of business cycles, and the designer of inventory and distribution controls that allowed him to stabilize employment in his own firm. Later labeled by John Ken-

16

neth Galbraith as perhaps "the most interesting businessman in the United States," Dennison provided evidence of the possibilities of enlightened management, although he also irritated other Boston businessmen, who thought him to be coddling his workers.

From the second conference on unemployment came the publication of a *Practical Program for the Prevention of Unemployment*, which embraced not only Dennison's ideas but those that were now characteristic of such leading technocratic reformers as Van Kleeck and Commons. It called for countercyclical public works planning, unemployment insurance, and the creation of a network of employment exchanges. In addition, and not surprisingly, it urged the regularization of employment by individual managers.[25]

All this, however, was but a foretaste of what was to come. For it would be the war, with its labor shortages and mounting costs, that popularized scientific management and encouraged explicit formulations of its relation to employment. And it was here that Harlow Person, who would become president of the Taylor Society during the 1920s, took the lead, arguing that scientific management could turn firms requiring constant attention into smoothly flowing operations. And when they were freed from the need for day-to-day oversight, the administrators of these firms might devote more of their attention to long-run policies designed to stabilize relationships both within and between various industries.[26]

There would always, Person conceded, be some degree of unemployment under capitalism. But given the collective militance of industrial workers, the growing pressures for unemployment insurance, and the rising costs of retraining, it was no longer true that capitalists benefited from a large reserve population of the unemployed or from seasonal and cyclical layoffs. Unemployment, as traditionalists had believed, might once have been a spur to growth and productivity, but it was now becoming a drag.

Thus as it was reconceptualized, unemployment was being transformed, at least for technocratic professionals, from a

17

systemic inevitability to an anomaly having no place in a capitalism subjected to technocratic direction. This transformation, moreover, was occurring not just among the new social workers and engineer-administrators. It was also taking place within the most explicitly technocratic of the several strains of modern economics, American Institutionalism.[27]

IV

Never a coherent school of thought, institutional economics arose late in the nineteenth century in opposition to the prevailing theory's shallow assumptions about human motivation and its ahistorical, unscientific (read un-Darwinian) presumption of the universality of capitalist institutions. Convinced that classical economics was inadequate and that much of the neoclassical synthesis was useless for understanding modern economic problems, the institutionalists raised strong objections to their profession's drift into what seemed to them irrelevance.[28]

The major figures in the movement were Thorstein Veblen, Wesley Mitchell, and John Commons. For Veblen there was much to be learned from the biological and anthropological sciences. Profoundly affected by Darwinism, he rejected neoclassical assumptions as narrow and unmindful of the power of culture, arguing instead for an "evolutionary" economics founded on an appreciation of cultural development and explicitly recognizing the role of economic interests, forces, and institutions in shaping economic behavior. Commons, for whom neoclassicism was similarly flawed, would go on to become a major force behind the legitimation of unions and the management reform movement. And Mitchell, who was Veblen's most gifted student, was to gain fame for his pioneering work in the measurement and analysis of business cycles. For our story, he was the most important of the three.[29]

From Veblen, Mitchell had absorbed a belief in cultural relativism, a skepticism of prevailing theory, and an awareness of the dichotomy between pecuniary interests and those of

18

rational production. But unlike Veblen, who rejected reform-ism for iconoclasm, Mitchell would eventually emerge as a major figure in the efforts to create macroeconomic stabilizers. Although his cycle analysis provided a powerful illumination of the way capitalist motivations produced booms and busts, he was also convinced that there were qualitative alterations in the economic structure, and that these might eventually make the social control of business cycles possible. Such a conviction would underlie his direction of the National Bureau of Economic Research in the 1920s.[30]

By the time that Mitchell's *Business Cycles* appeared in 1913, there was already much analysis of the dynamics underlying the ebb and flow of economic activity. But unlike earlier in-vestigators, Mitchell made extensive and detailed efforts to determine how closely the theoretical explanations fitted the "actual experience" revealed in the empirical data. And from such studies he drew conclusions that had a threefold signif-icance. His work, first of all, destroyed the commonplace no-tion that depressions (or expansions, for that matter) were deviations from "normality." Instead he argued that fluctua-tion was an unceasing process without beginning or end, and that it arose not from economic activity per se but from eco-nomic activity operating under a capitalist money economy. Second, his findings allowed mass unemployment, whether cyclical or seasonal, to be seen as the product of decisions made in business firms, and hence as something most likely to be remedied at the level of the firm. And finally, his data sug-gested that the reserve population of the unemployed, rather than being a spur to growth, tended to generate upward pres-sures on business costs. Thus, in effect, Mitchell was offering statistical and historical corroboration for a problem scientific managers were just then beginning to address.[31]

V

As their work with the American Association for Labor Leg-islation indicated, economists, social workers, scientific managers, and other technocratic reformers had moved by 1917 toward a common redefinition of unemployment and the beginnings of a common program. They had taken significant strides toward reconceptualizing the problem and their relationship to it, and in doing so they had advanced their professional identities along explicitly technocratic lines.

But while the work of Van Kleeck, Dennison, Person, and Mitchell suggested the potential of technocratic management, the chasm between vision and data competence remained awesome. It would take time and much patient empirical work, it seemed, before this chasm could be bridged. Moreover, stronger and more sophisticated political alliances with management, labor, and government groups would have to be forged before technocratic potential could move beyond the margins and into the mainstream of political and economic development. Fortunately for the young social scientists, World War I was the perfect vehicle for achieving these ends.

CHAPTER 2

Technocratic Mobilization, 1917–1918

> The War has revealed a younger intelligentsia . . . immensely ready for the executive ordering of events.
> —Randolph Bourne[1]

Randolph Bourne, more than most, understood in 1917 that modern war furthered not only the interests of the state but those of the intellectual classes as well. As Merle Curti would later note, these classes were already in the war before the nation had formally entered it. And it was only later, after much death and suffering, and after the Faustian quality of the bargain had become apparent, that their patriotic zeal and their admiration for war-induced unities and efficiencies would cool. But in the America of 1917, with the century still young and unrevealed, it was not difficult for the leaders of scientific management, institutional economics, and scientific social work to feel an almost visceral anticipation of the possibilities inherent in the war system.[2]

America's managerial culture flourished in the hothouse mobilization of 1917 and 1918. Where market chaos, unemployment, and social strife had helped to galvanize prewar technocratic progressivism, the war's acute demands brought it to the center of the stage and created an environment highly conducive to the growth of planning institutions and technocratic machinery. After all, a warring nation required basic information if it was to order, route, and coordinate its operations. And there were new roles to play for those who could generate and certify this information, especially for those who had spearheaded the social surveys, statistical analyses, and managerial reforms of the prewar years. The nation as a whole needed their kinds of skills, perspectives, and commitments, and many of them looked upon the unfolding conflict as a watershed, an opening to new opportunities. After the war, wrote the economist-statistician Allyn Young, "we shall realize, as we have not in the past, the possibilities of doing things on a national scale, of rationally adapting the mechanism of national life to fit national ends." He was not alone in believing that there could be peacetime equivalents to the war's planning institutions.[3]

More specifically, the bureaucratic structures of the war period, part private and part public, contributed to the managerialism that followed in at least four ways. First, they allowed the new social scientists to establish themselves as "disinterested professionals" serving a public cause, as embodiments, in other words, of the "service ideal," a long-honored test of professionalism and a way of bridging the gulf between the scientist as observer and the scientist as planner. Second, this convergence of private, associational interest with a transcendent "national" interest typified and reinforced a larger paradox of the period. On the one hand, the war encouraged unified and ferociously political behavior that held consequences not only for foreign enemies but for the domestic constellation of power and domination. On the other, it fueled the pretension that a society at war is one that has risen above politics and has need, so long as their behavior does not undercut this pretension, of decision-makers whose claims to social leadership are similarly "apolitical."

Third, the war mobilization introduced the technocratic approach and world view to a broad range of government, labor, and business leaders, thus creating a network of personal and professional associations that could become a planning constituency. And fourth, the system supported a significant data-gathering effort, which helped to reduce the gap between vision and competence and make technocratic professionals appear socially useful. Although it was of negligible value until the latter months of the war, this fresh knowledge of the nation's component parts suggested new possibilities for planning through the "eyes" of statistics.

II

As the heady swirl of "national consciousness" brought social scientists flocking to Washington, they responded somewhat differently to their new situation. Some, such as social worker Mary Van Kleeck and engineer Morris Cooke, plunged forward, apparently confident that their individual, professional, and public responsibilities coincided. But others, particularly the economists, faced more troubling ambiguities, for theirs was as yet a profession without a clear professional identity, uncomfortably balanced between the need to fashion a "disinterested" science and the equally pressing imperative to prove its utility in the public arena. Long torn between "advocacy and objectivity," they would experience a similar tension in their roles as generators of information for the war system.[4]

The engineers were among the first technocrats to be organized for war service. As the "preparedness" movement gained momentum in 1915, a Committee on Industrial Preparedness was organized within the Naval Consulting Board, a precursor of the Council of National Defense. The committee, staffed chiefly by engineers, was headed by the automotive engineer and standardization enthusiast, Howard Coffin, and as its major project it got the leading engineering societies to undertake an inventory of the nation's industrial resources. The aim in doing so was threefold. The committee hoped, first, to arrive at an approximate estimate of America's munitions capacity. Second, it sought to prepare businessmen for the imminent conversion of their plants to war production, and third, it wanted to construct an "industrial reserve" of skilled workmen who would be exempted from a military draft in order to further productivity in war industries.

By late 1916 not much had been accomplished along any of these lines, primarily because there was a lack of war enthusiasm among many engineers and businessmen. A good deal of the information that was gathered was too vague and unfocused to be of much value; and professional engineering societies, despite their desire to serve as "social orderers," were ill equipped to secure the business behavior they thought desirable. Still, despite its failure, the industrial inventory was important if only because it attempted to achieve a higher level of data competence, and, as Robert Cuff has noted, because it pointed to the possibility of technocratic professions acting to legitimate closer relations between business and government.[5]

Still other engineers, like the Taylorite revisionists Cooke and Dennison, who were leaders in the "human engineering" and personnel management movements, used the opportunity presented by the war to organize employment-management training courses on college campuses. Others of similar predisposition, including the statistician Roger Babson and the public works apostle Otto Mallery, joined the Information and Education Service of the War Labor Administration. There, "personnel science" was pursued with a vengeance as workers were propagandized, lectured, and exhorted to subordinate themselves to the war effort.[6]

For social work, the war led to similar efforts to generate new information, particularly in the areas of working conditions and the status of women workers. In addition, the general social dislocation produced by the mobilization of both troops and workers placed unprecedented demands on welfare agencies, one result being increased efforts to bring order and efficiency to relief and welfare work through new federations of philanthropic and charitable organizations. These federations, which emphasized the coordination of fund-raising and the distribution of services, coalesced in the war chest drives that tied local relief efforts to national appeals.[7]

During the war years, Mary Van Kleeck was again instrumental in advancing the data competence and technocratic claims of the social work profession. She had pushed hard prior to the war for the creation of a federal women's bureau in the Labor Department and had been joined in this campaign by the National Women's Trade Union League, since 1903 a vigorous force for the organization of female workers. The need for a women's bureau was self-evident, Van Kleeck felt, and flowed logically from her work up to that point. "Certainly we need facts," she insisted. "We must know more about minimum wage laws, the extent of night work and its results, the employment of married women in industry, and the health effects of dangerous processes." For Van Kleeck, the establishment of a women's bureau was a necessary step toward the formulation of a coherent, national attack on the problems of women in industry.[8]

To this end she responded eagerly to Morris Cooke's call for help in studying the possibilities of employing women in the government warehouses. In 1916 Cooke had become associated with the Council of National Defense. He subsequently became the chairman of its Storage Committee, and in 1917 he turned to Van Kleeck. Her investigations led to the establishment of a Bureau of Women's Work in the War Department, the formulation of protective standards for men as well as women, and a fuller view of the nature and status of the work force. In association with Cooke, Van Kleeck was also able to establish a Women in Industry Service in the Department of Labor. This was created in July 1918 and was the forerunner of the Women's Bureau in the Labor Department, an agency established by statute in June 1920.[9]

Van Kleeck saw the war as an opportunity to advance the eight-hour day, the minimum wage, and the concept of equal pay for equal work, all of which had been advocated by labor reformers for years. But at the same time, the war's unusual demand for labor threatened to wreck what fragile gains had already been made in these areas. She was particularly worried about the survival of protective legislation as well as the threat to the entire labor force should the rapid substitution of women for men lead to a drop in wage rates. "The problem is how to meet the immediate necessity for increased production through more extensive employment of women," she argued, "while preventing the repeal of night-work laws and at the same time regulating the night shifts of women in plants working on war materials in states which have no laws against night work."[10]

To meet the situation, Van Kleeck suggested the creation of a system of "war permits" to be issued to plants for specified periods through the War or Navy Departments. The enforcement and administration of this system would fall to the Women in Industry Service. Although unhappy at the prospect of encouraging night work for women, Van Kleeck and her allies in the American Federation of Labor and the American Association for Labor Legislation foresaw advantages in the permit system. For if it were backed by the government, such a system might actually further the campaign for the eight-hour day and equal pay for equal work.[11]

In their war work, both Van Kleeck and Cooke had reaffirmed their convictions concerning the inseparability of management reform, professional reponsibility, and social welfare. A similar affirmation characterized the war years for a variety of technocrats drawn from the disciplines of sociology, political science, and psychology. But it was the more ambiguous experience of the economists, operating now along the statistical frontiers of the mobilization, that was especially significant in the story we are attempting to reconstruct. It was from these activities and the heritage left by them that much of the subsequent optimism about planning capabilities and a managerial capitalism would spring.[12]

III

The wartime experience was initially characterized by frustrations and difficulties. It was the experience, so Grosvenor Clarkson wrote, of people who were "blinded because they had not developed eyes." "Their work," he added, "gave them eyes, whereas their eyes should have selected their work." Others agreed with this view. "The war," wrote Wesley Mitchell, "revealed the defects of the federal machinery for collecting statistics with startling suddenness." It also presented totally new problems for national administrators, creating, in the words of Allyn Young, "a situation in which we find ourselves in urgent need of a complete inventory of our national assets

26

and . . . industrial activities." In addition, it raised the problem of "relative urgency," of "priority in the widest sense"; and as a "conflict of directed masses—of aggregates," it cried out for statistical analyses and ways of thought that were as yet poorly developed and meagerly informed. Thus data-gathering became a top priority. But it could not be effective without informed planning to guide it and an organization to analyze the data, spell out its implications for the economic system as a whole, and make the results useful to administrators.[13]

Plagued by outdated, haphazard, contradictory, and generally inadequate statistics that were furnished by the equally inadequate and understaffed bureaus established prior to 1917, the mobilization was slow to overcome these frustrations and difficulties. More often than not, enthusiasm and luck had to suffice. And until midsummer of 1918, efforts to correct the situation seemed to produce little more than wasted time, new bottlenecks, and duplication of effort.

One possible exception was the work of the Statistical Division of the Council of National Defense. Under Leonard P. Ayres, former director of the Division of Statistics at the Russell Sage Foundation, this agency was successful in gathering valuable information for the Army; and subsequently, as a part of the Army General Staff, it would become the chief intelligence and interpretive arm of the American Expeditionary Force. Nevertheless, Ayres' work was an anomaly. The rest was a sea of confusion, a condition that would persist until a series of developments in the early months of 1918 ushered in a new stage of the mobilization, one that would feature a centralization of statistical functions and the emergence of Edwin F. Gay and Wesley Mitchell as the technocratic point men of a reorganized war effort.[14]

A major factor that was responsible for the new developments was a shipping crisis that led to the creation in February 1918 of a Division of Planning and Statistics by the United States Shipping Board. The crisis was rooted in a lack of ships to handle the greatly expanded commerce with the Allies, but it became especially severe after the battlefield reverses of late

1917 made it clear that American troops must be transported to Europe as rapidly as possible. Victorious on the Italian and Russian fronts, the Central Powers were massing their forces for a major offensive in France, and only a rapid expansion of the American presence in Europe seemed capable of saving the situation. With this in mind, the Army had turned to the Shipping Board with requests for vast increases in allotted tonnage—so vast, in fact, that granting them threatened to disrupt essential commerce and make it impossible to import vitally needed raw materials.[15]

Clearly it was crucial to establish a coordinative mechanism to sort out these conflicting requirements in the least costly manner. In an effort to create such a mechanism, Edward N. Hurley, chairman of the Shipping Board and a prewar advocate of business and government cooperation, asked Edwin Gay, dean of the Harvard Business School and an economic historian, to collect information on the Army's requirements, the volume of ship space consumed by nonessential imports, and the nature of the available ships. Gay agreed to do so and shortly thereafter became the head of the new Division of Planning and Statistics.[16]

Joining Gay in the new agency were the economist Wesley Mitchell and the managerial reformer Henry S. Dennison, the latter already associated with Gay through his work for Arch Shaw's Commercial Economy Board and his part in developing the curriculum of the Harvard Business School. With the aid of Mitchell and Dennison, Gay set out to unify into one mechanism the statistical work that was going on at the Shipping Board, the War Industries Board, and the War Trade Board. And in the weeks that followed he had a substantial degree of success.[17]

One struggle in which the new statistical analysis proved to be decisive was that between Gay and P.A.S. Franklin, the chairman of a new ship control committee that had been created to divert tonnage from nonessential imports to the transportation of American troops and military supplies. As president of the International Mercantile Marine Company, Franklin

28

tried to use his position to strengthen American shipping interests in Latin American markets, an action that necessarily meant fewer ships for the Army. In countering this, it was Gay's statistics that suggested "a disquieting lack of approximation" between the number of ships necessary for required imports and the number actually in use. In fact, they revealed "a large excess tonnage over trade needs" in the commerce between the United States and the east coast of South America, a discrepancy Franklin was eventually forced to correct. At first he was defiant, insisting that he was justified in looking after "the interests of American trade on the East Coast." But after the War Trade Board, the War Industries Board, and the American Mission to the Allied Maritime Commission had all backed Gay, the tonnage was diverted.[18]

The mounting reputation of Gay's agency made him the logical choice to head a further move toward the centralization of statistical activities. Thus in June 1918 he organized and became the head of the Planning and Statistics Division for the War Industries Board. And when President Wilson asked board chairman Bernard Baruch to produce a monthly "conspectus" of all the government's war work, Gay also became the head of the Central Bureau of Planning and Statistics, operating as an independent agency directly under the president. The new bureau represented the "peak" statistical division of the mobilization, becoming its "seer and prophet" for the duration, coordinating over a thousand employees engaged in research and statistical analysis, and, as the agency responsible for giving the president a concise picture of the entire economy, becoming the closest approximation to a "central statistical commission." During the latter stages of the war it set up a clearinghouse of statistical work, organized liaisons with the statistical staffs of all the war boards, and centralized the data production process for the entire war bureaucracy. By war's end, Wesley Mitchell recalled, "we were in a fair way to develop for the first time a systematic organization of federal statistics." By then, too, the economists of the mobilization had taken significant steps toward reducing the gap between vision and competence. Their war work had introduced them to a wide array of "men of affairs," encouraging the identification of professional advancement with public service. And while it did not entirely resolve the professional tensions that had nagged at them for nearly a generation, the mobilization, as we shall see, helped to make those tensions increasingly irrelevant.[19]

IV

Throughout the war, economist-statisticians like Mitchell and Young had argued that much of the duplication and most of the problems they faced could have been foreseen and prevented if only a centralized statistical bureau had been organized at the beginning of the hostilities. This was something that both the American Statistical Association and the American Economic Association had tried to promote through their committees on federal statistics. Neither had had much success, partly due to an absence of persistence, but also, it seems, because of a professional ambivalence that prevented them from throwing their collective weight behind public activities.[20]

This ambivalence was a reflection of the conflicting impulses that had dominated modern American economics since its birth. As organized in 1885, the American Economic Association (AEA) had been the creature of a rising generation of German-trained students who were committed to fashioning a useful science. In Bismarck's Germany, where they had taken their Ph.D.'s, their teachers had created a "historical" school of economics in order to build a "positive" state, a school deliberately designed as an alternative to Britain's neoclassical approach to economic study. But unfortunately for the young Americans, the only place where English ideas were taken more seriously than in England was the United States. In America, an antistatist political culture had been buttressed for generations by an amateur "moral philosophy" distilled from Smith and Ricardo. And it was in America too that the neoclassicists, Marshall and Jevons, gained their warmest following. In contrast to the German-trained group, a number of American economists were attracted by the development of a marginal utility calculus, a mathematized ordering of market relations that further reinforced inherited prejudices even as it seemed to suggest the dawn of a new age of consumption.[21]

The young profession soon found itself torn between alternative paths to professional identity. One road called for "objectivity" or a rigid abstinence from partisanship, while the other visualized science as an instrument of reform, insisting that an "objective" profession was one "that professes nothing." Faced with this divergence, the AEA was forced to adopt a constitutional provision against taking stands on public issues in an effort to promote professional unity.[22]

The involvement of economists in war work at first heightened their factional tension. Although many were ready to put their skills and training at the disposal of the government and justify this as "national service," in no profession was there as successful a resistance to collective, professional endorsement of the government's program. Thus economists who urged closer organizational ties to the mobilization were stymied by the executive committee of the AEA. Indeed, the closest the AEA ever came to serving as an arm of the war government was in the support it gave to war research and war placement and the near endorsement it mustered for the Treasury Department's Thrift Campaign.[23]

In the immediate postwar period the AEA would also refuse to sponsor an economic research institute, an act that was yet another reaffirmation of its nonpartisanship. However, this did not mean that economists as professionals would now remove themselves from practical affairs. On the contrary, the participation of the profession's leading lights in war work had clearly given it a higher standing in the eyes of "men of affairs." In fact, war chieftains like Bernard Baruch, Herbert Hoover, and Robert Brookings were increasingly disposed to regard economists and other social technicians as necessary fixtures in an emerging managerial order.[24]

Thus the war had helped to blur the traditional distinction

between advocacy and impartiality. It had enabled economists to demonstrate the utility of their techniques, to fuse science and service, and in the end to establish their professional identity along explicitly technocratic lines. In this way, the war marked the eclipse of the older view, which had sought to forge an identity and social standing by remaining aloof from political questions.

In the troubled months of reconstruction to come, the fragile planning capacities just achieved seemed more necessary than ever. At first, Gay and Mitchell fought to save the Central Bureau and to institutionalize it as a type of guidance apparatus within the executive branch. But the momentum of retrenchment and President Wilson's preoccupation with foreign matters would doom this plan, leading Gay and Mitchell to turn to the task of shaping peacetime equivalents for the war mechanisms, building especially on the organizational experience and data-gathering operations of 1917 and 1918. In the chapters to follow, we will examine not only this transition from war to reconstruction but also the crystallization of a technocratic critique and a planning constituency, as well as the emergence of new private planning institutions organized to act on a particular conception of the public interest.

CHAPTER 3

Ideas of Technocratic
Reconstruction, 1919

Histories of the World War's aftermath in America have traditionally concentrated on the three R's of retrenchment, reaction, and red scare. But the years 1919, 1920, and 1921 were also characterized by a debate over a fourth R, reconstruction, that would exert substantial influence over the shape of modern managerial culture. It was a debate formulated largely in technocratic terms and driven especially by the war-sharpened visions of mobilized social scientists and their managerial patrons. The wartime achievements had seemingly turned collaboration among social scientists and functional leaders into a virtue. And so, energized by what they judged to have been a successful demonstration of their capacities as planners, social scientists now looked upon the postwar period as containing an opportunity to be seized.[1]

Through the war machinery, it was argued, the nation had moved toward greater productivity, better labor conditions, and a viable system of priority planning, all of which constituted evidence of "progress." And for many this movement also validated what a number of engineers, social workers, and economists had been saying during the pre-war period, namely that mismanagement of material and labor processes lay at the root of economic and social instability. Now in the postwar period this critique would be elaborated through the medium of reconstruction into a broad-gauged strategy of social reform and profession building, to be achieved through new technocratic institutions resembling those of the war years.

Two interrelated problems, however, continued to plague those who envisioned this form of reconstruction. One was the prospect of renewed conflict over the distribution of national wealth and income; the other was the gnawing scientific illegitimacy of social science. Successful implementation of policy, so those involved came to feel, would thus require a further expansion of technocratic data and authority, an expansion that, at one and the same time, could lead to more wealth and income for everyone, to a narrowing of the gap between technocratic vision and competence, and to a higher and more secure status for social science.

Implicit within this strategy was the need to fashion peacetime substitutes for the war mobilization's alliances between social scientists and managerial elites, both to subsidize data-building and to legitimate and regularize technocratic authority. Social scientists would struggle to define the terms of such novel alliances throughout 1919, but it would not be until 1920 and 1921 and the creation of the National Bureau of Economic Research and the Federated American Engineering Societies that the terms of the modern bargain between social science and capitalism would begin to become clear.

II

The idea of reconstruction was part of the baggage of mobilization. By 1917, the French, British, and Germans had all set up reconstruction commissions, although in America there was an intitial reluctance to do so, for fear that this would detract from the war build-up. But by early 1918, congressional initiatives and informal symposia on the issue had begun to appear, and by summer the Council of National Defense was engaged in a study of postwar "readjustment." Its study reflected the mixture of foreboding and expectancy that was characteristic of most contemporary thinking on the matter. The war, it concluded, had altered prevailing habits, rules, markets, and aspirations, heightening the probability of postwar dislocation but making it impossible to turn back. As council publicist Grosvenor Clarkson put it, "Any view of the subject is futile, stupid, which does not go along with the understanding that little in our national life is to be the same after the war." Yet war-induced changes, it was also held, were equipping America with new managerial capabilities, making it possible to deal with the future through "mechanisms of readjustment." In this view, as Secretary of Commerce William Redfield declared, "many of the problems of production for war are the problems of production for peace as well."[2]

Still, as the end of the war neared, the likelihood of a federally sponsored peace industries board diminished. The president's interest in such matters, never strong, virtually ceased, while at the same time congressional and public opposition to extensions of the war apparatus mounted. Wilson's dissolution of the War Industries Board in December 1918 sealed the issue, signaling that the adaptation of the war's technocratic achievements to peacetime purposes would thereafter fall to private groups.[3]

Whether under a peace industries board or some private substitute, men like Edwin Gay and Wesley Mitchell seemed determined to preserve as much of the war's planning and statistical apparatus as possible. "There is a need of establishing some center for the study of after-the-war problems," Gay wrote in October 1918. And while the post-armistice rush of retrenchment initially threatened to destroy the Central Bureau of Planning and Statistics, Wilson's decision to make it the statistical agency of the American delegation to the peace conference saved it for the time being. It also gave Gay, Mitchell, and their staff some time to prepare a brief for the bureau's preservation.[4]

Even before Wilson's decision, Edmund E. Day, a Harvard economist serving on the bureau's staff, outlined several avenues of "possible development" that in his view would insure bureau's "usefulness" during demobilization. The studies already underway, he urged, including those pertaining to the world shipping situation and to labor conditions in the United States, should be rapidly completed. In addition, there should be new studies of European relief needs and of the war organization, the latter with an eye to transferring some sections to permanent government agencies while creating wholly new divisions out of others. Above all, Day argued that the bureau should have a role in public policymaking during "the difficult period of demobilization." To this end, it should, he suggested, inaugurate a "continuing canvass" of business conditions in the United States, one that might later be turned over to the Federal Reserve Board. "If possible," he added, "the Clearing House should be strengthened and its permanency assured," either "by alliance with some permanent Government office" or by establishing the bureau "as a permanent extra-departmental Central Statistical Office." The "Clearing House" he referred to was the agency that was processing and interpreting all the statistical operations of the war organization, and the future that Day envisioned for it was one that Gay would champion and seek to realize. In his terminology, it represented the "proper outgrowth" of the "Central Bureau idea."[5]

While seeking a role in demobilization planning, Gay and his staff also drew up a memorandum arguing for the "imperative necessity" of designating an authoritative and exclusive source of economic data for the American delegation to the peace conference. "Cables from Paris," it was declared, already showed signs of "great confusion in estimates of economic conditions." In the future such questions as "the economic value of certain territory, the needs of given countries, the available supplies to meet these needs, [and] the shipping which may be available" would all require estimates that would "carry conviction as to the justness of our attitude." And if these were to be made, American representatives must have the services of the only government organization qualified to provide the necessary economic data, namely the Central Bureau. Apparently, Wilson was convinced. Before sailing for Paris, he made the bureau a part of the organization to negotiate the peace.[6]

Wilson was not interested, however, in creating a similar organization for domestic reconstruction. Nor was Bernard Baruch, perhaps one of the few whose influence could have made a difference. Baruch adamantly refused to extend War

Industries Board support of the Central Bureau beyond January 1, 1919, a move that only increased Gay's irritation with those who could not see the value of a permanent planning and statistical agency. On December 27, he vented his anger at Baruch in a conference lasting nearly two hours, a meeting he later characterized as a "disgraceful performance, childish."[7]

Upon Wilson's return in March 1919, Gay again took his case to the president, emphasizing the usefulness of the bureau during the war, its present contributions to demobilization, and its value to the "peace time requirements of the Government." Encouraged by the fact that Wilson "was in the habit of reading regularly" the Central Bureau's weekly conspectus of government activities, Gay proposed that the agency be permanently attached to the executive office, where it could, "without departmental bias," furnish the president with needed information, enhance his capacity to control executive agencies, and become part of the machinery required for a national budget system. The president responded with a promise to seek congressional support for the continuation of the bureau. But Congress was not sympathetic, and the Central Bureau, along with most other survivors of the war system, ended operations in mid-June of 1919.[8]

The Central Bureau's demise was not surprising, given the clamor at the time for retrenchment and Wilson's preoccupation with foreign problems. However, the president's determination to leave "readjustment" to the individual actions of "spirited businessmen and self-reliant laborers" did not produce happy results. For in the year following the war, an economy that had seemed to be moving toward greater productivity, better management, and heightened stability instead fluctuated wildly from a condition of depressed markets and labor glut to one of hyperinflation and disruptive industrial warfare. Suddenly, the structure upon which technocratic progressives had pinned their hopes stood strangely disordered. It was within this larger context of forsaken federal planning, postwar gyrations, and disparity between technical potential and social reality that technocratic social scientists took the idea of reconstruction as their own.[9]

III

Although the fundamental ideas of technocratic reconstruction gestated throughout 1918, they achieved their clearest expression in two technocratic manifestos that were issued within weeks of the war's end. For the economists and statisticians, Richmond, Virginia, was a convenient site for the December 1918 joint meeting of the American Economic Association (AEA) and the American Statistical Association (ASA). The city was chosen for its proximity to Washington and hence to the many members of both associations who were winding up their war work in the capital. And in the programs of the conventions there was also a clear reflection of the deep involvement of both economists and statisticians in the recent conflict. Virtually every paper and discussion dealt with some aspect of the war, but by far the most important element of the meetings was the simultaneous delivery of presidential addresses by Wesley Mitchell (ASA) and Irving Fisher (AEA).[10]

In rhetoric brimming with self-consciousness and anticipation, Fisher spoke of a world that awaited rebuilding, of a "world reconstruction" that would be largely economic, and of a profession that would "probably have more opportunity to satisfy" its constructive impulses than would "other departments of human thought." Economists, he continued, should approach the potential of a "new world" by being mindful of the opportunities and duties before them, for the promise of that new world could never be realized if it were haphazardly built—particularly by the economists, who were among its rightful architects. Certain of a continuing struggle over the distribution of the nation's wealth, Fisher implied that the economists' major task lay in devising a mechanism of "readjustment." By this means they might occupy an "enviable position" as the logical arbiters of the impending class struggle.

But to do so they must jealously guard their independence and impartiality.[11]

Fisher's address was important because it pointed to an intersection of economic technique and professional aspirations with resurgent class conflict and likely demands for social guidance, implicitly identifying an enlarged political influence for the profession with advances in social technique. But it was Mitchell who offered the clearest analysis of the promise and weakness of technocratic social science. As his address made clear, the war had intensified his long-held faith in the technocratic potential of statistical knowledge, as well as his doubts about the worth of unplanned reform and his concern for the scientific weakness of the social sciences. As he saw it now, postwar dislocations, together with the failures of earlier reforms and the immaturity of social science, would demand a new strategy "to protect our future," one specifically addressed to the task of building a social science capable of harmonizing social relations within a modern capitalist order.[12]

"The war," Mitchell explained, "led to the use of statistics, not only as a record of what had happened, but also as a vital factor in planning what should be done." It had thus revealed not only the potential for social direction but the unprogressive nature of what passed for radical or reform movements. "Most of us are reformers of some kind," he noted. But reform "by agitation or class struggle is a jerky way of moving forward. Are we not intelligent enough to devise a steadier and more certain method of progress?"[13]

Underlying Mitchell's address were three fundamental aspects of the technocratic faith that had been developing over the last decade and a half. There was, first of all, an implicit acceptance of the permanency and flexibility of corporate capitalism. Although Mitchell was dissatisfied with the social costs it imposed, he felt these to be the result of poor organization and ignorance, and thus susceptible to intelligent management. Second, he was convinced that such broad social management depended on a precise comprehension of social processes, the lack of which was hindering the efforts of contemporary social reformers. And finally, he believed that social science was potentially capable of providing the data needed for planned reform, but that the young disciplines suffered from a severe lag between vision and competence, and thus from an internal crisis of scientific legitimacy.[14]

For Mitchell, this world view had in fact been well developed by the time he published *Business Cycles* in 1913. "We putter with philanthropy and coquette with reform," he wrote to Lucy Sprague, soon to be his wife, "and try to do what little we may to alleviate at retail the suffering and deprivation which our social organization creates at wholesale." What was needed, he continued, was "sure knowledge of the causal interconnections between social phenomena." After all, industrial and medical progress had been spurred by just such an appreciation of causality within physics, chemistry, and medicine. "But in all matters of social organization we remain backward; it is not lack of will that impedes progress, but lack of knowledge. . . . The progress of medical science has . . . come from the laboratories. . . . So must it be in other subjects. If we are ever to have an economics of use in guiding our efforts at social reconstruction, it must come from men who find some way of resolving the vital social problems into simpler elements."[15]

For Mitchell this had come to mean the recasting of hypotheses in terms that allowed for precise statistical illumination and verification. In his view, this was the only way in which both science and social progress could be advanced. "Such topics as the economic serviceability of advertising, the reactions of an unstable price level upon production, the effect of various systems of public regulation," he wrote, would "be treated with incisive vigor as we become able to make the indispensable measurements." And these empirical measurements were in turn indispensable to fashioning a "constructive criticism" of capitalism, one "which may guide the efforts of our children to make that marvelously flexible form of organization better fitted to their needs."[16]

To the assembled statisticians Mitchell suggested, much as Fisher had to the economists, an implicit linkage between imminent social upheaval and the development of technocratic social science. The world, as he portrayed it, was now an especially dangerous place, and America an especially troubled society. "We know," he declared, "that men who can read and vote make restless citizens in a state where their rewards do not satisfy their sense of justice. And such is the present state of affairs with millions of aggressive Americans. They can be counted on to change things by turmoil if things are not changed by method." Hence, the modern world was one in which the maintenance of harmonious social relations required a much more exact knowledge of social fact. Only in this manner could there "develop some way of carrying on the infinitely complicated processes of modern industry and interchange day by day, despite all tedium and fatigue, and yet . . . keep ourselves interested in our work and contented with the division of the product. That is a task of supreme difficulty—a task that calls for intelligent experimenting and detailed planning rather then for agitation and class struggle."[17]

And again, as he had since 1911, Mitchell called for the "progressive" strategies of physical science and industry to be brought into the social realm. In the former, he noted, "we rely, and with success, upon quantitative analysis to point the way; and we advance because we are constantly improving and applying such analysis." But in this respect the social sciences, "the best hope for solving our social problems," remained pitifully weak. They were "immature, speculative, filled with controversies," and overly concerned with what "ought to be" rather than "what is." If their potential was to be realized, they must concentrate on developing "the progressive features of the physical sciences"; and in the expansion of social statistics, Mitchell thought, they were beginning to develop in the right direction. This kind of study showed "forthright progress in knowledge of fact, in technique of analysis, and in refinement of results." It was "amenable to mathematical formulation," "capable of forecasting group phenomena," and "objective." A statistician was "usually either right or wrong, and his successors can demonstrate which." Nor were statisticians "con-

41

tinually beginning their science all over again by developing new viewpoints." "Where one investigator stops, the next investigator begins with larger collections of data, with extensions into fresh fields, or with more powerful methods of analysis."[18]

IV

Mitchell's and Fisher's heady assessments of the potential of scientific social direction were shared in the immediate postwar period by social scientists like Henry Jones Ford, who recalled with approval the contributions of political scientists to the war effort. In fact, speaking at the 1919 convention of the American Political Science Association, Ford went so far as to state that the application of expert knowledge to public service was one of the most encouraging aspects of the war. As he put it, "the new and great resources which the state has acquired through the progress of science and the amassing of expert knowledge" had been of practical and impressive value. And now that the war was over, the work of political science was just beginning. "The main task," Ford continued, "is to clear away the wreck and put things in running order again. Political science can help with its stock of information about forms of government, principles of organization, [and] systems of jurisprudence."[19]

For psychologists, the war had also provided an opportunity to demonstrate technique and a spur to professional growth. Formally represented within the National Research Council since its inception, psychologists had linked themselves to the war effort through more than a dozen committees of the American Psychological Association, each one functioning in an area of specialization applicable to military needs. As part of the resulting operations, such men as Robert M. Yerkes, Walter Dill Scott, and the young Beardsley Ruml had organized the Army's mammoth intelligence testing operations, setting significant precedents for the wide use of such devices by corporate managers after the war. Thus in the immediate postwar period, the fusion of psychological testing and business needs would spawn the new science of personnel management. And among the several consulting firms set up to market these new-found capacities was one organized by Scott and Ruml. Through this development, the work of psychologists in 1917 and 1918, it can be argued, constituted a "war gift to industry."[20]

Next to the economists and statisticians, however, it would be the engineers and social workers who would contribute most to the translation of technocratic critique into peacetime practice through the idea of reconstruction. The war had introduced engineers to the notion of treating the nation as an "engineering problem," and this they were continuing to do. "Although hostilities in Europe are over," wrote F. Herbert Snow, "warfare against waste and inefficiency has only begun." Like Snow, Herbert Hoover was confident that the war had "vindicated the scientific attitude in dealing with problems of social organization" and had thus marked the beginning of a new age requiring comprehensive rationalization of industrial life. In the view of C. R. Richards, "the necessity for speeding up production" had "attracted the attention of the whole civilized world to the need of a scientific basis for everything of an industrial nature."[21]

Such self-conscious assessments of professional mission typified postwar engineering thought. They were part of a movement that would eventually culminate in the creation of the Federated American Engineering Societies and its study of waste in industry. And accompanying them was a growing acceptance of the definition of waste set forth by such Taylorite revisionists as Henry Dennison, Harlow Person, and Morris Cooke. Their "broader approach" to the "man question," with its emphasis on the efficiencies to be gained through lower labor turnover, less unemployment, and better worker morale, was becoming part of the agenda of technocratic reconstruction; and since it promised labor benefits and tended to blame management for social wastes and inefficiency, it was not without a degree of acceptance in labor circles. Thus in the warming relations between Morris Cooke and Samuel Gompers there were hints of a major rapprochement between two groups and two approaches to industrial affairs that had been bitterly antagonistic only a few years earlier.[22]

Social work generated a critique and a reconstruction agenda that were more concrete than those of any other profession, partly perhaps because it had laid claim to the term "reconstruction" ever since *The Survey* magazine had launched a series on war and reconstruction in 1915. As peace approached, the magazine had created a department on reconstruction, intensified its dedication to turning war's lessons to the "common advanatage," and called a "Conference on Demobilization." This was attended in late November 1918 by over a hundred social workers, and out of it came a program much like the prewar platform of the American Association for Labor Legislation. It called, among other things, for a permanent Federal Employment Service, a continued Women in Industry Service, and a cabinet department to coordinate countercyclical expenditures on public works.[23]

In what followed, Mary Van Kleeck was a leading figure. For her the war had applied an acid test to social thought and practice, effectively cutting the present from the past and opening up new opportunities for the rebuilding of a fragmented society through technocratic means. "Reconstruction," she wrote in early 1919, was not "restoration." It required a recognition of "new forces," "new ideas," and, above all, a "new spirit," one demanding "not merely fairer conditions of labor, but a fairer share for labor in determining its own conditions." The central task ahead was the building of an industrial democracy with "power rather than reward" as its guiding standard. In line with this, given the effects of war mobilization on traditionally weak labor groups, their rightful claims would have to be acknowledged. Only then could "the test of the new spirit" be met.[24]

To this end, Van Kleeck not only helped formulate the reconstruction programs of the Woman in Industry Service and the Women's Trade Union League—programs that called for the adoption of such measures as the eight-hour day, equal pay for equal work, guarantees of collective bargaining, and the appointment of women as personnel managers—but also advocated a three-point program of her own that envisioned a strengthened labor force as critical to higher productivity. The first step toward comprehensive reconstruction, she argued, lay in the formulation and enforcement of standards "already demonstrated to be attainable and desirable" by the war. The second involved strengthening the national system of labor exchanges so as to match workers with jobs and make it easier to determine the causes of persistent unemployment. Finally, the third step necessitated the securing of collective bargaining rights and the education of male workers concerning their stake in wage rates for women. To allow the wartime gains of women workers to be undermined would, in Van Kleeck's view, amount to a catastrophe for national living standards, particularly now that good working conditions had proved their value as "mechanisms of efficiency."[25]

V

For technocratic professionals the great task of 1919 was to institutionalize their prescriptive capacities within the fluid nexus between government and business managers. And while fractious internal debates and the pursuit of futile policies characterized some of their efforts, a number of important steps were in fact taken.

Many engineers, for example, considered professional unification as the first step toward a national reconstruction based on engineering leadership. Progress in this area had been slow, since old rivalries persisted, and thus a consensus was difficult to achieve. However, in the fall of 1919 there emerged a potent and unifying force in the person of Herbert Hoover. As an engineer deeply committed to reconstruction through the application to society of engineering principles, and as an internationally acclaimed war chieftain and humanitarian, Hoover's reputation was such that he was able, almost single-handedly, to push his profession toward the type of organization that would give it a new kind of national leadership.

Hoover's call to action was set forth in a series of addresses delivered in late 1919 and early 1920. In these, even though he was not himself a recognizable Taylorite, he advocated a program of national reconstruction that was founded on the familiar Taylorite themes of waste elimination and maximized production. Convinced that insufficient productivity was at the root of social conflict, he called for a national campaign to reduce waste and increase production, a campaign very similar to the one that he would eventually direct as commerce secretary in the Harding cabinet. In presenting this program, Hoover was contributing, as were other engineers, economists, and social workers, to the construction of a managerial consensus on malproduction as the major obstacle to social cohesion.[26]

Hoover was not unaware of inequalities and injustice in the distribution of social rewards, but he saw little prospect for social betterment in premature redistributive schemes that could only further antagonize class relations and thus further hamper productivity. This, he felt, was the critical issue. "We have long since realized that the basis of an advancing civilization must be a high and growing standard of living for all the people, not for a single class," he would later write. "To all practical souls there is little use in quarreling over the share of each of us until we have something to divide."[27]

Consequently, Hoover would continue to reiterate his belief that increased production was the most pressing issue on the American agenda. And invariably he would link this issue to the broad conception of waste elimination that was emerging as central to the technocratic view of reconstruction. Thus, any hindrance to production, including employer-labor conflict and unemployment, was by definition a form of waste and something to be "eliminated." In Hoover's view, this could not be done through the further disenfranchisement of labor, for down that path lay only more class hatred and reduced productivity. Instead his belief that "the maximum of production cannot be obtained without the elimination of waste" became a rallying cry for the foundation of a new social consensus on the rock of economic growth. "There is no solution short of community of interest," he told the San Francisco Commercial Club on October 9, 1919. "We must begin by creating, somehow and somewhere, a solidarity of interest in every section of the people conducting our industrial machine. The worker, the administrator, and the employer are absolutely interdependent on one another in this task of securing the maximum of production and a better division of its results."[28]

On another front, Mary Van Kleeck was also reconceptualizing social work in terms of reconstruction. By the fall of 1919 she had already helped launch a series of investigations into contemporary experiments in organizing employer-worker relations. And in a remarkable memorandum, prepared in October for the Russell Sage Foundation, she called for a rededication of the joint efforts of philanthropy and social work to the task of creating an industrial sociology that would be capable of informing and guiding managerial decisions.[29]

The severity of postwar dislocations, she wrote in her memorandum, was such that "a new analysis" of the foundation's mission was imperative. For if the present situation constituted "an awakening," it seemed to her to be an "awakening of the blind," who were unable to see that the war had destroyed popular faith in established institutions and had made new approaches to industrial relations inevitable. Among workers, Van Kleeck added, there was "acute industrial unrest, stirred to the depths by the economic pressure of rising costs and the psychological effects of a world-wide discontent with existing contrasts between the economic power of a few and the precarious hold of the many in the economic organization." And among managers she saw a "keen anxiety due to inadequacy in production and numerous difficulties in dealing with labor." In the resulting climate, both the "destructive radical" and the "obstructive reactionary" were thriving. Thus it was imperative that the attention of the public at large be focused on "a sober, disinterested plan of action," which, given the Foundation's

47

reputation for disinterestedness and accuracy, it had a "unique opportunity" to underwrite.[30]

What was needed now, Van Kleeck felt, was an even more explicitly technocratic conception of the foundation's function, one that would involve the translation of heightened data competence into material that could be of immediate use to industrial managers. "Research and investigation," she wrote, "continue to be the chief tools of the Foundation in its relation to industry." But the "new situation" seemed to require "modification in the use of information gathered through investigation." Not only was it "probable that, in view of the rapid changes and the urgency of the present crisis, publications should be issued more promptly in the form of pamphlets and articles," but there was also a need to consider using the foundation's data "not only for public education but in direct application to the needs of an employing organization or a group of workers." To this end, Van Kleeck suggested that the foundation consider creating a new Bureau of Information within her Division of Industrial Studies, one that would provide "expert counsel for employers, workers, state officials or others who desire assistance in applying the experience of others to their own immediate problems."[31]

VI

In an attempt to close the circle of these early efforts at technocratic reconstruction, we must return in the end to the economics profession, where in the wake of the Central Bureau's dissolution new approaches to technocratic planning emerged, the most important of which were the efforts to create a nongovernmental institute for economic research. Unlike the Central Bureau, such an enterprise could be fitted into the antistatist climate. In the eyes of men like Arch Shaw, Henry Dennison, and others who shared Wesley Mitchell's view of these matters, this institute could develop economic research along the lines that had proved so fruitful for the physical and medical sciences. In other words, it could provide researchers in the field with the needed "equipment" and collective organization through which the profusion of unordered data generated by a complex and troubled economy could be made intelligible, an achievement that lone, uncoordinated researches could never hope to accomplish.[32]

Irving Fisher had advocated such an institute in his presidential address of December 1918, and between then and the summer of 1919 the social crisis of demobilization had made the search for economic intelligibility and control even more insistent. Thus while calls for industrial parliaments, company unions, Plumb Plans, and corporate welfarism proliferated, a small but significant strain of thought, strategically situated within powerful foundations, rising professions, and certain sectors of business and government, was looking to social science for the answer. In this view, social science could not only undertake the intellectual expeditions necessary; it could also, if properly delimited, help to legitimate efforts to "solve" intractable political problems through administrative mechanisms.[33]

In May 1919 Fisher followed up on his December suggestion. In the interval, several businessmen had approached him with ideas for a research institute, suggesting that the initiative come from academic economists. Fisher was amenable, and he now circulated a letter among AEA members asking for suggestions on possible research goals and organizational structure. In the letter he noted that "the further development of the science of economics depends on the close cooperation between economists, businessmen, and representatives of labor," and that the primary object of any research institute should be closer relations among these important groups.[34]

Fisher's preference was for a quasi-independent organization that would be privately funded through corporate subscriptions and would rely upon the AEA for the selection and administration of projects. He was somewhat leery, to be sure, about involving the association in this way, probably for fear of compromising its long-held prohibition against taking a stand on issues of public moment. He had, after all, already cautioned economists about the need to preserve their impartial status. But the envisioned institute, he conceded, "would be the child of the American Economic Association in a sense," and the association, he thought, should have representation on its board of directors, hold a veto over all appointments and projects, and "exercise such a function as the Senate of the United States exercises in regard to appointments by the President." Without at least this much AEA participation, Fisher feared, the institute would fail to attract financial sponsors.[35]

From Fisher's initiative came a committee of those interested in the project, and from the committee came recommendations that the AEA proceed along essentially the same lines that Fisher had suggested. In its deliberations the committee emphasized five points that constitute one of the period's clearest expressions of the case for nonstatist technocratic planning. First, the committee noted that lone researches were inadequate in the face of the "comprehensive character" of contemporary problems. Second, it recognized "a desire for scientific guidance" from "employers' associations, labor organizations, commercial organizations, legislatures, etc." Third, it took note of how recent developments were fast increasing "the sum of available data of value to economists." Fourth, it acknowledged the effects of the war, both in producing a "vast amount of data awaiting interpretation" and in bringing "urgent calls for guidance." And finally, it pointed to the fresh wave of enthusiasm among economists for the "methods of inductive science." This, it observed, had "awakened a desire for greater opportunity to employ these methods."[36]

The committee's report reflected Fisher's cautious enthusiasms, particularly his desire to "create a distinctive organization," thus relieving the association of a responsibility that it was "not properly organized to discharge." Moreover, it refracted the image of a technocratic constituency, one actively seeking fresh ways to tie its critique to policymaking. It did not, however, lead directly to an economic research institute. That job was left to another group of technocratic enthusiasts working along a parallel track, a group led by Edwin F. Gay and Wesley Mitchell, which was eventually successful in producing the National Bureau of Economic Research.[37]

CHAPTER 4

Institutions of Technocratic Reconstruction, 1920–1921

The goal of sustained economic growth as a cure for distributive conflict was first institutionalized in the countercyclical planning apparatus of the 1920s. But behind this, as previous chapters have noted, was a view of reconstruction that linked the expansion of planning capabilities and social data to the containment of class conflict and the realization of a productivity capable of meeting popular expectations. To bring about this expansion a variety of institutions had been envisioned, and in 1920 two major ones, the Federated American Engineering Societies (FAES) and the National Bureau of Economic Research (NBER), became realities. Their initial studies of industrial waste and national income produced evidence of a postwar productivity crisis, contributed to the formation of a managerial consensus on the social costs of mismanagement and malproduction, and thus acted as transitional vehicles between war corporatism and New Era macroeconomic management.

The significance of what was happening in 1920 and 1921 has been largely ignored by modern historians. But seen in retrospect, the new institutions were clearly portents of things to come, since they contained the rudiments of the modern managerial constellation of business, foundation, social science, and government elites. Because of this, they facilitated the transfer of public policymaking from the political to the administrative arena, a process that had begun a generation earlier with the rise of the modern corporation. They also provided the framework within which the production of social knowledge was made routine, thus launching a substantial

51

subsidization of the data competence and scientific legitimacy of social science.

This chapter will examine the formation and significance of these new institutions, looking in particular at the rise during this period of philanthropy's modern role as financial sponsor, organizer, and protector of technocratic organizations. The most important instance of this came with the sponsorship of the National Bureau by the Commonwealth and Carnegie funds. And primarily within the National Bureau the period also witnessed the institutionalization of a "technocratic bargain" between social science and those seeking to replace political processes with capitalist planning. Social science thus became a partner in the structure through which depoliticization was to be achieved. It did so by implicitly accepting the primacy of capitalist norms and subordinating its public function and professional identity to the task of building the data competence necessary to coordinate and improve the existing system. As it became institutionalized, this technocratic bargain helped to legitimate both an emerging managerial capitalism and the rising technocratic professions. It allowed elites serving capitalist purposes to appear as scientifically enlightened "public men," and it gave the technocratic professions a sphere in which they were recognized as useful and authoritative.

II

The National Bureau's origins lay in the preoccupation of prewar progressives and would-be technocratic reformers with the compostion and distribution of the national income. According to their way of thinking, industrial disputes could not be settled fairly or a healthy society built without first establishing a consensus on the facts of the nation's wealth and income. It was this sort of analysis of wages, rents, and prices— key components of national income—that Edwin Gay had hoped to organize in 1914.[1]

As noted previously, Gay's reputation as a technocrat had been rising since the establishment of the Harvard Business

School in 1908. As the school's first dean, he had allied himself with Henry Dennison in statewide industrial inquiries, and in 1911 had presided over the new Massachusetts branch of the American Association for Labor Legislation. He was also the man who persuaded Frederick W. Taylor to lecture at the business school, calling Taylor's scientific management "the most important advance in industry since the invention of the factory system." And with Arch Shaw, Gay had also organized the Harvard Bureau of Business Research to analyze the marketing end of local businesses.[2]

Consequently, in 1913, when Jerome Greene asked for suggestions on formulating institutions for the advancement of social science, Gay was receptive. Greene, a former secretary of the Harvard Corporation and at that time the director of the Rockefeller Institute for Medical Research, was convinced that an economic research institute similar to the Rockefeller organization, one with an independent board of directors, research chief, and all necessary funds and facilities, could do for the social sciences what the Rockefeller Institute had already done for medical science. Encouraged by Gay's favorable response, Greene, in March 1914, organized an exploratory committee with Gay serving as chairman. In June this committee produced a memorandum calling for an impartial investigation of the "basic facts" of wages, prices, rents, and other components of the national income.[3]

Wesley Mitchell was Gay's choice for project director, but with the beginning of the European war the project was temporarily shelved. It was not until April 1916 that it resurfaced, this time under different auspices, but still led by Mitchell and Gay. The new sponsor was Malcolm C. Rorty, an electrical engineer and statistician with AT&T, who had sought out Gay with the proposition of AT&T rent data as a lure. Mitchell had then promised to formulate a research program if Rorty could persuade other men of reputation to join, if he could raise the necessary funds, and if he could recruit a board of directors representing a sufficiently broad spectrum of responsible opinion. The latter was necessary, Mitchell felt, if the project's findings were to "carry weight."[4]

It was Rorty's belief that a knowledge of the distribution of the national income was "of vital consequence" to almost every social and economic problem and was particularly important for the "industrial readjustment that will necessarily arise during and after the present war." He was successful, moreover, in recruiting luminaries for the proposed institute that would seek out this knowledge. On the list, in addition to Gay and Mitchell, were John R. Commons of Wisconsin, then president of the AEA; Allyn Young of Cornell, then president of the ASA; N. I. Stone, a statistician, conservative socialist, employment manager, and associate of the newly created Brookings Institute for Government Research; and John P. Frey, a conservative trade union leader and editor of the *International Molder's Journal*.[5]

"The Committee," so a statement of its purpose declared, would "concern itself wholly with matters of fact." It would advance "no conclusions or theories," would assume "no obligation to any subscriber," and would thus maintain the "impartiality of attitude" that was an essential element in the undertaking. Then, as later, an overriding desire to fashion "disinterested" institutions of research and guidance proceeded in train with self-conscious aspirations for status and influence over policymaking. And also then, as later, a number of philanthropic and corporate leaders viewed institutions that could establish scientific claims of disinterestedness and professionalism as potential producers not only of economic intelligence but of better coordination and greater social legitimacy for the organizational hierarchies of a corporate capitalism.[6]

Again the war intervened, forcing the dissolution of the committee and its proposed undertaking. But in August 1919, in the midst of the reconstruction debates, it again resurfaced, still under the sponsorship of Rorty but now allied with the United Americans, a New York City association of bankers and professional men engaged in a campaign "of education in opposition to Bolshevism." Rorty saw in the United Americans an opportunity "for the necessary preliminary financial support" to get the project off the ground. For its part, the organization wanted to borrow some of Rorty's social scientists to aid in its campaign.[7]

Such ties did not sit well with some of those whom Rorty had previously enlisted. To Stone, for example, they seemed to violate the basic principle "that the Bureau was to have distinctly the character of a research organization, wholly disconnected from any work of propaganda." Its purpose, he insisted, was "to get at facts which are difficult to obtain and which require scientific research and dispassionate careful study." And its board of directors, he continued, must be composed of members of both radical and conservative organizations, thereby creating a body of facts that all could accept "as a premise." Commons agreed; and John Frey, in a letter to Rorty, also called for a return to the original conception. "If this committee had been able to take up its work when it was first being formed," he declared, "it is probable that we would have some most valuable data at the present time when data of this character would be of more value than ever before."[8]

The importance of this episode lies not so much in the proposed link between the committee and the United Americans, for the comments of Frey, Stone, and Commons quickly disabused Rorty of that enthusiasm and nothing more was heard of it. More important was the clarification of ends and means that was prompted by Rorty's indiscretion. Obviously the overriding concern of technocratic intellectuals, as it had been before the war, was still to find ways of creating what their society would accept as "impartial bodies" of technocratic competence. Thus to the extent that Rorty rankled his colleagues, he also stimulated a reaffirmation of both the possibility of constructing such institutions and the necessity of fashioning their organizational structure in such a way that continuous and automatic impartiality could be claimed. This task would soon preoccupy the organizers of the National Bureau.

More immediately, however, Rorty took steps that not only guaranteed the birth of the bureau but also marked the beginning of the postwar linkage of philanthropy and social science for the purpose of inaugurating routine and continuous technocratic planning. On August 9, he turned for support to the new Commonwealth Fund, chartered in 1918 as a foundation through which the Stephen Harkness fortune might "do something for the welfare of mankind." Under its first director, Yale historian Max Farrand, the fund's mission remained highly flexible, and it seemed possible that, in addition to its appropriations for European relief work, it might help to launch an economic research institute.[9]

In correspondence with Farrand and his assistant, Samuel C. Fairley, Rorty outlined his plans, reiterated his associates' insistence on the "absolute" independence and impartiality of the project, and explained how the proposed bureau should be organized so as to secure and maintain a science-based objectivity. "The Bureau," he wrote, "must be tied into certain at least semi-permanent popular and governmental institutions, such as the American Economic Association, the American Statistical Association, the U.S. Chamber of Commerce, the U.S. Department of Labor, the Federal Reserve Board, leading universities, etc." To do this, its initial corps of directors should ask such institutions for additional nominations to the directing board. Once these ties had been established, he felt, "it would be very difficult for anyone to claim that any particular institution or interest had established the Bureau."[10]

To emphasize the disinterested character of the enterprise, Rorty also made plain his intention to "detach himself wholly" from the bureau once it was well established. Initially, if the Commonwealth Fund would provide financial support, he would take action to charter and incorporate the bureau, begin an active endowment campaign, and organize the research apparatus. But having done these things, he would then sever all connections with the new agency.[11]

Farrand was receptive to Rorty's proposal, offering to support the bureau's first two years. However, he and his associates felt that the success of the undertaking would probably depend in large measure upon the persons who composed the initial organization. To insure that the quality of the personnel remained high, they insisted "that if the group of men originally named were modified in any way, any new names suggested should be approved by the [Fund's] Executive Committee and the General Director."[12]

With this assurance of support, Rorty then drew up the bylaws and a charter of incorporation. By mid-November his diligence had won Mitchell's praise, and in mid-December Farrand submitted the proposal to his board. In doing so, he argued that the undertaking was "probably . . . the most important step that has yet been suggested for the inauguration of a plan to obtain a body of facts that will be acceptable to all parties." It was, in his eyes, "as great a service as any which the Commonwealth Fund could render," and the fund, he thought, stood to gain substantial credit should it "adopt" such a promising infant at its birth. "Three things stand out," he concluded: "The need for such an organization—improbability of duplication—and the high calibre of its personnel." On December 16, 1919, a somewhat skeptical Commonwealth Fund board of directors bowed to Farrand's persistence and voted to underwrite the NBER with a one-year grant of $20,000.[13]

Farrand's insistence on the need for such an organization might have been impelled by the failure that year of other efforts to moderate industrial strife and establish mechanisms of social cooperation. President Wilson's First and Second Industrial Conferences of September and December, called against the background of a nationwide steel strike and aggressive union-busting, had not been able to solve the postwar "labor problem" or overcome prevailing class antipathies. Although plans for industrial tribunals, industrial "democracy," and collective bargaining guarantees had been suggested and discussed, none had provided the basis for industrial peace. And such failures no doubt made the idea of an institution capable of transcending contending interests through a unique claim to scientific objectivity particularly attractive.[14]

January and February of 1920 were taken up with debate and revision of the bureau's bylaws and charter. Of particular importance, then as before, was the problem of securing and maintaining a "scientific attitude." And while Rorty's original plan for a board composed of directors-by-appointment as well as self-sustaining members remained the basic format, it was now decided, in response to objections from the Commonwealth Fund regarding political appointees, that there were to be no representatives from government agencies. In addition to the ten original directors (including Rorty, Mitchell, Gay, Stone, Frey, Young, T. S. Adams, Elwood Mead, John Commons, and J. E. Sterret "of Price Waterhouse & Co."), a director each was to be nominated by the American Economic Association, the American Statistical Association, the American Federation of Labor, the Chamber of Commerce of the United States, the Engineering Council, the American Bar Association, the American Bankers Association, the American Federation of Farm Bureaus, and the National Industrial Conference Board.[15]

With the recruitment of Harry W. Laidler to the board in early February, Rorty resigned as a director but stayed on as secretary-treasurer. Laidler, another "conservative socialist" who, according to Rorty, was held in "high repute by Prof. Mitchell," was seen as an addition who would "strengthen the carrying power of the Bureau's findings." As Oswald Knauth, a student of Mitchell's and the bureau's first secretary pointed out, the bureau's leadership at the time was "especially aware that it would not alone be sufficient to determine the facts, but that it was even more important to have the facts accepted and believed after they had once been ascertained." There was a need, in other words, to establish a "weight" with the narrowly defined public the bureau hoped to cultivate—the business, labor, and government managers whose activities would be rationalized, harmonized, and made legitimate through their acceptance of the bureau's technocratic prescriptions.[16]

III

In late February 1920, with the election of Gay as president, Frey as vice president, and Mitchell as research director, the National Bureau was incorporated and took steps to organize the long-promised analysis of the composition and distribution of the national income. Throughout the events leading to the bureau's formation, national income analysis had been seen as the key to unlocking the answers "to almost every important political and social problem." It was the kind of analysis, so the argument ran, best capable of producing speedy results and of generating the fundamental data without which more specialized studies could not proceed.[17]

Mitchell had hoped for some time to organize the bureau's research program around questions that were, first, of primary social importance, and second, capable of the statistical resolution needed to surmount social science's internal crisis of scientific legitimacy. These criteria were met when it was declared that the bureau's first major project would be that which later led to the publication of *Income in the United States, Its Amount and Distribution, 1909–1919*. Not only would this be the most sophisticated assessment of the national income yet produced, it would also be the first comprehensive survey of the war's influence on the volume, composition, and distribution of that national income. And in its most important conclusion, the study would imply that it was the national income's insufficient volume and distorted composition, rather than its distribution, that was the most pressing issue facing the country.[18]

"We have set our hearts on getting the very best men available," Mitchell wrote to Max Farrand of the Commonwealth Fund in March 1920, "and we find that the two men whom ... we regard the most promising have both said they would like to join us." These two were Frederick Macaulay, a mathematical statistician, and Willford I. King, a student of national income data, both well respected within their professions. King and Scott Nearing had had the field of national income studies

59

virtually to themselves in the prewar years and in 1915 King had published *The Wealth and Income of the People of the United States*, a study whose estimates he would later change somewhat, but which was still a remarkable work. Little is known of its methodology, but its conclusions were not far from meeting later standards, no small achievement in light of the fact that King had woven his estimates from an eclectic mix of "1901 worker survey data, 1902 Chicago wages, 1914 tax returns on top incomes, Wisconsin state income tax returns, and other odds and ends." Such was the brash vision of the social scientists gathered up by Wesley Mitchell.[19]

Shortly thereafter, Oswald W. Knauth joined the research team, and on May 17, 1920, Mitchell opened its first meeting with a survey of the field and a discussion of the two ways in which the bureau's initial study might proceed. It could, he said, begin with a definition of national income and proceed with a search for materials to fit that definition. Or it could begin with a "very general notion" of national income, proceed to a search for data to fit this broader scheme, and "finally find out so far as possible precisely what income means in these data." This latter approach, so Mitchell thought, would prove "unquestionably the more fruitful."[20]

After setting out various methods of income estimation, Mitchell and his staff concluded that the mixed nature of their data—AT&T community rent figures, reports on professional salaries, census publications, income tax returns, and miscellaneous federal figures—demanded significant statistical controls. Consequently, they decided to produce two independent estimates from different bodies of data. Thus King was to calculate income from sources of production, while Knauth would estimate income received by the public. This, so Mitchell felt, would provide the best safeguard against error.[21]

Like the larger study itself, the specific questions to be pursued were determined by two criteria: the promise of reasonably accurate statistical solution and the ability to illuminate the economy as a moving system. Among the questions finally framed were:

What has been, year by year, the aggregate money income of the nation?

What part of the changes in the aggregate are due to fluctuations in prices and what part are due to fluctuations in the production of goods?

How is the aggregate income divided among individuals?

What proportion of the whole income goes to wage and salary earners?

What changes does this proportion undergo?

How does per capita income in the United States compare with that in other countries?

How has the average wage in different industries varied during the decade?

Which industries are increasing in importance and which are decreasing?

Beyond these specifics, however, lay the overriding question that Knauth posed in a November 1920 letter apprising the Commonwealth Fund of the study's progress. After outlining several of the study's objectives, Knauth concluded that the basic question was whether the income of the country was "so large as to make its proper distribution the primary source of public interest, or is the income so insufficient that its increase is the question of prime importance." Knauth went on to note that the reconstruction debate rested on this question, and that the lack of a definitive answer "blurs much of the present-day discussion."[22]

By June 1921 the two sets of independently derived estimates were sufficiently developed to allow comparison. "We felt not a little nervous when the day came," Mitchell would write later. "When the largest discrepancy in any one year proved to be only 7 percent we felt a marked increase of confidence in our work." Seven percent sounds like a large discrepancy, but in fact it reflected a real accomplishment since an inaccuracy of less than 10 percent in national income estimation was considered at the time to be an achievement of the highest order.[23]

Trumpeted as "the most exhaustive [study] ever made of the income question in this country," the first and summary volume of *Income in the United States* was published in 1921. Subsequently, a second volume offered a detailed explication of the methodology that had been used, and a third, *Distribution of Income by States in 1919*, broke down the data into smaller divisions. The general findings, made public on October 27, 1921, were along three lines. First, it was stated that the increase in national income from 34.4 billion dollars in 1913 to 61 billion in 1918 was largely due to price inflation. The increase in production had been much smaller, and a good deal of it had been in war rather than consumer goods. Second, the study showed that the per capita rise in individual income from $340 in 1910 to $586 in 1918 was worth only $372 in 1913 dollars. And third, it was found that while income distribution was severely inequitable, with the top 5 percent of income receivers getting 26 percent of the national income, the war had tended to diminish somewhat the share of this top 5 percent and had thus contributed to a leveling of the income structure.[24]

While it did not command wide public attention, the study drew praise from the social science and reform communities. Indeed, Jacob Hollander, a Johns Hopkins economist and an earlier opponent of proposals for an AEA-sponsored research institute, proclaimed that *Income in the United States* "ranks with the best [that] American economic scholarship is producing." In Hollander's view, not only had the National Bureau shown "what success can attend quantitative investigation into subjects that affect public welfare," but it had also established "the necessary starting point for all succeeding discussion" of economics and public policy.[25]

Professor Henry Seager of Columbia University was similarly impressed with the thoroughness and accuracy of the study. Writing in *The Survey*, he made particular note of the project's low estimation of recent productivity and concluded that "the moral of this is that in our continued efforts to bring about greater equality in the distribution of income we must be equally alert to the need of increasing production." The danger now, Seager felt, lay in the possibility that measures designed to alleviate inequality might curtail production, with the result that "instead of making the poor richer we may merely cause all to grow poorer together."[26]

The study's successful completion and reception had a two-fold significance for the National Bureau. It appeared, first of all, to vindicate Mitchell's research strategy, with its emphasis on cautious, painstaking empiricism applied to pressing public issues and designed to advance both the store of useful knowledge and the scientific status of social science. And second, it appeared, at least in the eyes of its proponents, to vindicate the bureau's novel organizational structure. The findings had "carrying power," and this could be attributed, at least in part, to the "disinterestedness" of those who paid for it and the endorsement of it by a governing body of directors from business, science, and labor.[27]

The study's broader social significance was also twofold. Corporate spokesmen would subsequently refer to its conclusions as evidence of modern capitalism's benign tendencies. But more important, and more immediately, *Income in the United States* represented a potent contribution to the elaboration of a technocratic critique of malproduction and to a social policy of economic growth. Taken together with the concurrent efforts of engineers to draw attention to waste as a critical factor in low productivity, it would further the formation of a managerial consensus envisioning rationalized management practices as the key to increased production.[28]

IV

"A great engineering dream has come true." So proclaimed Leon P. Alford, mechanical engineer and Taylorite, at the organization of the Federated American Engineering Societies in June 1920. "The earnest wish of many engineers to participate in public affairs," Alford observed, "to make their education, training, and experience serve society at large is on the road to realization."[29]

That this was so was due largely to Herbert Hoover. Through a series of major addresses in 1919 and 1920, Hoover had emerged as the chief spokesman for an engineering role in social reconstruction. In the process, he had achieved what Edwin Layton would later call "a remarkable synthesis of the various strands of engineering thought," so much so that he stood now, in Morris Cooke's eyes, as "the engineering method personified." It was no surprise, then, that at the initial meeting of the FAES, in November 1920, Hoover was unanimously elected its first president.[30]

Acting in line with his oft-stated conviction that low productivity stood as the chief obstacle to social stability and progress, Hoover took immediate steps to mobilize engineers for a campaign against malproduction. Having been authorized to organize a Committee on the Elimination of Waste in Industry, he turned for assistance to his chief lieutenant, Edward Eyre Hunt, who though not an engineer, was a disciple of scientific management. A member of the Harvard class of 1910 that included Walter Lippmann and John Reed, Hunt was a poet and editor, and, together with Lippmann and Reed, had been active in the Harvard Socialist Club. He had served as a war correspondent in Europe, where he had joined Hoover's Committee for the Relief of Belgium. An energetic organizer, Hunt would act as Hoover's spear-carrier throughout the construction of the New Era planning apparatus.

Envisioning the new project as the first step in what should become a "comprehensive program to reduce economic waste and increase production," Hoover and Hunt chose Taylorite revisionists, for the most part, to staff the committee. They would follow the same procedure in organizing a subsequent FAES study of the twelve-hour day in continuous industries. And in both cases, their choice of associates made it clear that they shared the revisionists' broad conception of waste as any "deficiency in production."[31]

Hoover would soon direct his program of economic rationalization from the Commerce Department, but for the time being the creation of the FAES and the inauguration of the waste survey provided him with a platform from which to hammer home his analyses and prescriptions. Thus in several addresses in late 1920 and early 1921, he elaborated not only on the dangers of lagging productivity and the need for expert analysis in policymaking, but also on the potential of America's new economic organizations for meeting modern needs without sacrificing traditional liberties. In Hoover's view, the great task was to see that this potential was realized. For in an age traumatized by war and what he deemed to be antisocial political movements, poor economic performance could unleash forces that would lead to social disintegration and new forms of tyranny.[32]

For Hoover, as for most technocratic reformers, unemployment was the chief manifestation of the existing system's irrationality, the major source of malproduction, and thus the most important waste to be eliminated. "The intermittency of employment in the ebb and flow of economic tides, the ever present industrial conflicts by strike and lockout," he declared, "produce infinite wastes and great suffering," some of which would have to be tolerated but much of which could be reduced through new machinery for bringing organized economic groups into proper relation with each other and with the system as a whole. "Successful development of our economic system," Hoover observed, depends upon "whether we can turn the aspects of these great national associations towards coordination with each other in the solution of national economic problems." If this could be done, America would not only have developed "a new economic system, based neither on the capitalism of Adam Smith nor upon the socialism of Karl Marx," it would also "have given a priceless gift to the Twentieth Century."[33]

Hoover's analysis reflected the high degree of consensus then emerging among technocratic social scientists, labor leaders, and reformers. Like Mary Van Kleeck, Hoover considered strengthened federal and state employment and statistical services as well as collective bargaining guarantees to be essential to the attack on unemployment. And, like Wesley Mitchell and Henry Dennison, Hoover was troubled by the alienation and disenfranchisement already prevalent among American workers. For not only was this a barrier to greater efficiency and production, it also posed an ongoing threat to social development and thus to the routine stability of the economy. Thus to a significant extent, Hoover shared with Van Kleeck, Dennison, and Mitchell a recognition of the need to reduce employer domination over employees; and, like them, he looked toward extensions of technocratic authority as the most promising means of fashioning the necessary restructuring of industrial relationships. His program, moreover, was not unlike that of such trade union leaders as John P. Frey and Samuel Gompers, men who had embraced the central tenets of technocratic reconstruction as the surest means of advancing a limited array of labor goals within a hostile political climate. Frey, as we have seen, was a founding force behind the National Bureau. And Gompers, in the fall of 1920, lent his public support to Hoover's campaign against economic waste. The American Federation of Labor, he declared, would help in "bringing about such relations within industry as would establish a stable and equitable basis for production and would eliminate industrial waste."[34]

Conceived as a "reconnaissance survey of a limited field," the waste study got underway in early 1921. As envisioned by Hunt and Hoover, its purpose was to generate both an analysis and a set of remedial schemes as quickly as possible. And because of this, it became not so much an extensive engineering analysis as it did a vehicle for demonstrating the potential of such an analysis. The original plan called for a survey of ten industries and of the twelve-hour day, but the latter was soon dropped and the list of industries reduced to six. In all, some eighty engineers were employed, the heart of their activities consisting of data gathering through a standard questionnaire and evaluation form. Large amounts of data were generated, but since those involved used the forms in different ways, what was labeled as waste in one area was not always labeled as such in others.[35]

Completed in June 1921, the study pointed to the mismanagement of men, materials, and labor relations as the major sources of waste. But in what became its most controversial conclusion, it also ascribed to management most of the blame for inefficiency and malproduction. This was unsurprising given the composition of the committee and the tendency of Taylorite revisionists and others subscribing to the technocratic critique to insist on managerial solutions. But it surprised and angered the executive board of the FAES, which refused to accept what it judged to be an attack on business managers. Still, Hoover's reputation and a carefully worded introduction managed to get the study into print.[36]

As a technical achievement, *Waste in Industry* did not rank with *Income in the United States*. It did, however, contribute to the store of technocratic data competence and to the growing acceptability of technocratic analysis. According to Hunt, it not only "produced definite improvement in some of the industries covered," but its influence soon spread into numerous other industries. Taken together, both studies represented the initial successes of the new technocratic institutions of 1920 and 1921, and both would be used as intellectual fodder in the coming designs for countercyclical planning. In addition, both (although this was true to a greater extent of *Income in the United States*) were generated by organizations of visionary intellectuals whose efforts to build a science capable of social reconstruction also helped to produce the modern bargain between social science and managerial capitalism.[37]

V

To assert the existence of a bargain between technocratic social science and managerial capitalism, one that would effectively harness the main thrust of social science to managerial requirements, is not to trivialize or crudely reduce to the level of conspiracy the complexity of social science's modern de-

67

velopment. Nor does it necessarily impute unworthy motives to key figures in the story. On the other hand, it would be equally mistaken to deny the role played by consciousness and by purposeful intent operating within boundaries shaped by political power and possibility.

The technocratic bargain was struck in a political climate that was overshadowed by an ascendant, if severely troubled, capitalism, a fatally damaged left, and an intimidated labor movement. Thus the key factor was not so much business power but the near absence of a confident and organized opposition to such power. For in a political environment bereft of alternatives but beholden to egalitarian and decentralist ideals, political illegitimacy is highlighted and worsens the already severe problems of "rationalizing" difficult economic relations.[38]

Within this political context, professional economics enjoyed a precarious but strategic position. The war had mobilized the profession, demonstrated the value and potential of its technical capacities, and thrust it to the brink of broad social influence. Statistical techniques, in particular, had enabled economists to impose upon reality categories of empirical description crucial to the operation of a managerial economy. And by subsidizing the development of such techniques, the war system had advanced the technocratic identity of economics, thus elevating it into the vanguard of modern social science and making it the first of the new social disciplines to challenge and attempt to throw off older deductive paradigms.[39]

In addition, the war system had seemed to resolve the long-standing tensions between aspirations to political influence and aspirations to scientific status. In doing so, it had brought the profession into alliances with policy elites, which far from compromising its claims to a disinterested scientific status, had not only enhanced its data competence, and thus its scientific basis, but had also developed for it an appreciative managerial constituency through which it might be able to build both a stronger science and a broader social influence. The war system, in other words, had offered a temporary and artificial means of reconciling impulses that had seemed mutually exclusive for over a generation. And for technocratic leaders like Wesley Mitchell and Edwin Gay this was a critical development, for it suggested that a peace-time adaptation of the system could, at one and the same time, conduct inquiries that would reveal objective reality, design reform programs informed by this new understanding, and make the decisions necessary to implement such programs. In effect, the search for an "intelligent" reform would now rely less on public education and more upon informing the decisions of managerial elites.[40]

If the war system had suggested such a possibility, however, it had also revealed just how little economists knew of contemporary economic behavior and processes. Thus it had illuminated a crisis of scientific legitimacy within economics itself, a crisis that could be overcome only through a rapid expansion of verified data, built up through empirical testing of hypotheses about the workings of the existing economic system. In the postwar political context, subsidization of this data production came to depend upon the development of institutions through which social science would help to legitimate the peacetime functioning of managerial capitalism's corporate hierarchies. Such institutions held forth the promise of both scientific legitimacy and social influence; and in the minds of technocratic leaders, progress toward a better society, a progress that could be assured only through enlightened direction, depended on the attainment of both.

In the new technocratic institutions of 1920, then, one can find the crystallization of a mutually gratifying bargain between social science professionals and managerial elites. However, it was not, in any sense of the term, a sell-out. On the contrary, the leadership of American social science was sincere in its belief that institutionalized data-building would serve not only the interests of precarious professions but those of human welfare. And it is wise to remember that the professions involved were indeed precarious. Those who have criticized social science's subsequent preoccupation with data-building as an abandonment of its normative obligations have not appreciated the enormity of the internal legitimation crisis it faced during the 1920s. Yet if there was no sell-out, one must recognize that there was a subordination of social science that stemmed from its political weakness in the face of business power. Caught within such constraints, social science data production can proceed according to scientific norms and is theoretically available to all, but it will be most effectively employed by those institutions that subsidize, legitimate, and are most effectively mobilized to use such empiricism. In the case of the United States since 1920, these have been the institutions of a managerial capitalism.[41]

CHAPTER 5

Impulses Toward Techno-Corporatist
Stabilization, 1921–1922

The worst depression in thirty years broke out late in 1920, lending fresh urgency to the search for means to stabilize the economy and fashion a steady growth. At its trough in January 1921, following the most precipitous price collapse in American history, unemployment stood at nearly 12 percent. As in the prewar period, this problem would again bring forth designs for technocratic management. Now, however, this development would proceed within the newly established machinery of the President's Unemployment Conference, the brainchild of the new commerce secretary, Herbert Hoover, and an early and important triumph for his ideas concerning national economic reconstruction.

Hoover had entered the Harding cabinet in March 1921, after being assured that he could expect to exert considerable influence in all phases of economic policy. As noted previously, he was convinced that low productivity and economic mismanagement were fundamental threats to capitalist stability and social progress. To combat these intertwined disorders, he envisioned not only far-reaching programs of waste elimination and market expansion but also the creation of countercyclical mechanisms capable of producing the data and behavior needed to control business cycles and maintain macroeconomic stability.[1]

As conceived, this countercyclical planning would be undertaken through a technocratic constituency of foundations, social science professions, and new hybrids like the NBER, a constituency that by 1921 had already developed a social critique and ambitious, if still tentative, claims to social authority. This constituency, so Hoover thought, could perform func-

71

tions that government would not or should not undertake. Yet government, specifically the Commerce Department, could assist in the development and legitimation of the new planning apparatus. What Hoover envisioned was a form of statist action that was essentially corporatist in nature, one in which the government functioned to create an arena in which private institutions would be encouraged to act in a public capacity. In this sense, the committee system that would soon emerge from the Unemployment Conference of 1921 represented a kind of techno-corporatist state undertaking functions that government agencies were either unwilling or unable to perform.[2]

The technocratic bargain between social science and capitalism, as this chapter will attempt to show, was reinforced through government sponsorship of a corporatist arena within which the bargain's critical element, data-building, could be subsidized and more closely tied to the task of informing economic decision-makers. In addition, such state sponsorship institutionalized a public role for private technocratic and capitalist institutions, thus offering public legitimation of their claims to social authority as well as providing an opportunity to demonstrate the virtue of such claims.[3]

II

The central ideas and the particular shape of the counter-cyclical machinery that developed in the early 1920s owed much to three factors. One was Hoover's political philosophy and organizational experience. A second was Wesley Mitchell's agenda for the advance of social science as reflected in the employment of the NBER. And a third was the increasing willingness of the major foundations to support the development of social science and its application to public policy.

As the chief sponsor of such machinery, Hoover contributed the most to the setting of its ideological and organizational limits. As a technocrat concerned about the dearth of social data, he was committed to research and technocratic prescription. Yet as a foe of "statism" and "politicization," he also needed active agencies grounded in the private rather than the public sector—agencies that, in his mind, would operate similarly to the National Monetary Commission, whose studies had led to the creation of the Federal Reserve System, or to the more recent waste survey. In addition, Hoover's war relief activities had brought him into close contact with the major New York foundations, yielding a recognition of their ability to provide more than just financial sustenance. Perceptions of their "disinterestedness" would also be valuable, he seemed to think, in furthering an investigation's "carrying power" with the "business public." "I am a great believer in investigations of this type as a method of clearing the decks of erroneous ideas and restarting public thought in the proper channels," he told Henry S. Pritchett, president of the Carnegie Corporation of New York. "The great quality of such investigations," he continued, "is that they should be carried out under such auspices as guarantee not only the soundness of its [sic] collections but will carry weight with the entire community."[4]

At a more fundamental level, Hoover's political philosophy, as Ellis W. Hawley has noted, was essentially dialectical. It attempted to reconcile traditional American qualities of opportunity, mobility, and decentralization with the requirements of the new business system. And for Hoover this meant commitments that could best be realized by fashioning a framework within which microeconomic decisions could be so informed as to further the attainment of broad social goals.[5]

Consequently, Hoover was opposed to outright federal control or direction of economic activity. This, he thought, would lead America down the European blind alley of deadened opportunity and initiative, malproduction, and intensified class warfare. And, convinced that America had recently developed a range of voluntary, functional organizations that could be educated to embrace a larger, national sense of responsibility, he believed that an alternative to statist planning was available. Thus a public role for these private organizations and associations was for him an appropriate middle way between the

73

twin disasters of laissez-faire and bureaucratic coercion, a way that would promote both the systematic coordination needed to ensure growth and social progress and the widened opportunities and reliance upon voluntaristic cooperation that were necessary to maintain an open society.[6]

As conceived, however, this solution would require unprecedented activism within a sharply delimited portion of the public sector. Recognizing the private association as the critical institution of social development, public power would thus be used to speed up and coordinate an organizational phenomenon that had emerged spontaneously and logically within the recent American past. In other words, government's job was that of energizing, sponsoring, and informing an unfolding historical process, one whose eventual maturation would theoretically make governmental action obsolete.[7]

The second major figure shaping these developments was Wesley Mitchell, who, as we have seen, brought to the task a faith in the potential of social science, once it was properly subsidized, to generate the data necessary to inform the construction of intelligent public policy. Mitchell was convinced that the continuing study of business cycles held the possibility not only of realizing a true social science but of moving toward a truly technocratic economics. The analysis of an economy in motion, he believed, would generate a new data competence, which in turn would enhance both the status of the economic analysts and the potential for effective economic management.

As the NBER's income study neared completion, the organization had turned naturally to the idea of business cycle investigation, for no other subject seemed to offer such wide prospects for quantitative analysis, policy prescription, and macroeconomic understanding. In addition, from its very beginnings as the Committee on the Distribution of Income, the bureau's founders had, in the words of N. I. Stone, "thought of business cycles as the second project." Now, with another slump in progress, the wisdom of this conviction seemed even more apparent. "Business Cycles," Oswald Knauth wrote to Barry Smith of the Commonwealth Fund, "seems at present the most important field for investigation in economics."[8]

The third factor helping to shape the countercyclical machinery of the early 1920s was the increasing willingness of foundations to become involved in social research and social planning. As noted previously, this development had begun before the war and had gone furthest in the Russell Sage Foundation's subsidization of social work and industrial sociology. But despite these beginnings, such foundation activity was primarily a postwar phenomenon, resulting partly, it seemed, from the postwar sense of social dislocation and partly from the war-generated optimism about social science's potential for the future. Thus even those philanthropies that had been most successful in avoiding political involvement now found such insulation difficult; and for most the lines between "human welfare" and "social reconstruction" seemed less clear than ever before.[9]

There were also more philanthropies at work as new foundations and new managers for old foundations arose to take advantage of the opportunities opened by the war. These groups sought to link philanthropy more closely to an emerging managerial culture, to support the development of social science and new technocratic institutions, and thus to make philanthropy a more effective force for the private planning of public policy. The first and most notable instance of this, which took place immediately following the war, was the critical role played by the newly formed Commonwealth Fund and the Carnegie Corporation in launching the NBER.

In subsequent initiatives, the Commonwealth Fund would continue to play an important part, but its influence, as well as that of the Sage Foundation, was soon surpassed as a result of new leadership and a concomitant reorientation within the older and larger Rockefeller and Carnegie philanthropies. This reorientation was led by a number of men, among them Henry S. Pritchett and Frederick P. Keppel, but it was Beardsley Ruml's rise as a wizard of technocratic philanthropy, first at the Carnegie Corporation and then as head of the Laura Spelman Rockefeller Memorial, that did the most to make philanthropy a critical source of support for the development of social science and technocratic authority.[10]

From a convergence of these various forces came a vision of stabilizing activity that relied fundamentally on informing the makers of microeconomic decisions with the data and thinking of technocratic social scientists, the presumption being that, once so informed, microeconomic choice could be transformed into a countercyclical tool. If they could be armed with a larger view of their place in determining the shape and intensity of business cycles, so the argument ran, businessmen would tailor their investment, production, pricing, and distribution policies in such a way that speculative booms and deep deflations would soon be relics of a less enlightened era. Similarly, an invigorated trade association movement would also be needed, primarily to help organize and disseminate needed data and to bring pressure on the "backward" and "non-cooperative," especially in the more atomistic industries. But the critical point to the proponents of this type of countercyclical thinking was that it relied not so much on the ultimate coercion of statist or institutional power as it did on a mobilized and enlightened self-interest.[11]

This was, admittedly, not the sort of activity that can be easily fitted into the usual notions of what constitutes macroeconomic planning. But taken on its own terms and within its own logic, it was just that. It was also a fitting climax to a decade that had seen technocratic analysis and managerial institutions pass the twin trials of war and its dislocations with some measure of success. Hence the elaboration of an "associative state" in the 1920s was an indirect tribute to this success, for it amounted to conferral of public legitimacy on an expanded social authority exercised by private managerial elites and by technocratic experts who insisted on the social significance and perfectability of managerial decisions.[12]

III

Upon assuming office in 1921, Hoover busied himself with departmental reorganization, the assertion of jurisdictional claims, and the development of standardization, trade expansion, and statistical programs. The latter, in particular, became a major concern, partly perhaps because the waste in industry survey had recommended the formation of a comprehensive program of economic data production.

In any event, by reconvening the recently lapsed Advisory Committee on the Census, Hoover now brought Wesley Mitchell, Edwin Gay, and Allyn Young into active consultation with interested industry leaders. This was followed, in July 1921, by the launching of the Survey of Current Business, a monthly compendium of production, inventory, and sales data supplied by cooperating trade associations. Its inauguration marked the beginning of a new era in the production of federal economic statistics.[13]

As the slump worsened, Hoover went even further and approached Harding with a plan for a government-sponsored experiment in cooperative planning, one that would draw upon the model of wartime mobilization for peacetime purposes, this time to mobilize local relief activity. But from the outset, Hoover and his allies also looked upon the Unemployment Conference as the vehicle through which microeconomic regularization and a greater data competence might become instruments of macroeconomic stabilization.[14]

From the beginning, it was Hoover's intention to dominate the conference by setting the agenda, by determining in advance the conference's conclusions and recommendations, by carefully selecting the participants, and by demanding their unanimous asset to his program. To this end he formed, on September 21, an Economic Advisory Committee that was composed, for the most part, of AALL, Taylor Society, and NBER representatives. Included were John B. Andrews, George E. Barnett, Henry Dennison, Edwin Gay, Sam Lewisohn, Otto Mallery, Samuel McCune Lindsay, Wesley Mitchell, and Leo Wolman, all of whom shared with Hoover a basic faith in the social virtues of technocratic analysis and prescription.

The committee was then charged with hammering out a program that called for the measurement of unemployment and for measures to provide immediate relief, as well as for an examination of preventative measures. But in its preconference report to Hoover, it was this latter point, and particularly the opportunity to promote employment regularization, that the committee was clearly eager to pursue. Especially promising, the report concluded, was the chance to focus public and managerial attention on business cycle control and on the way this could be furthered through continuous operation, unemployment insurance, and more knowledge and coordination of labor markets.[15]

The conference that followed was intended to amplify and promote this program. By the time it adjourned on October 13, the participants were advocating stepped-up local and voluntary relief through the organization of mayors' coordinating committees, bemoaning the lack of reliable employment statistics, urging the creation of employment bureaus, and backing such remedies as the advance planning of public works, further elimination of waste, and regularization of employment. The confluence of Hoover's views with those of his Economic Advisory Committee, particularly Mitchell and Dennison, was never more apparent than in the conference's insistence that the business cycle could be controlled. "The worldwide scope and the long succession of business crises," the committee declared, "do not prove that the problem of controlling the business cycle is a hopeless one. On the contrary, this history, when examined in detail, proves that the problem can be solved at least in part." Industrial nations, the committee's report continued, had learned valuable lessons from past misfortune, lessons that already pointed to "incontestable progress toward diminishing the violence of business crises." And in a reference that both Hoover and Mitchell would return to again and again, the report noted that "the creation of the Federal Reserve System is a notable example of American achievement in this field. That measure prevented the crisis of 1920 from degenerating into panic. Having devised a method of mitigating the severity of crises, we can with good prospects of success turn our constructive efforts to the further problem of mitigating the severity of depressions."[16]

It appears that Mitchell was the major author of the conference's call for an investigation of business cycles and unemployment. As noted previously, it was Mitchell's work on business cycles that had cut through earlier assumptions of "normality" to reveal the intricate undulations of an organized money economy in pursuit of profit. Each phase of the cycle, Mitchell had argued, spurred its successor. Thus prosperity carried within it the germs of depression, notably in the form of costs rising against prices, strained credit resources, over-expansion, and speculation. For Mitchell, the key to preventing precipitous declines lay in first preventing the "feverish extremes" of prosperity, a notion that was now embodied in the conference report, one that would inform the subsequent Business Cycle Committee's whole approach to the issue. "It is the wastes, the miscalculations and the maladjustments grown rampant during booms that make inevitable the painful process of liquidation," the report noted. Hence, "the best time to act" was "at a fairly early stage in the growth of the boom."[17]

Hoover was pleased with the conference, judging it at least a partial advance and vindication of his reconstruction program. Thus before its adjournment he took steps to institutionalize the technocratic authority he had helped to invoke by creating a standing committee to oversee the implementation of the conference's recommendations. One of the standing committee's first acts was to authorize Hoover, its chairman, to appoint subcommittees for this purpose, beginning with the Committee on Unemployment and the Business Cycle. To a considerable degree, this initial committee was also the most important, for in conceptual and organizational terms it set the precedents for the subsequent elaboration of New Era planning.[18]

As in the case of the earlier waste survey, Hoover envisioned the inquiry to be undertaken by the business cycle committee not as "an isolated project, but [as] part of a comprehensive program to reduce economic waste and increase production." And he had several particular goals in mind. First, he wanted a "careful technical investigation" that could generate a much-needed mass of useful economic data. As Edgar Rickard, Hoover's liaison with the New York foundations put it, "Mr. Hoover and the Administration in general [are] very much handicapped . . . by the entire absence of facts with which to refute or support the exaggerated statements of the contending interests."[19]

Hoover wanted, in addition, to ensure that the committee and its findings carried "weight" with the managerial public. Consequently, he was adamant that the project neither be "dominated by pedantic economics" nor funded by the government. "It is extremely critical," Hoover wrote to Rickard on November 14, "that the matter should be carried out as a private undertaking under the guidance of . . . leading manufacturing and industrial leaders." Thus, even if congressional funding was available, Hoover believed it should be avoided. In his view, it would only detract from the committee's repute and influence.

Also involved in Hoover's considerations, and probably of greatest importance, was his desire "to eliminate from the American mind, if possible, a number of hallucinations transported from Europe." There was, he explained, "a great undercurrent of demand for governmental action in the matter of unemployment of the type of European countries." However, in his opinion, "a careful investigation" would "demonstrate that such methods are not applicable nor desirable to American life." In addition, he hoped that such an investigation would identify and promote an American alternative based on "some of the sound business and financial plans gradually emerging from American industry and the handling of public works."[20]

There seems little doubt that these goals and concerns guided Hoover's choice of committee members. As chairman, he secured the services of Owen D. Young of General Electric, a man who had served with him on Wilson's Second Industrial Conference and who was regarded as the prototypical enlightened industrialist. Other committee members were Clarence Mott Woolley of the American Radiator Corporation, Joseph

H. Defrees of the U.S. Chamber of Commerce, Matthew Woll of the American Federation of Labor, and Mary Van Kleeck of the Sage Foundation. And as committee secretary, Hoover installed E. E. Hunt, rounding off a group that clearly subscribed, at least for the time being, to Hoover's general outlook and strategy.[21]

While his aides worked the foundations, Hoover approached Gay and Mitchell in hopes of recruiting the NBER to perform the technical study. He had come by this time to hold both men in high regard, and Mitchell in particular had impressed him as the economist most qualified to help transform the Commerce Department into the nation's "economic interpreter." In July he had tried to recruit Mitchell as an economic advisor, stressing in his plea the numerous foreign and domestic matters "in which this department must give some voice" and arguing that he was much in need of the assurance that could come from sound economic analysis. "I feel," he had declared, "that you are the one man in the country who could adequately take care of this job." Although Mitchell had respectfully declined this offer, he was now amenable to Hoover's request that he "think out a method by which the prestige of the Unemployment Conference, the business judgment of large employers, and the technical equipment of the National Bureau" might be combined to give an investigation of business cycles and unemployment "maximum effectiveness."[22]

Given the bureau's own impending program of business cycle research, Mitchell thought Hoover's suggestion of cooperation "eminently wise." He was also plainly enthusiastic about the prospect, submitting to Hoover a preliminary plan of cooperation "without waiting to secure the formal approval of our Executive Committee," and expressing his willingness to put his staff at the disposal of Hoover's committee without charge. "Such an undertaking," he noted, "would mean to the Bureau no more than a change in the time-sequence of studies," which would be made in any event.[23]

Some of this enthusiasm may have been due to the prospects

for new funding that Mitchell saw in the undertaking. As of 1921, the bureau was having great difficulty raising enough money to secure matching grants from the Carnegie Corporation and the Commonwealth Fund, since those approached were reluctant to lend support "in advance of any actual publication." Thus it must have been with some relief that Mitchell and Gay greeted an alliance that would ensure additional funding for projects the bureau had intended to pursue anyway, funding that would necessitate, moreover, an enlarged staff and facilities. "To do a workmanlike job for the Standing Committee," Mitchell stressed, the bureau would need to add "an investigator competent to handle the engineering aspects of certain proposals for the mitigation of unemployment"; "consulting experts on legislative procedure and municipal administration"; "research assistants, stenographers, and computors"; and more office space and funds for traveling expenses.[24]

As eager as he was for an alliance with the business cycle committee, Mitchell also understood the benefits his organization could confer upon Hoover's project, and he was careful to bring these to Hoover's attention. "As a going concern with a staff of investigators already familiar with the problem of business cycles and the technique of statistical investigation," he noted, "we should be able to accomplish more satisfactory results in a brief time and at less expense than could be accomplished by a new and temporary organization." In addition, and of far greater importance in Mitchell's opinion, was the "carrying power" guaranteed by the bureau's novel structure. "We believe," he wrote, "that the character of the Board would prove a valuable asset in getting the results scrutinized by men of varied training, experience, and opinions, and also in getting the results accepted by the general public as impartial." The bureau, in other words, could offer the potent legitimation of "scientific disinterestedness" for the corporatist planning Hoover envisioned. While "debarred from making propaganda for any policy," it could provide "a well-organized and clearly stated report" that would go "a long way toward securing agreement upon the question of what ought to be done." And, as Mitchell put it, "by working in close touch with the . . . subcommittee, the Bureau would try to put its report in such form as would meet the needs of the body charged with formulating policies."[25]

At first, Mitchell and Hoover agreed that $25,000 would be sufficient to fund the committee's investigation, but the estimate was soon raised to $50,000, and this was the amount that Hoover requested from the foundations with whom Rickard had been doing advance work. By November, the Russell Sage, Carnegie, and Commonwealth organizations had all been approached, and Rickard had met personally with representatives of the latter two. From R. A. Franks of the Carnegie Corporation, who had been a personal assistant to Andrew Carnegie and was now on the corporation's executive committee, he had received strong encouragement. But from Barry Smith and Max Farrand of Commonwealth, there had been a less positive reaction. While each was personally sold, they cautioned that their trustees were not. Smith explained "that his Directors have not been too pleased with the results obtained by Mitchell's Committee." Moreover, he continued, they had little confidence in Hoover's plan for indicative stabilization. "They blankly state," Rickard recounted, "that even though our industries are advised as to the reasons for business depressions and are given the remedies that they will act on their own initiative which is chiefly that of getting ahead of their competitors."[26]

Hoover told Rickard to impress upon his Commonwealth contacts that influential businessmen, not economists, would dominate the committee. But aside from this, he ignored Commonwealth, preferring instead to concentrate on Carnegie, which had already demonstrated its technocratic sympathies by promising in May 1921 to underwrite the National Bureau for three years. Thus he asked Owen Young "to take the matter up with some of our friends"; and he himself approached Elihu Root, Carnegie's lawyer and advisor, and Henry Pritchett, the Carnegie Corporation's acting president. Both men were receptive, despite the already heavy obligations facing the corporation, and Hunt soon forwarded a formal request to Pritchett, one that generated a clarifying correspondence.[27]

Hunt explained that a Carnegie grant would "make effective a much larger sum of money than that directly expended" because the National Bureau and the Russell Sage Foundation had promised to donate their staff and facilities without charge, and because the Bureau of Railway Economics, the Harvard Committee on Economic Research, the New School for Social Research, and the Pennsylvania State Industrial Board had all promised their cooperation. In addition, Hunt's memorandum stressed the importance of the business cycle study as the third leg of a "comprehensive program to reduce economic waste and to increase production," a program "being carried forward by the cordial cooperation of several agencies, public and private." Hunt was convinced, so he told Pritchett, that the results already achieved in the program's two other legs, waste elimination and market expansion (particularly the speed with which the waste in industry study had been executed and its recommendations spread) justified support for the new venture. "It is the promptness and definiteness of past achievements, the eagerness with which the public has reached out for authoritative information presented under the auspices of impartial bodies, and the prospect of future cooperation from these bodies," Hunt concluded, that made it likely that a brief and intense investigation of business cycles could develop "a basis for wise practical action."[28]

But just as Malcolm Rorty's proposed alliance with the United Americans in 1919 prompted a restatement and clarification of the importance of "disinterestedness" to the success of the National Bureau, so too did Pritchett's reply elicit a similar clarification. However, this time it was the indispensability of both technical and philanthropic disinterestedness to the legitimacy of corporatist planning that was at issue. "There is one question," Pritchett wrote, "which the Trustees will perhaps ask me and which I do not find covered in your memorandum. That is, whether such expense as you indicate ought not to be paid for from the funds of the general government rather than from funds provided through individuals or charitable foundations." "We believe it is all important," Hunt replied on December 29 after conferring with Hoover, "that the study . . . be technically first-class, and that it be presented to the business public under the auspices of a disinterested group which will carry weight." Even if a government appropriation could be secured, Hunt continued, an investigation under state auspices "would have to be done under the burdensome conditions of routine Government work, with a personnel paid the salaries set by the Government." If this were the case, the study's quality would be jeopardized. And because "the presentation of the results, when obtained, would be under Government auspices," their stature would be reduced "at the moment they might be most effective in shaping business decisions." "If, as we believe," he wrote to Pritchett on January 25, 1922, "we are entering upon a fairly long period of declining prices and severe economic competition, the business public will be eager for such information . . . long after the usual period when improving business conditions divert public attention from these recurring hazards."[29]

IV

On February 9, 1922, with the Carnegie Corporation's grant of $50,000 to the business cycle committee, the three legs of Hooverian countercyclical planning were in place, and the focus now turned to organizing the committee's technical investigation. At issue in the negotiations that followed was the need to protect the National Bureau's scientific reputation while allowing the business cycle committee to have access to the resulting material. It was with both these goals in mind that Mitchell drew up a plan of investigation that the committee considered and approved at its first meeting. This took place in Washington on February 20.

Under the plan, Mitchell envisioned a three-part study. Part

85

I, a diagnosis of unemployment, would examine the sources, merits, and deficiencies of currently available employment statistics; the types of unemployment, with an eye to distinguishing those that resulted from the business cycle; the nature and extent of underemployment; and the accuracy of payroll statistics as an index of unemployment. Part II, the relationship of unemployment to the business cycle, would attempt a definition of cycles and their social costs. And Part III, a survey of proposed methods of preventing cyclical unemployment, would examine remedial proposals then current, including the long-range planning of construction and public works; the expansion of production stabilization programs; the various schemes of public, private, and trade-union unemployment insurance; and the possibility of improving the nation's system of employment offices and exchanges, business and government statistical services, and financial controls.[30]

As secretary to the committee, E. E. Hunt had circulated Mitchell's plan for criticism and comment prior to the February 20 meeting. In his view, it was "a fine outline from the point of view of pure research," but it lacked, so he told Owen D. Young, "the sort of pointing up which is a necessary spur to action." He recognized, of course, that the technical work was only a prelude to committee findings that would do such "pointing up." But still, his remark clearly revealed Hoover's conception of the committee's mission. For to Hoover, carefully executed technical investigation was desired, not so much for its own sake, but rather to strengthen the "carrying power" that would serve as the instrumentality for economic rationalization.

Hunt was also anxious that the committee quickly generate "a definite statement in simple terms of what the American businessman can do and what Governmental departments can do," lest the constructive momentum stemming from the unemployment conference dissipate. The point, he told Young, "is for continuing public education while the study is on. In a certain sense I feel less interest in the final report than in the progress reports and summaries which can be put out while the study is on."[31]

Developments in Congress probably added to Hunt's uneasiness about a loss of momentum. There the Kenyon Bill, a modest attempt to nudge the federal government toward a countercyclical public works program, was dying in the Senate. Originally introduced in 1919 by Senator William S. Kenyon of Iowa, the bill now had the support of Hoover's publicity apparatus. In a Commerce Department press release, Hunt had praised the measure, arguing that "if we can get the people of the nation into the habit of long-range planning of public works," then "we shall have established an important factor in any permanent program for combatting unemployment." In similar statements, Otto Mallery, a leading advocate of public works planning who had served as secretary of the unemployment conference's public works committee, described the potential latent in Kenyon's bill as "a force of the first magnitude," capable of making any "recurrence of such a period of waste and suffering as the present forever impossible." But despite this support it was clear by February that the bill was going nowhere. Notwithstanding its broad-based and essentially "harmless" nature, as Robert Littell described it in *The New Republic*, those senators who were not merely bored by the issue opposed its provisions for federal forecasting of business conditions as being a Hooverian power grab and an invitation to an economic scare. "I would rather postpone a panic until the time when God brings it," Senator Norris opined, "than to have Hoover entrusted with this power, and get the panic a year sooner. . . . We had better let God run it as in the past, and not take the power away from him and give it to Hoover."[32]

While arguing the need for "continuing public education," Hunt was also arranging for a preliminary survey of the methods currently being used to moderate the effects of cyclical fluctuations. Mitchell drew up a short questionnaire on the matter, and this was then circulated through a committee of the National Conference of Business Paper Editors headed by

Frederick Feiker of McGraw-Hill, the theory being that this group was in the best position to canvass quickly what the nation's businessmen were doing.

With this canvass underway, Hunt then turned to the business of implementing Mitchell's plan of study, and by early March nineteen investigators had been assigned to seventeen separate topics. Each substudy was to be completed by August, with the whole of the technical report ready for submission to the business cycle committee on or before August 20.[33]

On April 13 the committee again convened in Washington, meeting this time with business representatives in order to publicize its progressive and lay the groundwork for implementing its recommendations. Feiker's canvass had already turned up "a considerable number" of countercyclical schemes then being practiced by American firms, and the idea now, as Hunt and Mitchell saw it, was to build on these early results. Specifically, they hoped to bring together "representatives of trade associations to discuss with them the value of the study to their members, how best to popularize its results through the associations, and how we can obtain from the associations 'leads' as to stabilization of production and long-range planning of construction work." In opening the meeting, Hoover noted that employment regularization, whether through the planning afforded by statistical forecasting or through the balance wheel of public works, was "a subject which had been under discussion for twenty-five years" yet was still one that had "never been exhaustively examined." The business cycle committee, he said, "comprising as it does, some of the leading businessmen of the United States," was in itself a warranty of the seriousness of the question and the feeling on the part of the men who have dealt largely with industry that there may be some solution found that would be workable." Mitchell then followed Hoover and noted that the National Bureau's role was to develop the data that would make it possible for managers to reduce the waste and speculation characteristic of a boom's peak and thus prevent subsequent deflation. "Our concern is not with the best methods of mitigating the suffering which widespread unemployment causes after it is started," Mitchell pointed out, "but with the gathering of facts which throw light upon the possibility of preventing such periods from recurring in the future with the rough periodicity that they have in the past."[34]

As the technical studies neared completion, the Commerce Department's publicity apparatus was also gearing up to promote what Hoover in private conversations was calling "the most important economic investigation ever undertaken in this country." Newspaper stories, editorials, and feature articles in trade and technical journals were evidence, according to Hunt, of "a considerable amount of public attention." In preparation for the publicity that was to surround the committee's receipt of the study, and the beginnings of its deliberations over policy recommendations, Hunt requested suggestions from a number of those who were closely involved.

Wesley Mitchell, as he would do throughout the next several months, laid stress on the areas in which the technical investigations had yielded new and important data. Of particular significance in this regard, he thought, were the studies of the nature and scope of unemployment written by Willford I. King of the National Bureau, W. A. Berridge of Brown University, and Paul Brissenden of Columbia University. He then went on to outline four general kinds of remedies indicated by the studies. First, he said, were those that could be adopted by individual enterprises, among which were the various regularization procedures outlined in the reports of N. I. Stone on the stabilization of production in textiles, Sanford Thompson on the stabilization of both production and distribution across several industries, and Ernest Bradford on stabilization in the building trades. Second, came an overlapping set of proposals—drawing again on the work of Thompson and Bradford, but also on that of Julius Parmelee—that emphasized the possibilities for industry-wide stabilization through trade associations. Third, were the remedies requiring new legislation, among which were controversial proposals for monetary and banking reform, advance planning of public works, a new system of public employment offices, and various forms of unemployment insurance. And fourth, were upgraded statistical services. In Mitchell's view, Mary Van Kleeck's and Oswald Knauth's studies of business and employment statistics had made plain the extent of the deficiencies in this field. These deficiencies, he felt, would have to be corrected before progress could be made with any other kind of remedy.[35]

Stuart Rice of Columbia University and Otto Mallery also responded with a mix of general and specific suggestions, many of them drawn from their respective reports on the social effects of unemployment and the potential of public works planning. But John B. Andrews, secretary of the AALL and a member of the standing committee, made clear the limitations of the unemployment conference and the skepticism with which its work and that of the business cycle committee had come to be viewed by influential members of the reform community. The AALL, he reminded Hunt, had gone along with "the emergency program" because it "had been promised a continuing committee which would take up the long-range problem" of prevention. It had hoped that this would lead to a "straight-out, constructive, far-reaching program," one that, in his "cool judgement as a result of more than a dozen years of very intensive work," meant "the establishment by legislation of some kind of unemployment compensation which will place the financial burden upon the business managers and thereby keep them thinking about this problem" in good times as well as bad. But in Andrews' view it was now doubtful, given the composition and largely antistatist views of Hoover's business cycle committee, that the opportunity to advance such a program would be taken. As it turned out, Andrews had good reason to be concerned.[36]

CHAPTER 6

The Business Cycle Report and Its Aftermath, 1922–1923

By the summer of 1922, significant steps had been taken to institutionalize the public authority of technocratic and business planners. Their ability to fashion an enlightened managerialism, so the argument ran, would be instrumental in generating steady productivity and higher living standards. Thus part of the business cycle committee's job, as Hoover saw it, was to disabuse Americans of any lingering fascination with statist proposals. But as the committee members met to draft their recommendations in the late summer and fall of 1922, their deliberations were punctuated by serious divisions over this question, by institutional rivalries that threatened the project's claims to technocratic "disinterestedness," and by accompanying episodes of subterfuge and pettiness. It was only with considerable difficulty that these differences would be surmounted so that the resulting action could become another affirmation of the potential for indicative planning within a corporatist arena dominated by allegedly enlightened business managers.

At its first meeting from August 7 through 9, the committee seemed to feel inundated by the technical reports. The chairman, Owen Young, "did not believe the Committee was going to get anywhere by reading the vast amount of material." He doubted, moreover, that it should rush into print with a set of recommendations without first sounding out business and labor groups. For even if the committee's recommendations constituted a program potentially capable of preventing depressions, Young feared that such a program would not amount to much without some preliminary education of "the people who are effective in putting it into operation." In other words, there would have to be a "scheme" for involving labor, financial, and trade groups in the committee's deliberations, thus setting the state for a more effective translation of committee recommendations into business practice.

The need to fashion some kind of mechanism along these lines was important, Young concluded, because "our difficulty is overcoming inertia." Consequently, the committee forwarded to Hoover a proposal under which the drafting of a program would be delayed until relevant groups could express their opinions on the practical application of the regularization schemes discussed in the technical reports. Hoover thought this a fine idea. As a result, the recommendations were postponed and a referendum was undertaken by Hunt.

When Hunt approached trade association executives and trade press editors for help in organizing the referendum, he discovered that most felt no single set of questions could adequately cover the range of industries to be surveyed. Consequently, while Hunt's preliminary canvass turned up much informal and apparently positive reaction to the committee's work, it did not lead to the type of referendum he had originally envisioned. However, instead of waiting on such a survey, the committee eventually decided to go ahead with the report and ask for responses to it. Accordingly, Elliott Goodwin of the U.S. Chamber of Commerce helped Hunt to prepare an instrument for securing these responses, constructing it so as to try to stimulate debate on regularization strategies.[1]

While working along these lines, Hunt was also busy drafting preliminary proposals to be considered at the committee's October meeting. To this task, he brought a basic allegiance to Hoover's combination of antistatism and activist promotion of public roles for private groups. Like Hoover, he could support such measures as the Kenyon Bill while opposing "statist" insurance schemes or the use of government power to implement employment plans. On this he differed from J. B. Andrews or committee member Mary Van Kleeck, both of whom saw a degree of federal coercion as being necessary to correct imbalances and injustices, and also from Wesley Mitchell, who

92

wanted the committee to endorse the desirability of public as well as private insurance schemes. Hunt's only differences from Hoover, as it appears from what evidence is available, were in his willingness to consider state insurance as a topic worthy of future deliberation and in his support for a federal public works fund.[2]

As he wrote his preliminary draft of recommendations, Hunt must also have been aware that all committee members were in general agreement with the Mitchell thesis, namely that cyclical extremes could be controlled and that the best chance for such control lay in preventing the waste and speculation characteristic of the boom's peak. On this and on the fundamental importance of microeconomic decisions, they tended to be of one mind. But on such issues as a public works reserve and the appropriate role for the Federal Reserve System, they were less so. And on the issue of unemployment insurance, as their meeting at Chicago's South Shore Country Club on October 2 and 3 would make clear, there were serious divisions.[3]

Before the meeting, Hunt's tentative draft of recommendations was circulated among the committee. Having read it, Stuart M. Crocker, Young's General Electric assistant, proceeded to forward a copy to Wallace Donham, Dean of the Harvard Business School. Crocker, it seems, thought Harvard, his alma mater, should have a larger role in the operation. By September he had struck up an alliance with Donham designed to further this objective and also, it would appear, to protect Young's reputation from being tarnished by his association with a committee whose recommendations might embrace dangerous forms of statism. This alliance would continue, quietly and unknown to most of the committee, throughout the duration of the project, and it would soon involve the Harvard Bureau of Business Research in rivalry and friction with the National Bureau of Economic Research.[4]

Donham thought little of Hunt's draft recommendations or of the NBER-sponsored studies upon which they were based. As Crocker wrote to Hunt in September, Donham, "had noticed we were retaining Wesley Mitchell as one of our experts and wondered whether we had consulted Professor [Charles J.] Bullock," the chairman of the Harvard Bureau of Business Research. "It was Dean Donham's opinion," Crocker continued, "that Professor Bullock is the best authority in the United States" on business cycles.

Donham's views were also clear in a ten-page memorandum written for Young. "This material in its present form," he wrote, "is material which I do not believe you should make yourself responsible for." The technical studies, he thought, were weak and unscientific, consisting of little more than "a succession of magazine articles written (1) by economists who write from the economic standpoint in such form as to make the material of little value to the businessman, or, (2) by businessmen and engineers who know nothing of economics." The report, on the whole, he continued, was "superficial," "inconsistent," "incoherent," "tinged with propaganda, particularly along the lines of compulsory state insurance," "almost entirely free from a factual basis for a research foundation," and "frequently unsound." Furthermore, he intimated that Mitchell should bear much of the responsibility for these shortcomings. "Many of these defects," he declared, "could have been cured by editorial supervision," although no amount of this could have made "the job anything other than an extremely superficial one."[5]

In addition, Donham wanted Young to understand the relevance and quality of Harvard's work in this area. He had, he said, given "Mr. Crocker some of our own plans for research with the idea of indicating some ways in which the problems might be approached." And finally, he emphasized not only how Young's "authority and position" might give "unsound conclusions . . . unsupported by research an improper emphasis" but also the need for Young to be particularly careful to dissociate himself from any advocacy of government intervention through public works reserves, unemployment insurance, or statistical production.[6]

It is somewhat difficult today to understand the intensity of these arguments, particularly since Hunt, Hoover, Mitchell,

94

and Donham were all emphatic in their belief that managerial prerogatives must be maintained and that improved economic intelligence would benefit not only the individual manager but the cause of cyclical stabilization. Donham, it would appear, was upset with what he may have regarded as the National Bureau's arrogance in taking on such a large subject in a six-month study, and with Mitchell's insistence that the resulting research had broken new ground. And beyond this, he seems to have genuinely believed that any government intervention, even in the form of adjusting the expenditure of existing appropriations to the rhythms of the business cycle, would lead to socialism, regardless of whose auspices it was invoked under. With so much at stake, he apparently felt that his critique had to be stern and thorough.[7]

These objections would surface in muted tones in Young's direction of the Chicago meeting. The chairman, echoing Donham, began by asking Mitchell whether the bureau's studies were not really a series of articles expressing each author's views. "Inevitably," replied Mitchell. But he went on to note that not only had the bureau articles "contributed very substantial new facts," but that taken together they constituted "the fullest attempt ever made" to understand how the business cycle might be controlled.[8]

That Young did not accept all of Donham's strictures was equally evident. On the issue of a public works reserve fund, for example, he remained supportive despite the possibility that "we will all be accused of being Socialists as a result of it." He then raised the issue of unemployment benefits, wondering whether they were even a proper subject for the committee's consideration. In this, he was reinforced by Joseph Defrees and Matthew Woll. However, Mitchell spoke up in defense of unemployment benefits, arguing that they "had a very definite relation to the whole question" of unemployment and the business cycle. "Providing you can make an unemployment benefit scheme work," he explained, "it is one of the distinguished important possible remedies for the business depression . . . for, of course, one of the difficulties in business depression is that retail trade is restricted by people who are forced to cut down on their purchases."

On this subject, Mary Van Kleeck provided further arguments that went beyond Mitchell's concerns with mitigating the severity of deflation. As she had been doing for more than a decade, she again proclaimed that the value of unemployment insurance lay in the incentives it provided for the regularization of investment and production. "Where are you going to get the punch for advance planning," she asked, without such programs? "Businessmen should look after the problem of unemployment in advance to get ready for the depression."[9]

Following further discussion, the committee decided to have Hunt revise the recommendations. In doing so, he was to note, in particular, the antisocial effects of wasteful competition at the peak of the boom. And it was agreed that he would enlist the aid of Sprague of Harvard in drafting the committee's banking recommendations.

Crocker thought the Chicago meeting a great success. "Mr. Young," he reported to Donham, "was exceedingly pleased" to be forearmed with Donham's memorandum. And Donham, he knew, would be "much interested" in seeing the revised recommendations when they were "finally written up by Mr. Hunt." "The amusing part of it," he continued, was that Young had done "just exactly what I thought he would do." He had told Hunt that "one of the reasons why he had changed his views on certain subjects and desired that they should be changed accordingly in the recommendations" was because of suggestions made by Crocker, a statement that had caused Hunt to take notice and thereafter show him "proper respect." "Nothing," he added, "was said to indicate where the information really came from."

Subsequently, Crocker also made it clear that he intended not only to protect Young's interests but to advance those of the Harvard Bureau of Business Research. Upon learning of Hunt's plans to visit the business school, he wrote to Donham emphasizing "that Mr. Hunt knows nothing of my trip to Cambridge and conferences with you and your associates." And in a bid to strengthen his position, he arranged another trip and a series of meetings at the business school both for himself and for Mary Van Kleeck.

Apparently, Van Kleeck had her own reasons for visiting Harvard. There is no evidence that she knew of or was taking part in the Donham-Crocker collaboration. But still, Crocker would subsequently report that "Miss Van Kleeck was very much impressed with the work that was being done at Harvard—so much so that it is not much of an effort on my part to see that very proper recognition is made throughout the report of the work that is being done in Cambridge."[10]

By late December, few were happy with the state of the business cycle committee's recommendations. Hunt, to be sure, had made revisions in the earlier draft, and these had been circulated. But there was no unanimity among those who commented on them. On one side, such men as Harlow Person, Morris Cooke, Leon P. Alford, and John Commons believed that Hunt was now on the mark, particularly in his insistence that the businessman, while ultimately "responsible for the exaggeration of the boom," acted "primarily as a link in an endless chain" and was "almost inevitably forced to unsocial action." Profits, Hunt had pointed out, were not the only factors determining business judgment. The businessman wanted "above everything else to maintain his relative position in his industry"; and while he was "not anxious to run up inventories or to take the risks of plant expansion and other investments at inflated prices," the alternative often appeared to be a sacrifice of "what he believes to be his place in the trade." It was a dilemma "inherent in our competitive system," and this meant, in Hunt's view, that "cooperation rather than competition" was "the only way to meet this difficulty and so to hold down the peak of the boom." Competition, he concluded, while normal and healthy at most times, could become antisocial at a certain point in the movement of the business cycle. When it did so, "society" must consider the problem of curbing it.[11]

On the other side, Edwin Gay and Charles Bullock took

97

issue with this whole line of argument. Bullock thought its premises incorrect, while Gay pointed to the experiences of businessmen like Dennison as an example of the extent to which managers were "not under any compulsion of an iron law to expand unduly when everyone else expands unduly." Gay thought, too, that Hunt's emphasis on social control was dangerously open-ended and failed to take into account "the limited degree of cooperation which is now possible" without statist intervention. Was there, demanded Gay, to be enlightened trade association action, guided by "a better diffusion of fuller statistics?" Or was the committee suggesting something beyond this? Did it "envisage a new economic order something on the plan of Guild Socialism?"

Both Donham and O.M.W. Sprague were also adamantly opposed to the Hunt draft. Not only did Donham take issue, as Bullock and Gay had, with the premise that businessmen were trapped in a competitive vise, he was also, and predictably, very upset with what he interpreted to be the draft's continued advocacy of government intervention. "Fundamentally," he wrote to Crocker, "I am personally so far at variance with the emphasis and the reasoning of the memorandum that I think it is both unsound and particularly dangerous. . . . If I were Mr. Young, I should not wish to be connected with the statement in its present form."[12]

Faced with this schism among the economists, a chastened Young began considering its potential impact on both the referendum and on other forms of group consultation upon which implementation of the report would depend. It was necessary, he argued in early November, to see if some consensus among economic experts could not be reached. These, after all, were the people that trade, labor, and financial groups would "necessarily consult before starting active work"; and if they should "state that the report in certain phases is not right, this might discourage action by these groups of men whom we hope to get to work on these problems of national importance." In addition, Young went on to suggest that in light of Hunt's recent appointment as secretary of the United States Coal

Commission, it might be best for Crocker to take over the job of discussing the committee's recommendations with the economists.

Hunt thought Young's suggestions worthwhile, confessing his own dissatisfaction with the present state of the committee's proposals. He also expressed his admiration for the value of the criticism already received from various economists, including those at Harvard. Thus, with his acquiescence, Crocker moved to seize the opportunity and develop a larger role for Harvard and its Bureau of Business Research. The way was now open, he felt, for a "different approach," and it was time, so he wrote to Van Kleeck on November 24, "to tell Mr. Hunt what we are doing."[13]

Van Kleeck's reasons for supporting Crocker's moves are not very clear. Apparently, she had been genuinely impressed by the quality of the personnel and work at Harvard, by its early commitment to field work, and by its long-standing studies of cyclical behavior. Also important, to her mind, was Harvard's emphasis on practical application and service to the businessman through its consulting arm, the Harvard Economic Service. This was precisely the orientation Van Kleeck was trying to bring to the Industrial Studies Division of the Russell Sage Foundation, and in the area that most concerned her, statistical production and application, the Harvard Bureau seemed to have found an effective and workable method. Under Donham, it has supported government collection of statistics but had argued that interpretation was more properly left to a nonpolitical body standing between the state and the individual businessman. It was an approach quite similar to Van Kleeck's own vision, in which apolitical social data would be applied in scientifically informed field work.[14]

In any event, Van Kleeck now collaborated with Crocker in drawing up a new draft of recommendations, one in which the work at Harvard was given a prominent place. But, perhaps reflecting Van Kleeck's senior role in the partnership, it also emphasized the sort of expanded government responsibility for data collection, coordination among departments, and statistical leadership that she had been advocating for some time. There is no record that Donham ever saw the draft, but one can only wonder at his response.

It was now Hunt's turn to raise the specter of statism. "This particular draft," he wrote to Crocker, "throws its main emphasis on governmental action, discusses this action in highly technical terms of administrative detail, and leaves me with the feeling that I, as a businessman, can pass the buck to the government because, until the government feeds me with a lot of statistics, there is little that I can do." He realized, he said, that this was what Crocker had intended. But, he protested, "there is absolutely nothing in this for the businessman to do." Moreover, there was little or nothing in the draft on the regularization programs already developed by individual firms, on the countercyclical value of unemployment reserves, or on the need to avoid speculative behavior—all of which had been explored in the NBER and the waste in industry studies, and all of which had been demonstrated as practical by such businessmen as Henry Dennison.

In addition, and perhaps of greatest importance, Hunt saw the Crocker-Van Kleeck memorandum as a threat to the fragile technocratic authority of the business cycle committee, and hence to the "weight" and "carrying power" of its findings. In effect, he argued, it had rejected the work of a research body whose governing structures guaranteed its "impartiality," and had substituted for this the work of an agency lacking such guarantees and openly offering itself as a "commercial service" for hire. "I think it unwise," he wrote, "to harp on a single group such as the Harvard group in the way that you have." Not only would this hurt the committee's prospects for attaining the general approval of the economics profession; it would also confront the committee with a mass of new material to consider, thus substantially delaying its progress. And even if that material was to be supplemented with other work, Hunt continued, it would "lay the Committee open to the charge of bias or carelessness or both." He realized, he added, that Crocker was in favor of "the complete separation of the Mitchell report from the Committee's recommendations." But, as he saw it, the project had always been envisioned as one comprising two distinct halves—first, the technical report, and second, the committee's proposals. "A skillfully phrased disclaimer," he insisted, was all that the committee would need to make clear that it was not responsible for the various views of the authors of the National Bureau reports.[15]

As this correspondence was taking place, Crocker was also arranging for the promised meeting between the committee and the economists. This was scheduled for the annual convention of the American Economic Association, which was to be held in Chicago in December. At this meeting, both Hunt and Van Kleeck would make clear that while they might disagree over the benefits and dangers inherent in the committee's collaboration with the Harvard Bureau, they still shared a belief in the importance of "scientific" and "impartial" research agencies to the development of countercyclical planning.

II

The scheduled meeting, convened on December 28, revealed wide support among economists for the committee's purpose and for its emphasis on microeconomic regularization as the key to macroeconomic stabilization. What debate there was arose over the importance of financial tools as a method of cyclical control, the one area the committee had chosen to skirt.

In opening the meeting, Hunt sketched the committee's brief history, its modest accomplishments, and its latent potential as the beginning of a larger program of indicative planning. "Now that the study is made," he said, "no one feels anything but a scientific skepticism about the whole subject." Yet the conviction had grown "that the extremes of the business cycle can be controlled; that there are relationships in this field which are now beginning to be clearer than they were a few years back; and that, above all, the responsibility for action can be designated and a rough outline of formal action which is probably desirable can be indicated." Mr. Hoover, Hunt informed his audience, "feels that this particular investigation is one of the most important, if not the most important, investigation that has been undertaken in this country."[16]

Speaking after Hunt, the self-effacing Wesley Mitchell described how NBER investigators had undertaken "to do an alleged piece of scientific investigation under conditions which made it impossible to satisfy themselves." And in an oblique bow to Van Kleeck, Mitchell noted that the "member of the Business Cycle Committee who has had experience in carrying on investigations gave more vigorous expression to the feeling which they had all had about the undesirability of trying to get a fair basis for wide social policies in a hurry." The job would have been impossible, Mitchell concluded, had it not been for the generous cooperation of individuals and organizations who came together under the NBER's umbrella. He then went on to outline the contents of the report's three parts, reiterating, in particular, his conviction that although far from exhaustive, the NBER studies marked a significant advance in what was known about the subject.[17]

Mary Van Kleeck then took the opportunity to remind the audience that unemployment was the committee's fundamental concern and that its interest in business cycle control stemmed from its determination to mitigate the unemployment problem. The committee's job, she said, was "to peer in through the windows of the laboratories of the economists" in order to better inform its function as a "connecting link" between economic research and the business community. In other words, its object was not to push a program of its own, but to "get the subject into manageable shape for consideration by a much wider group than has considered it before."

Unlike Mitchell, however, Van Kleeck did not think the National Bureau studies had broken new ground. "The Committee does not feel that as a committee it has been able to add to the knowledge of the subject," she noted, "but it does feel that it is in a position to formulate what is known." It has drawn the conclusion, she observed, that "combinations of business conditions" are responsible for the phases of the business cycle. "If this be true," she went on, "and if those business conditions are in the control of businessmen, then it is legitimate to put to businessmen the question, is it practicable for you to change your policies and practices so that that particular combination of circumstances will not lead us to extreme fluctuations of the business cycle?" As for the assembled economists, Van Kleeck continued, the committee also had one fundamental question: "Is it justifiable to say that it is possible to reduce the extremes?"[18]

In concluding her remarks, Van Kleeck summarized the committee's current recommendations, noting in particular the need for more and better statistics and for research institutions capable of interpreting statistical data, and, in an obvious bow to the Harvard Bureau, noting also the important role universities could play in sponsoring "neutral, scientific, impartial agencies for research." In collaboration with Mitchell and Joseph Defrees, she then went over the several questions for workers, engineers, businessmen, managers of public utilities, and bankers that constituted the committee's proposed referendum. Following this, the meeting was opened to discussion.[19]

As previously noted, the major debate was over the issue of financial tools, particularly over the degree to which such tools could be effective, and over the position that the committee should take on the question. A number of economists, of course, were on record as insisting that credit controls were essential to any countercyclical program. But the complexity of the issue and the likely need for legislation to implement new financial controls had discouraged the committee from pursuing the topic. It had, after all, been given only a limited mandate, one that called, above all, for research and recommendations useful to individual business managers. And since managers could do little to modify the nation's financial system, the committee had felt justified in sidestepping the issue.

Mitchell was instrumental in this, but his own research on

103

price movements and on the recent depression had encouraged him to believe that "the longest strides" toward "controlling booms" might be taken through proper use of the banking system. Such research as had been done, he explained, indicated that "a large part of the business cycle's ills" were "due to the fact that after we have attained capacity production on the up grade we go on and increase prices further, increase haste and waste, but do not increase the production of serviceable commodities." This was due to unwise credit policies. Thus he believed that the proposed referendum should lay great emphasis on the possibility of credit control and should strive to obtain suggestions from all concerned. Since a meaningful countercyclical program had to be enacted on a national scale, and since "the single solitary point on which all industries touch is the banks," he concluded that a system that combined credit restraints with unemployment insurance reserves might well prove to be the most effective brake on hyperexpansion.[20]

Irving Fisher agreed with Mitchell. "The solution to this problem," he declared, was "legislation to improve banking practice." This was borne out by experience in Europe; and in his view "if the government would lay down an administrative ruling authorizing banks to utilize rate of discount to the end of keeping the level of prices as stable as possible, much would be accomplished." "The Federal Reserve Board," he argued, "would act on this hint."

In subsequent discussion, a variety of views were expressed. Joseph Defrees, to begin with, was opposed to any kind of stabilization legislation. This, he felt, was the job of the gold standard and, given America's tremendous reserves of war-gotten gold, it was the banks' duty to lend despite the inflationary consequences. Harold G. Moulton, director of the new Brookings Institute for Economic Research, then spoke up, acknowledging the importance of the financial issue, but urging the committee to stick to its decision to treat the question peripherally. There was no great urgency to this matter, he felt, and hence the committee should simply discuss the problem in a brief chapter and leave its resolution "for later developments." In addition, there were suggestions from Mitchell and Young as well as from Moulton that the committee approach the American Bankers' Association for help in formulating a countercyclical banking policy.[21]

The most remarkable aspect of the meeting was the near unanimity of the participants on the idea of altering microeconomic management in such a way as to further macroeconomic stabilization. "The employers of the country, the businessmen," said John Commons, "are the only people who can stabilize employment, and it is up to them to do it if they don't want to see repeated in this country an approach toward what is going on in Europe." Moreover, he thought, it was the businessmen who would have to take the lead in insisting that the nation's banks contribute to stability. There was, he warned, much at stake. There was "an undercurrent of feeling of envy, revenge, or something" that seemed to him "quite ominous," an undercurrent that was "true of both organized and unorganized labor." Managers, he believed, must be shaken from their traditional sense of helplessness in the face of a cycle larger than themselves and their operations. They must "be educated to the fact that they alone are responsible for the business cycle"; and if they were at all wise, he felt, they would support legislation not only for credit management but for a system of unemployment compensation that would compel their colleagues to "accept the burden of stabilization."[22]

John Maurice Clark and Walter W. Stewart also expressed faith in microeconomic strategies; and it was the general consensus on this that Crocker emphasized in his post-conference telegram to Owen Young. "Friendly controversy joined in by all sixteen professors finally ending in general agreement," he wired. "Moreover," he concluded, the "Committee has made just so many more friendly supporters of their report." The meeting, in Crocker's view anyway, had admirably served Owen Young's purpose.[23]

It had served other purposes as well. For Van Kleeck, Hunt, and Mitchell, it had helped to put the business cycle committee's work in perspective and had contributed to the "clarification" of issues needing further research and hence to the development of social science. (Mitchell and Van Kleeck, among others, had been arguing for some time that just such a clarification and demarcation of areas capable of yielding empirical knowledge was critical to the advance of the discipline.) For Hunt and Mitchell, the committee's emphasis on the potential for forecasting, once statistical competence had been improved, was a step toward a technocratic social science that might someday be capable of erasing the business cycle altogether.

"If we could foresee the business cycle," Mitchell was now persuaded, "there would be none." In that case, business managers would take appropriate steps to protect themselves from impending overexpansion and by doing so would reduce the likelihood of subsequent deflation. As Hunt saw it, if this proposition were true, then the "idea of voluntary action" by informed managers, which the business cycle committee was about to test, should have a "great deal of validity." Like Mitchell, Hunt was optimistic about statistical forecasting as a remedy for the business cycle, although he seems to have been aware of the possibility that informed voluntary action by private bodies might be insufficient.[24]

On January 27, 1923, the business cycle committee held its final meeting, convening this time at General Electric's New York offices and inviting Hoover to attend. Prior to the meeting, there had been some fear that Hoover and Hunt were bent on rushing the committee into approval of the report without further discussion, but this did not prove to be the case. Instead, the report was discussed, and on the matter of data collection and research the discussion was particularly lively. Hoover, for instance, argued strongly for maintaining a distinction between the collection of fundamental data by the government and the interpretation of that data by private research bodies. There was a real danger, he felt, of compromising the collection of industrial data if commercial research and forecasting organizations were allowed unlimited access to statistics gathered by the government. Van Kleeck agreed, arguing that the "one agency that could collect fundamental statistics was the Government." More than any other member of the committee, she was pushing for a strong plank on this, determined not to allow private forecasters to interfere with such an important undertaking. Still, neither she nor Hoover wanted to discourage "impartial" economic research carried on by universities or by agencies like the NBER. In her view, this was "interpretive" research into "special problems," as opposed to the less salutary commercial forecasting.[25]

On April 2 the business cycle committee released its summary recommendations to the press, and shortly thereafter those same recommendations, along with an accompanying questionnaire and technical study, were published by McGraw-Hill under the title *Business Cycles and Unemployment*. As expected, in its public pronouncement the committee stressed the importance of the dissemination of statistical information if business cycles were ever to be brought under control. It emphasized as well the need to use public and private construction funds as a balance wheel, noting the critical role the Federal Reserve might play in moderating the cycle's course. But it was microeconomic regularization that remained at the heart of its recommendations. "The first point of attack on the problem," it declared, "must be more informed action by individual businessmen in periods of rising markets in order that excessive expansion may be prevented and the extent of the decline reduced." In his introduction to the report, Hoover called it "a definite advance in economic thought," and a major step toward stability. It did not "suggest panaceas or economic revolution," he noted, but sought instead to educate individual businessmen to a broader view of their role in the cycle so that their "consequent widened vision as to approaching dangers will greatly contribute to stability."[26]

Public reaction to the business cycle study was mixed, with business and social science reviewers expressing approval while the reform community announced its unhappiness with the report's failure to endorse compulsory unemployment insurance. The report "is good so far as it goes," wrote *The New Republic*, but in prescribing remedies the committee had stuck to "minor palliatives," an action showing "that American business leaders are not yet ready to grapple seriously with the problem of depression." "When they are," it continued, "they will come out squarely for a program of unemployment insurance that will compel the periods of expansion to assume the burden of easing off the hardships of the ensuing depression."[27]

On the other hand, W. C. Clark, writing in *The Journal of the American Statistical Association*, found the study to be "an authoritative and exceedingly valuable compilation of fact and opinion." Both he and Willard Hotchkiss of the Taylor Society were particularly impressed with Mitchell's and the NBER's contribution. The bureau, Clark noted, "had again placed us heavily in its debt." And John Commons, writing in the *American Review*, thought the report might contribute to a needed change in "the public psychology," one that would lead Americans to "do the things necessary to stop these cycles of prosperity and depression."[28]

Business editors like Arch Shaw of *System* borrowed freely from the business cycle study; and *Forbes* magazine, after pronouncing it an "excellent report," offered its pages to Owen Young. In them, it suggested, he might tell the magazine's readers, "a great many of whom are of the employer class, just what you and your committee would most like to impress upon them." It was "anxious to cooperate," it declared, "in bringing about your aims and purposes."[29]

In a May letter to the Carnegie Corporation, Hunt announced that the report's publisher, McGraw-Hill, was "tremendously pleased" with the book's early sales and "proud" to have published it. In addition, "a booklet containing 31 editorials" had been sent to "10,000 newspapers—dailies, weeklies, semi-weeklies, and to hundreds of class and trade journals." Seventeen news stories had been sent to national lists. Special stories had been placed with the Science Service, *The Nation's Business, Delineator, Collier's, World's Work, The Sur-*

vey, the syndicates, and a number of religious, agricultural, fraternal, and women's federation magazines, and 4,800 matrices had gone to morning, afternoon, and Sunday newspapers. "Clippings are already running into the thousands," Hunt added, and "the success of the preliminary publicity appears phenomenal." The Federal Reserve Board was even quoting from the study in its May bulletin, urging bankers to follow up on the committee's recommendations.[30]

For both Hoover and Young, the business cycle study was vindicated by its apparent influence over business behavior. "When Mr. Hoover asked me to accept the Chairmanship," Young told Elihu Root of the Carnegie Corporation, "I had great misgivings as to whether any study of such a sprawling subject . . . would have any appreciable effect." And given the fact that it was finished in a period of recovery and rising employment, he had feared that it would "attract but little attention and have but little influence." Yet on both these points, he admitted, "I was wrong." On the contrary, the report had an unusually wide circulation among "thinking men" in business and labor circles. And, "as it turned out, the issuance of the report could not have been better timed. Business managers had very fresh in their minds the disastrous experiences of the sharp depression of 1920 and the early part of 1921. They were apprehensive of the tremendous upward swing of the latter part of 1922 and the early months of 1923, because they feared the consequent reaction." "Personally," he continued, "I believe that the peak of this upward swing was largely cut off by the publicity given to the Business Cycle Report." For the first time, he thought, "we have had . . . cooperation both by business managers and by labor leaders in trying to prevent a disastrous peak," and the result would be "fairly good but not booming business for a considerable period.[31]

In October, Hoover sent 809 editorial clippings to Frederick P. Keppel, the new president of the Carnegie Corporation. "I have never known of an economic investigation which had anywhere near so much attention," he reported, "and, as you will notice from the editorials, the attention is practically invariably favorable." The press, he noted, "continue to refer to this idea of business cycles and the technical papers indicate that most businessmen have accepted it substantially as gospel." And echoing Young, he pointed out the report's "striking" effect on business planning. "My opinion and that of Owen D. Young," he said, "is that the peak of the dangerous upward swing which started last Spring was largely cut off by reason of this report."[32]

It is impossible to assess with any precision the truth of Hoover's and Young's conclusions. It seems likely, however, that they overstated by a very large margin the extent to which the study actually influenced business behavior. It is true that businesses cut production throughout the summer of 1923, seeking to reduce excessive inventories. And it is also likely that the blanket coverage of the committee's recommendations in the mass and trade press could have contributed to this and thus to the mildness of the subsequent recession in 1924. But more important, it would appear, was the creation in June 1922 of an Open Market Committee to manage the purchase and sale of government securities by federal reserve banks. For by the summer of 1923 over $500 million in government bonds had been sold, thus reducing purchasing power substantially and compelling producers to take steps to protect themselves.

Still, this was just the sort of financial action the business cycle committee had hoped to encourage and eventually see made routine. And to the extent that the committee's propaganda acted to educate businessmen and bankers to the potential such financial steps held for moderating the swings of the cycle, it can be said in support of Young and Hoover that the committee prepared the business community to react with more than usual dispatch to the Federal Reserve actions.[33]

What matters most, however, is that Hoover, Young, and their associates thought their work had set the stage for countercyclical management, that it had, in particular, pointed to the need for better economic data as a precondition for stabilization. Even if Wesley Mitchell exaggerated the empirical contributions of the NBER-sponsored study, the business cycle committee had contributed to the advancement of data competence and to the technocratic bargain within which it would be generated.

CHAPTER 7

The Advance of Techno-Corporatist Legitimation, 1924–1927

By the mid-1920s, the business cycle committee's apparent success in moderating boom and recession had given its ideas and supporters a new standing. Business cycles, it seemed, were amenable to control; and having taken much of the credit for allegedly controlling one, those involved in the committee's operations proceeded to consolidate and strengthen their positions. On one level this took the form of subsidiary expeditions into sick and badly organized industries such as construction and coal. On a second level, it brought further development of mutually reinforcing ideas and commitments within social science and business institutions. Thus in the years from 1924 through 1927, the spread of business regularization activities, the increasingly technocratic orientation of the social sciences, and the intensification of philanthropy's commitment to social science and policy research were all manifestations of a continued effort to legitimate an expanding public role for private managerial institutions.[1]

The new standing for technocratic authority meant wider acceptance of its social critique and its macroeconomic pretensions, and the coinciding takeoff of the post-1924 boom contributed powerfully to this development. It also encouraged a shift in the calculus of modern legitimation, for macroeconomic performance was now increasingly cast as a major test of legitimate authority, just as the expanding domain of a scientifically "enlightened" managerialism was justified by assigning it the primary responsibility for the movement toward greater economic abundance. In this respect, the period foreshadowed more recent equations of managerial development with national progress. It is the distillation of these developments into a distinctly managerial ideology—the ideological product of the technocratic bargain—that is the subject of this chapter.

II

Within social science, three developments were much in evidence during the mid-1920s. One was continued data building through organizations linking the state and business with the new professions. In this manner, the gap between vision and competence was being reduced and internal legitimation tensions were being eased. A second was the growth of specialized empirical research, which in operation hastened the decline of older deductive paradigms and the capacity that these had once had to hold the social sciences together. A third development, deriving in part from the other two, was the movement toward a new interdisciplinary synthesis, one that sought to reintegrate the social sciences along more explicitly technocratic lines.[2]

The growth of a legitimating data base stood out most clearly in economics, where the issue had been sharpest. There, so Wesley Mitchell noted in December 1924, the spread of research organizations supported by "officials, businessmen, and philanthropists" had done much to improve the professional standing of economists, who now had at their disposal "a more powerful technique and more opportunities to get assistance." In the future, he thought, the "endowment of economic research" might well become "as favorite an enterprise of public spirit as the endowment of medical research." At Harvard, Warren M. Persons expressed similar views. "Comparing the data now available with those available previous to 1919," Persons wrote in 1925, "one finds that there has been a pronounced addition during the last six years."[3]

In Mitchell's case, moreover, there was a clear understanding that an organizational society both facilitates and requires technocratic empiricism and direction. "Institutions standardize behavior," he wrote, "and thereby facilitate statistical procedure." Hence, as the scientific status of economics rose through subsidized data-building, it would turn increasingly, as the physical sciences had before it, toward the manipulation of its subject matter. "As in other sciences we desire knowledge mainly as an instrument of control," Mitchell asserted. "Control means the alluring possibility of shaping the evolution of economic life. . . . It is this possibility, of which we catch fleeting glimpses in our sanguine moments, that grips us."[4]

Nor was Mitchell alone in his predilections for a science of observation and control. "I do not think that most people realize the gathering force of the renaissance of economic thought we are having in this country," Rexford G. Tugwell wrote in his introduction to *The Trend of Economics* (1924), a work he regarded as a "manifesto of the younger generation," even though the contributing essayists were neither all young nor all easily identified as institutionalists. Among the contributors were Morris Copeland, Frank Knight, A. B. Wolfe, Sumner Slichter, Frederick C. Mills, Paul Douglas, George Soule, and J. M. Clark, representing in Tugwell's words, "both deductivists and inductivists, . . . neo-classicists and institutionalists, . . . marginalist logicians and experimentalists." As Tugwell saw it, all of these schools were now "merging" as never before, "in a common stream flowing to a common sea." Thus nothing less than "the possibility of a remade world" was now at hand.[5]

But the empiricism and the careful data-building that were fueling such pretensions were also having disintegrative and fragmentizing effects. They were part of a general movement toward specialization that was rupturing the habitual boundaries of inquiry and unraveling the threads tying one social science to another. Throughout the social sciences, behaviorists and inductivists were now generating and verifying new data, but in the process they were destroying the grand syntheses that had long guided social inquiry. Their researches were becoming ever more specialized, conducted now by increasingly isolated investigators operating within highly differentiated fields of inquiry. One result of this, according to William

F. Ogburn and Alexander Goldenweiser, was the spread of "greater ignorance as well as greater knowledge." "Increasing specialization," they wrote, was "part of the great accumulation process in social knowledge." Yet "this accumulation process" was so great that it had become "exceedingly difficult for any one individual to become well oriented in the general field of the social sciences."[6]

The disintegration of earlier unities and the spread of a worrisome chaos were particularly prominent themes at mid-decade. For some they constituted a major threat to the advance of social knowledge, since without a guiding purpose or coherent strategy the social sciences might find themselves working at cross purposes, unable to communicate with one another through the fog of their terminologies. But for others—among them such figures as Mitchell, Tugwell, Van Kleeck, and Ruml—the shattering of the older syntheses was a step forward. The possibilities now existed, they argued, for a true science of society, for the creation through intensive empiricism of a new foundation upon which a modern synthesis of social knowledge could be erected. In their eyes, moreover, this new unity was already emerging and finding expression in the shared concern of all groups with human and institutional behavior. As Mitchell put it, "what Jeremy Bentham's idea that all our actions are determined by pleasure and pain once did to provide a common program for jurists, economists, psychologists, penologists, and educators may be done again by the idea that all these groups, together with the political scientists, sociologists, anthropologists, and historians, are engaged in the study of human behavior; a common method—the quantitative analysis of behavior records; and a common aspiration—to devise ways of experimenting upon behavior."[7]

What was needed now, the argument frequently ran, was an appreciation of the "interrelationships" among the social sciences and, implicitly, of the "interdependence" of the social world under observation and manipulation. Needed also were mechanisms to further "cooperation" toward these ends and a means of establishing such mechanisms. Attempting to meet

115

these goals was the new Social Science Research Council (SSRC). Underwritten by philanthropy, in much the same way as the National Bureau and the business cycle study had been earlier, it represented the latest step in the extension and consolidation of technocratic authority.[8]

The SSRC was the brainchild of University of Chicago political scientist Charles E. Merriam. But also joining him as its leading lights were Wesley Mitchell and Beardsley Ruml, the latter functioning now as the director of the Laura Spelman Rockefeller Memorial, an agency that between 1923 and 1930 would spend over $40 million to subsidize social science research. Like Merriam and Mitchell, Ruml was interested in both science-building and synthesis.

Merriam's great concerns, as expressed in 1921 and 1922, had been with the lack of "objective" study in political science and with the tendency of the various social sciences to become isolated from one another, to adopt different stances toward empiricism, and thus to undermine the standing and influence of social science as a whole. To remedy these defects, he had recommended a new coordinating body capable of generating the university and foundation support necessary to sponsor an explicitly technocratic reintegration of the social sciences. In theory, such an agency would do for the social sciences what the National Research Council had done for the physical sciences, acting, as Louis Wirth put it, "as an important catalytic agent, . . . stimulating research, encouraging the improvement of scientific method, and facilitating interdisciplinary communication and cooperation."[9]

As initially founded in 1923, the SSRC was the joint creature of the American Political Science Association, the American Economic Association, and the American Sociological Society. But by 1925 its governing body also included representatives from the American Psychological Association, the American Statistical Association, the American Anthropological Association, and the American Historical Association. Together, these professional groups were making joint efforts to improve government statistics; they were supporting cooperative research

116

on migration; and they were engaging in a joint analysis of research methods and their complementarity throughout the social sciences. The overriding purpose of the SSRC was to foster an appreciation of the essential unity and interdependence of social reality and thus of the need for an equally interdependent social science. But implicit in the whole effort was an assumption that social science's generalizations must first be restated so as to make them amenable to quantitative verification.[10]

The ideal, in other words, was a social science capable of the kind of analysis "so common in the natural sciences, where the same subject is attacked by a variety of research workers simultaneously from various angles, where the same question is subjected to repeated investigations, and where comparative studies are the order of the day." Only in this way, so the thinking ran, could the acquisition of data competence lead to the kind of knowledge needed for continuous social management. "Social scientists have come into possession of data on a scale and of a degree of reliability," Wirth would later write, "that could scarcely have been imagined" without the aid of such an organization.[11]

III

As noted previously, these developments in the social sciences were dependent on the continued and rapidly escalating support given by philanthropy. And as a provider of such support, no institution was more important than the Laura Spelman Rockefeller Memorial. While the Carnegie Corporation, the Russell Sage Foundation, and such smaller funds as the Commonwealth remained active in the field, the Rockefeller Memorial was alone in dedicating itself to the systematic "upbuilding" of social science. Between 1918 and 1930, it funded such agencies as the National Bureau, the SSRC, and the Brookings Institution, and was responsible for much of the nearly fortyfold increase in philanthropic support of social science during this period. Behind this escalation, more responsible for it than anyone else, stood the imposing and improbable presence of Beardsley Ruml.[12]

Described by Robert Maynard Hutchins as "the founder of the social sciences in America," Ruml was responsible for transforming the Laura Spelman Rockefeller Memorial from a moribund and ill-defined fund into a potent technocratic institution. A psychometrician by training, Ruml had been among the technocratic elect during the war, and he now shared with Mitchell, Merriam, Van Kleeck, and others a commitment to technocratic science-building. As noted earlier, Ruml had already helped to secure Carnegie Corporation support for the National Bureau; and as assistant to Carnegie's president, James R. Angell, he had impressed Abraham Flexner of the Rockefeller Foundation's General Education Board. When Angell left the Carnegie Corporation to become president of Yale, Flexner brought Ruml to work for the Rockefellers, and in 1922, at the age of twenty-six, he became director of the Laura Spelman Rockefeller Memorial. The memorial's trustees, it seems, looked upon Ruml only as an interim director, confident that the memorial was soon to be absorbed by the larger Rockefeller Foundation. Hence they were surprised when Ruml, the "inflated office boy," as Alva Johnston described him, offered in October 1922 a ten-year plan for memorial support of the social sciences.[13]

Ruml's general memorandum of October 1922 stands as a remarkable document in the history of social science and American planning. Like the Fisher and Mitchell addresses of December 1918, it was a technocratic manifesto, calling not only for a usable social science but for a large and continuous philanthropic commitment toward making such a science a reality. Ruml's vision was of a *technocratic* social science, one able to inform the deliberations of business and government managers. By helping to create it, and by helping to form linkages between social science and managerial institutions, he believed the memorial would contribute both to the development of a nonstatist public planning and to the creation of new public roles for scientifically informed private managers.

118

In the memorandum, Ruml insisted that the social sciences deserved support not out of "an academic interest," but because it had become "more and more clearly recognized that unless means are found of meeting the complex social problems that are so rapidly developing, our increasing control of physical forces may prove increasingly destructive of human values." Nor was the support needed something that could be undertaken as a part of "a single year's activity." Instead it was "the work of a period of years, perhaps a decade," since the "basic need" involved was not one that existed "as a result of temporary conditions or accidental circumstances," or that might "soon pass through normal social and political development."

Such a program, moreover, would be the surest means of advancing social welfare, the field in which the memorial had made its earliest donations. Real advances there required, as a first step, "the production of a body of substantiated and widely accepted generalizations as to human capacities and motives and as to the behavior of human beings as individuals and in groups." According to Ruml, those in the field were "embarrassed" by the lack of such knowledge and were greatly handicapped in attaining the ends they sought. The situation, in his view, was as though "engineers were at work without an adequate development in the sciences of physics and chemistry, or as though physicians were practicing in the absence of the medical sciences."

Continuing his analysis, Ruml concluded that the current state of affairs in the social sciences was the result of three factors. One was their youth. "Only since the middle of the nineteenth century," he pointed out, "have human beings in their conscious capacities been considered a part of the natural order, and their capacities and behavior subject to study by experimental or even inductive methods." Wilhelm Wundt's psychological laboratory, the first of its kind, had been established in Leipzig only fifty years earlier, and "as important an instrument for social research as the coefficient of correlation" was less than forty years old. Furthermore, the beginnings of efforts to measure "general intelligence" and other human traits were "to be found largely within the present century." The second factor was the intractable nature of the subject matter—the fact, in other words, that human society, behavior, and institutions could not "be brought into the laboratory for study" and that important forces could not be "controlled and experimented with" but had to be "observed if, when and as operative." And third, there was the fact that the institutional home of the young social science professions, the university, was neither equipped nor properly organized to sustain the social research needed to build scientific competence. According to Ruml, academic "facilities for the collection and tabulation of data" were "meager," and the "requirements of classroom instruction limit markedly the possibilities of contact with social phenomena." As a result, production from the universities was "largely deductive and speculative, on the basis of secondhand observations, documentary evidence and anecdotal material." It was small wonder, then, that the social engineer found his science to be "abstract and remote, of little help to him in the solution of his problems."

As Ruml saw it, there were four major ways in which the memorial could help to meet this pressing need "for knowledge of social forces," a need that was felt not only "by social welfare organizations, but by business and industry, and by agencies of government as well." These included: first, "the definition and marking off within the field as a whole of a certain class of related problems upon which emphasis will be placed"; second, "the opening up of possibilities of contact for scientists with concrete social phenomena and the provision of facilities for the collection and evaluation of data"; third, the attraction to the field of more "highly able men"; and fourth, "the provision of ways and means for the general dissemination of the knowledge that is secured and for its utilization practically in the advancement of social welfare."[14]

Ruml's first point, the demarcation of areas of research amenable to quantitative technique, echoed the thinking of Van Kleeck, Hunt, Merriam, and Mitchell. His fourth point, the construction of what he would later term a "social technology" in which managerial institutions would be more closely tied to the growing data competence of social science, was set forth only in the most general terms, but would soon rise in importance in his thinking. The third point, the recruiting and support of more social scientists, complemented what appears to have been his chief concern at the time, namely his second point, the subsidization of data-building. And in regard to this, Ruml enunciated three subordinate principles.[15]

He argued, first of all, that the university, provided it was properly equipped and organized to sustain social research, should be the base for those who were engaged in gathering and interpreting new data. In the past, academic production had been "meager" and "deductive," but this could be changed through systematic support. In Ruml's opinion, the university as an institution offered researchers numerous advantages. Thus "the stability of the organization, the presence of a wide range of professional opinion, the existence of scholarly and scientific standards of work, [and] recognized and reasonably effective channels of inter-university communication," all made for "a favorable environment of investigation."

Second, Ruml held that a promising, if still difficult, possibility for advancing research lay in bringing about "closer associations among the various social sciences, and in creating better means for cooperative work." This, of course, was one of the impulses behind the formation of the SSRC and its attempts at technocratic reintegration of the social sciences. Finally, Ruml advocated a role for philanthropy not unlike that played by government in Hoover's techno-corporatist state. The memorial, he argued, should act as an energizer of existing institutions, stimulating and assisting them to meet research needs. Only where no existing institution seemed "suitable" should it consider creating a new one.

Ruml also believed that the memorial must always work through a mediating institution, thus remaining insulated from specific researches. This would protect the foundation from political controversy, particularly that aroused by the "outcome of any specific piece of research"—a touchy matter with

Rockefeller philanthropies because of the "abuse and vituperation" heaped on their industrial relations investigation following the Ludlow Massacre. Such insulation would encourage perceptions of philanthropy's "disinterestedness," thus protecting it from political criticism and accountability at a time when it was in reality expanding its political function. In addition, Ruml pointed out, working through an established institution would help to maintain an indefinite "continuance of interest in a group of related problems," providing a kind of data and knowledge accumulation that could not be attained through ad hoc committees or projects.

Among the first practical steps the memorial might take, Ruml argued, were grants of aid that would allow research universities to upgrade their facilities, inaugurate fellowship programs, and improve the state of scholarly journals and similar publications. Even such tentative steps, he was convinced, would produce quick and desirable results. Not only would they bring a "great increase in our knowledge of social forces," there would also be an improvement in the standing of social sciences and in the ability to use such knowledge "practically." Experience seemed to indicate, he continued, "that the results of investigations in the social sciences, where they are conducted by obviously impartial scientific agencies, and where these results are generally accepted by scientific men, come to play a definite and wholesome part in the thinking of people generally."[16]

Throughout the next several years, the memorial's commitment to social-science building expanded well beyond its first "extremely tentative" steps. Increasingly, its earliest commitments to particular projects in particular institutions were supplemented by the expansion of fellowships, research facilities, and opportunities for cooperative research. And by mid-decade "the usefulness" of the work being supported was becoming clear. "Among other things," it was noted, "we have seen the Mayor of Chicago call on the University of Chicago for an extensive investigation of municipal employment" and the "Governor of North Carolina request the University of

North Carolina to study and report on crime and delinquency in that state."

By 1926 Ruml was confident that "great good" had resulted from the memorial's "advancement of social science." Not only was the scientific legitimacy of the social sciences being enhanced by "the quality of studies produced," but their influence in the world of affairs was also rising fast. Thus the "increasing demand of public and private bodies for scientific analysis of problems of social consequence" suggested the important role institutions like the memorial could play in forging links between social science and managerial institutions.[17]

IV

Perhaps the clearest expression of how social scientists and business managers were engaged in mutual legitimation could be found in the mid-decade rise and spread of the business regularization movement. For in the ideology that accompanied and was being used to promote this movement, a new set of "enlightened" business managers, armed with new and "scientific" social tools, were allegedly erecting a superior economic order, one now capable of continuous expansion and sustained prosperity. To dismiss this as self-serving propaganda, which much of it undoubtedly was, is to miss the emergence of a set of ideas that could and would be used to enhance public acceptance of and dependence on private managerial authority.[18]

The roots of the regularization movement lay in prewar stabilization schemes like those of Henry S. Dennison, but much of the mid-decade impetus for it came from the business cycle committee's promotion of microeconomic stabilization measures and from the accompanying promotional efforts of the Commerce Department. This was because regularization, understood as managerial production and sales strategies that could reduce fluctuations in employment and business activity, had now become a major plank in the Hooverian program for macroeconomic management. And the implementation of it, in theory anyway, required a merger of social science and business organization, the two complementary halves of a "new capitalism."

The promotion of regularization, moreover, did coincide with unprecedented prosperity, leading to unwarranted assumptions that the first was the cause of the second. Although there is little evidence that this was actually the case, it was purported to be so; and to one degree or another, Hoover, Mitchell, Van Kleeck, Dennison, Ruml, Owen Young, and others managed to convince themselves that science was rationalizing business and socializing it to a larger public purpose. For them management was being ideologically legitimated by the most modern of standards, while the techno-corporatist bodies from which these standards had sprung were finding confirmation of their technocratic powers, and a significant measure of their social legitimacy, in the objective performance of the economy.[19]

It is important to state clearly that techno-corporatist planning and the regularization movement probably had little to do with New Era prosperity. Nevertheless, the modern managerialism they represented did prosper through its close association with good times, thereby encouraging a shift in the definition of legitimate social authority to one more appropriate to a depoliticized system. In the eyes of many, there was a continuum that ran from technocratic analysis through managerialism to abundance.

This was the argument advanced in an outpouring of regularization literature from 1924 on. It was the theme, for example, in Lionel Edie's *The Stabilization of Business* (1923), in Sam Lewisohn and Ernest Draper's *Can Business Prevent Unemployment?* (1925), in Herman Feldman's *The Regularization of Employment* (1925), and in Stuart Chase's *The Tragedy of Waste* (1926). It was also the theme in a variety of articles appearing in business and reform periodicals, especially *The Survey*, the *American Labor Legislation Review*, *System*, the *Bulletin of the Taylor Society*, and *Factory and Industrial Management*. All were part of an effort "to influence the behavior of thousands of managers" and by doing so to resolve macroeconomic problems through the scientific making of microeconomic decisions.[20]

In terms of action, regularization remained a minority movement, confined to "reform-minded" businessmen and found chiefly in larger and more profitable firms. As Evan Metcalf notes, "stabilization" was every businessman's goal, but to many the word meant "simply the reduction of uncertainty from any source." For those in the less profitable and hyper-competitive industries, it frequently meant some form of antitrust revision, although such revision was also seen by some as necessary to permit regularization programs to be installed in healthier industries.[21]

Yet even if a relatively few practiced regularization, the movement did enjoy the official sponsorship of the Unemployment Conference and did, as a result of the business cycle committee's work, command the widespread attention of business leaders and groups. Proponents could point to a number of companies who had achieved a degree of production and employment stability through conscious manipulation of their inventories and order backlogs; and this could be depicted as the leading edge of a new kind of managerial practice capable of applying social science so as to serve the public interest.[22]

Also contributing to such perceptions during the period were several other developments, one of which was the notion that social work as well as social science was now undergoing a mutually beneficial merger with business management. "Industry is being invaded by social work," Mary Van Kleeck wrote in 1922, with the result that the professional authority of both management and social work had been improved. "The management engineer and the social worker," she asserted, "have found cooperation necessary"; and this she concluded, was "highly desirable to the success of each group" and critical to a "professionalization" that depended upon a group's ability to facilitate the social effectiveness of other professions. "Only as social workers are prepared consciously to formulate their experience as a guide for the practice of others," she pointed out, "can they lay claim to the possession of technique."[23]

Still another contribution to the "new managerialism" came from business educators and from engineering schools who were turning their attention to the training of "engineers-as-managers." In the process, business and engineering curricula were upgraded to include social science training. Now enjoying wider currency, particularly in these training institutions and among the business leaders who were associated with them, was the idea that just as American business had learned to progress through bold experimentation in material matters, so it must learn to adopt "any modern device" that might "bring about better workers, better citizens, better morale." Sam A. Lewisohn, E. A. Filene, Henry Dennison, Gerard Swope, and Owen Young consistently expressed such sentiments. "You are not afraid of new inventions and new engineering in your physical plants," Young indicated to a trade group in 1926. "May I suggest that invention, improved engineering and courage to take the road are needed now in the social more than in the physical sciences?"

In addition, Mary Van Kleeck, Harlow Person, and Henry Dennison affirmed social science's intrinsic value to business management through the proceedings of the Taylor Society. "Can the market be understood without using the methods of the social sciences?" Van Kleeck asked. And pointing with approval to a statement by S. A. Courtis of the University of Michigan, which suggested that "the supreme value of research" lay "in the power of truth to harmonize conflict of human opinion and make cooperation possible," she argued, "that social research in industry may be more than a method of discovery confined to a research department." Rather, it could be "the motivating spirit and attitude of the organization."[24]

Similarly, Henry Dennison continued to articulate the case for a "new managerialism," enlightened now by the informing powers of social science, and therefore capable of delivering wide social benefits. "The greatest single service any man can give to the business world just now," he asserted in an address to the Bureau of Personnel Administration, "is to do his bit in advancing business management and technique toward a professional status." Accepting Van Kleeck's notion of an interpenetration of social science and management resulting in the improved social authority of each, he looked to the professionalization of management as the best hope of ending "unsatisfactory relationships between employer and employee" and of achieving a "more effective distribution of material wealth."[25]

Dennison was also confident that business had already progressed well along the path to professionalization. The U.S. Chamber of Commerce's recent adoption of a national code of ethics, he insisted, had been "called for by thousands of people" and represented more than a public relations smoke screen. "It signifies," he declared, "the development and stabilization of the business situation and its passing out of the individualist state." Providing further testimony of this, he argued, were the related movements toward professional business training and the establishment of closer links to social science. "We see around us," he said, "growing up at an astonishing rate," not only "special schools and programs for business education" but also engineering programs that were making a "very specific effort" to combine engineering training with "business management instruction," with a new "research and experimentation progressing in the fields of scientific management, scientific merchandising, scientific selling, [and] scientific organization," and with steady development of such "auxiliary sciences" as "economic history, statistics, [and] industrial psychology."

As a result, Dennison argued, there was a clearer understanding of such things as trade restriction, business cycles, and employee capabilities; and in the light of this understanding, managerial functions were being redefined. They were being "marked off" into specialties and either "lifted into science-based professions" or developed in ways that would eventually mean their transformation into such professions. Thus

127

the new manager was becoming a professional, increasingly dependent on social research and economic analysis, and with the aid of such "professional research agencies . . . as the Russell Sage Foundation" was engaged in the kind of fact-gathering and use that met professional tests in regard to "the use of scientific methods."[26]

Through a number of channels, then, perceptions were being created of a new managerial authority, an authority informed by social science and legitimated both by its scientific quality and by the ability of the fusion of science and management to enhance productivity and bring economic abundance. In such thinking, the ultimate test of the industrial order was, as Mary Van Kleeck put it in 1926, the "effect on the standards of life." And while Van Kleeck continued to worry about modern capitalism's potential for bureaucratic domination and its tendency toward an impersonal standardization that would erode individual autonomy and destroy even the promise of "community," she, like other technocratic social scientists, saw the key to preventing this nightmare in even closer links between social science and business institutions. Passionately committed to the development of "social truths" as a precondition for social justice, she saw modern capitalism as a "network of relationships" in which "control is possible," but in which that same control would depend on "the quality of the scientific perception" made available to social managers.[27]

That this technocratic vision was now more and more linked to a model of social management in which private groups were being encouraged to assume public roles attests to the potency of techno-corporatist ideas in the flush of New Era prosperity. But it also suggests the difficulty such ideas might face when economic breakdown followed prosperity, and when the expanded authority of private interests encouraged not the desired harmonization of society but its fragmentation.

CHAPTER 8

Toward a Technique of Balance, 1927–1929

"There is nothing like it in economic history," Herbert Hoover said in 1927 of America's recent prosperity. Indeed, so stunning had been the generally stable expansion since 1921 that America had become the world's marvel. General strikes, debt and exchange difficulties, and recurrent depression had continued to plague Europe, but the United States was experiencing steadily rising wages, increased mechanization and output, and rising living standards. And these were acting as a magnet, drawing to America dozens of investigators and numerous missions of exploration intent upon searching out the sources and unlocking the mysteries of this new kind of economy.[1]

As Hoover and his associates saw it, however, there was no real mystery. To be sure, they admitted to an uncomfortably high degree of ignorance concerning the precise factors underlying America's prosperity, but they were also convinced that their indicative planning machinery had played an important part in that prosperity. "Why," E. E. Hunt asked rhetorically, "have we not built up unmanageable inventories, why have commodity prices remained steady, why have we had a phenomenal and uninterrupted period of high production and consumption since 1921?" Much of the answer, he thought, lay in the extraordinary progress made by business management. As a result of this progress, American business had collectively practiced a "self-restraint" that had helped to prevent the kind of speculative fever that always preceded depression; and the fact that business had been systematically informed about economic conditions and encouraged to take

129

such action marked "an absolutely unprecedented achievement."[2]

Because of these triumphs, Hoover and his associates also argued, it was time to reactivate the apparatus of the unemployment conference and the business cycle committee. There was a need, they insisted, to assess the depths of the change and the progress that the country had made since the depression of 1921. As Hoover put it, "We need to know more about the foundations of our prosperity and how to maintain it." For from such knowledge could come new social machinery and guidance systems capable of maintaining and extending the country's prosperity.[3]

What was needed, in particular, was an intensive investigation of recent economic developments similar to those underway in Britain and Germany. But unlike the European surveys, the American study should be directed not at things gone awry but at things gone well. And, also unlike them, it should be not a creature of legislation supported by government funds but rather "a continuation and amplification" of the Committee on Business Cycles and Unemployment, "made under the same auspices, utilizing the same agencies, and following the same methods." Since these agencies and methods had demonstrated their effectiveness, their apparatus should now be redeployed as the first step toward building an ongoing "technique of balance."[4]

Also underlying Hoover's call for such an investigation was some concern that the unprecedented nature and peculiarities of the current prosperity might be concealing dangerous developments. One "outstanding peculiarity," Wesley Mitchell had noted, was "that we are doing profitable business in most industries with a slowly declining price level." Another development, much in the public eye, was that such important sectors as agriculture, textiles, and coal had remained depressed amidst the general expansion. "We appear to have made real progress," Hunt would say, "but we need to examine the situation carefully to know whether this has been in part fortuitous and so to determine if our present assumptions are sound or fallacious."[5]

The result was the Committee on Recent Economic Changes, organized late in 1927 as another expression of techno-corporatist thought and of the "new managerialism" that had emerged in the wake of the business cycle study. This committee's new study was to be more than just another exercise in data production; rather, it was designed to hasten new organizational linkages, encourage a further fusion of social science and business management, and provide an elaboration of technocratic claims to social authority. It was to be a manifestation, moreover, of Hoover's confidence in the value of his indicative apparatus and in the possibility, now that prosperity had been won, of elevating such machinery into a force for continuous national planning.

Yet if the new investigation was an expression of Hooverian planning at high tide, it was also undertaken in the face of some skepticism in the technocratic constituency through which it was to operate. Here Mary Van Kleeck played a central role, for by 1927 the evidence of rising unemployment within the general prosperity had made her increasingly skeptical of the Hooverian approach. Her dissent would grow more and more vigorous from 1927 on, and it was a dissent that could not easily be dismissed since she had, after all, been one of the leading lights in the pre-1927 operations. The fact that she was now a critic and was not to be a member of the Committee on Recent Economic Changes symbolized and foreshadowed the breakdown of what had once been a technocratic consensus.

II

The year 1927 brought with it a mild recession, one in which sales temporarily slumped, manufacturing output rose more slowly, and wholesale prices fell by more than 4 percent. But few at the time saw this as a sign of any real danger, particularly since there had been no serious inventory backlogs in advance

131

of the slump. Nor was there much doubt that "full-fledged prosperity" would soon return. Wesley Mitchell, while noting the onset of a recession, thought "that the declining price level must tend to maintain the rather conservative spirit which American enterprisers have exhibited since their terrorising losses in 1921." This, he believed, combined with the fact "that most of our business prophets have been telling people to prepare for a recession," should help to sustain business activity and prevent "the accumulation of the type of strains which have put the closure upon most of our booms."[6]

E. E. Hunt was also confident that stable growth could be maintained. The influence of Secretary Hoover and the business cycle committee, he insisted, were the key factors that had led to "a remarkable strengthening of our economic statistics . . . and a very great enlargement of their use by businessmen." As a result, "conservative policies" had prevailed, and "we have had a sustained level of prosperity which is without parallel in our economic history." "Ups and downs of the business cycle," he conceded, would "doubtless continue." But there was "reason to believe that the more violent and destructive extremes" had been "definitely curtailed."[7]

"We have in Hoover," so Hunt had been saying, "a unique personality. He is in command of a great Government department. He has the confidence of organized labor. He has the confidence of those who are in control of American industry." And around him, so Hunt thought, there had developed "a national program" of "reconstruction," one that had begun with the waste survey of 1921 and was now ready, following new studies and investigations, to fashion still more effective tools for guiding and stimulating socially desirable business activity.[8]

In Hunt's mind, the time had almost arrived "when genuine scientific national planning" could be undertaken. And to this subject he had been giving a good deal of thought, envisioning, in particular, a "National Planning Board" established as a "private or at most semi-public body," composed of senior "public men," and surrounded and enlightened by "a per-

manent staff skilled in economic and engineering investigations." The board's purpose, so Hunt reasoned, would be "to
submit to the public not simply basic facts, but plans of action,"
thus meeting the public "need for authoritative, disinterested,
and continuous national planning."[9]

In 1927 Mary Van Kleeck also looked forward to a new
national economic survey. But, unlike Hunt, she was motivated
more by skepticism than optimism. "Are we economically as
sound as Republican orators tell us we are?" she asked. Were
their claims really borne out by employment data and earning
figures? And could one rely upon what those "in power politically" were saying about "the contents of the dinner pail?"

Van Kleeck was dubious, particularly in view of a report on
unemployment statistics prepared by a committee of the
American Statistical Association and published by the Russell
Sage Foundation. This demonstrated, she thought, that there
was much work to be done before the data collected by business
and government could be fully trusted and used for "wise
planning and good management." Thus, as a step toward ac-
cumulating fuller and more reliable information, she supported a resolution introduced by Senator David Walsh of
Massachusetts calling for "a nation-wide investigation of the
economic state of the country."[10]

Employment data, so Van Kleeck argued, were the most
useful form of business statistics, not only because they illuminated "both sides of the economic balance—production on
the one hand and final purchase on the other," but also because
they provided the best indices of social welfare. This was true,
she felt, in Massachusetts, the state having the longest and
most extensive record of such data, where the record now
revealed a decline in both wages and employment. What 1927
might bring, she admitted, was "impossible to predict." But
the figures already collected by the Massachusetts Department
of Labor and Industries showed that in January, as compared
with December, employment and earnings had decreased. The
employment level had fallen by .7 percent, aggregate payroll
by 2.3 percent, and average weekly earnings per capita by 1.7

133

percent. It could be argued, she continued, that this was not characteristic of the nation as a whole, at least on the basis of the data compiled by the Federal Bureau of Labor Statistics. But, on the other hand, "not a single state in the South" collected such data, nor did the nation as a whole have adequate information, particularly in regard to employment in agriculture, mining, and the building trades. This would have to be gathered before anyone could claim to have the "comprehensive view" of economic activity needed to assess the soundness of prosperity and make that prosperity real for all.[11]

By late 1927 Van Kleeck's criticism had grown sharper. And as it did she urged American labor to take a more active part in publicizing the economy's deficiencies. Reiterating her earlier warnings against taking too literally the economic assessments of those in political power, she now suggested that "the trade unions can keep before the public the facts about unemployment." If the labor movement refused to accept this responsibility, she warned, "the public is in danger of being deceived." Already "the common impression on conditions here, as it is reflected, for instance, in reports of foreign delegations, is that everybody is prosperous and every worker employed at high wages." In her view, to the extent that "we fall short of the standard reflected in this impression," it was "disastrous not to make the facts known."[12]

The time had come, she said now, to ask whether the problem of stabilizing employment should any longer be left "to business leaders looking upon it as primarily a problem of industrial management." She was suggesting, in other words, that the linkage between the goals of industrial and employment stabilization, a linkage that had informed and underlain her war work and her participation in the business cycle study, should no longer be made. "Employment and unemployment," she argued, "are not merely subheads under stabilization of industry, but need their own spokesmen and their own students." While it was true, she added, "that in the long run business as a whole should be made stable and secure," it was "by no means true that all groups at all times have equal interest in stabilizing the economic machinery." A few, she noted, "profit by instability"; and furthermore, what was thought of as "stability" did not always mean security for the individual worker. For example, a given industry's employment schedule might feature too little work at the beginning of the year and overwork at the end, yet still result in a satisfactory annual performance. "Business stability," she concluded, "is important to the workers, but the workers themselves must be actively engaged in study and action to make employment secure." This was "the responsibility of the trade unions." And it was the responsibility of social scientists, she had now decided, to see that "the power of science should not be used only for the technical developments of industry." It must "be used also to help labor achieve greater independence and more power."[13]

III

The Committee on Recent Economic Changes, "a conspicuous example of private initiative with government collaboration," was to be "another effort to carry over into the field of National policy making the knowledge of the experts." So said E. E. Hunt; and in organizing the study, Hoover and Hunt sought first to reactivate the funding and research legs that had supported the business cycle committee's inquiries. Once again, the National Bureau was called upon, its directors approving its participation "unanimously." Also "thoroughly convinced" of the project's worth, so much so that they were "very keen to tackle it," were Edwin Gay and Wesley Mitchell. Remarking on the "very peculiar course" of economic activity since 1923, they noted again the "depressed condition of agriculture, the difficulties of many of our most important customers, and the milder troubles encountered by certain of our manufacturing industries." These, Gay and Mitchell pointed out, existed within a "condition of prosperity," the duration of which was "perhaps unexampled for this country save under the impetus of war demand during the Civil War and the World Wars [*sic*]."[14]

Testifying to the fundamental importance of technocratic investigations of this sort, Gay and Mitchell noted that "whether one thinks in terms of business prosperity or of social welfare," knowledge of the new prosperity's roots was essential. Was it rooted, they asked, in "fortuitous circumstances?" Or was it the product of "policies adopted by Government agencies such as the Department of Commerce and the Federal Reserve Board?" What part had scientific management and the business regularization movement played? Could "wise planning" maintain prosperity "indefinitely"? Or was prosperity itself "quietly producing conditions which will inevitably terminate" in depression? "If so," Gay and Mitchell asked, "can any measures be devised which will check or perhaps prevent the threatened decline?"[15]

Its concern with such questions, in their opinion, meant that "the proposed investigation possesses a measure of scientific interest and practical significance scarcely matched by any past undertaking of a similar sort." It would utilize scientific methods to study "economic fundamentals"; and it would, so Gay and Mitchell noted, develop a new capability for cooperation between research and policy-making agencies. In particular, the National Bureau would be working with "the Department of Commerce, the Institute of Economics, the Food Research Institute, [and] men connected with the Harvard Graduate School of Business Administration, the Columbia School of Business, and . . . departments of economics in several institutions." All of these would have roles to play; and together they would seek to ascertain whether "our curious current prosperity" had been due primarily to a more informed business management and "whether a continuation and development of the new practices can be made to sustain the economic income of the country as a whole indefinitely upon the unexampled levels which have been reached."[16]

It should be noted, in addition, that Gay and Mitchell were anxious to maintain the quasi-public standing that the National

Bureau had acquired during the earlier business cycle study. By 1927, Gay could note that "the Bureau stands in high estimation among economists; our friends among leading business men have ceased to speak of it as a promising 'experiment.'" As a way of maintaining this reputation, influence, and "carrying power," a new alliance with Hoover seemed made to order. The bureau's leaders, wrote George O. May, a bureau director and Price Waterhouse executive, "feel it is highly desirable to link it up with Hoover; . . . the controlling argument in their minds is that it is necessary to have some such public backing, and that it is necessary to get the cooperation of the Department of Commerce."

Beyond this, Mitchell and Gay also feared that "if the Bureau attempted to tackle the job without some strong individual or committee associated with the project it would be impossible to get the effective and cheap cooperation" upon which they were counting, with the result that costs "might easily be doubled." And finally, they had been pleased with Hunt's performance as secretary of the business cycle study and were eager to work with him again. "They are satisfied," May wrote, "that Hunt is the right man to take immediate charge," that he would allow the bureau and no one else to direct the study, and that he understood the importance of maintaining and protecting the bureau's impartiality. "They tell me," May continued, that during the business cycle study "when some conflict arose between committee views and the scientific view, Hunt took a very satisfactory stand on the scientific side although he had to run counter to some very influential people in doing so." Furthermore, he concluded, "they say he is an excellent man at carrying out a program in accordance with a time schedule and a budget."[17]

May's views, contained in a letter to Frederick P. Keppel, president of the Carnegie Corporation, were intended to persuade that organization's directors to approve Hoover's request for funding. In conjunction both with this appeal and with one to the Rockefellers' Spelman fund, Hoover reiterated his arguments concerning the demonstrated influence of the business cycle study and the need to reactivate its machinery in order to secure further improvements in national economic management. "An examination of recent economic changes," he wrote, "will lay the foundation for an overhauling of some of our basic statistics and for the strengthening of our industrial, commercial, and financial policy, looking toward further steadying of business and reduction of unemployment." Such an investigation, he added, would be larger and more extensive than the business cycle study because of the significant expansion of scientific competence. This, he said with some pride, would make possible the "collaboration of many organizations," whose prior investigations would make available "large contributions of material from both Governmental and private sources." As a part of this enlarged machinery, he envisioned once again a sponsoring committee composed of the "leaders of the business and economic groups" of the nation and charged with presiding over and receiving the National Bureau's technical study. "This should insure a practical direction to the study," he contended, "and the promotion of a sound program of action."[18]

In Hoover's mind, a realistic timetable for the study was one starting in January 1928 and making the results available by the spring of 1929. The costs, so Mitchell and Gay estimated, would be about $155,000. Accordingly, Hoover wanted the Carnegie and Spelman funds to contribute $75,000 each. At the latter the decision to do so came without much difficulty, but at the Carnegie Corporation there was considerable resistance, partly because its directors were trying to retrench to compensate for what they saw as overly generous past donations. "Might it not be advisable," asked Carnegie director Russell M. Leffingwell, soon to be one of Hoover's harshest critics, "to decline participation in the proposed study on the ground that the Corporation during the past decade has carried its full share of economic research activities . . . and cannot see its way clear now to assume a new 'Economic' obligation?"[19]

In view of such sentiments, Carnegie president Frederick P. Keppel turned for advice to Harold G. Moulton, director of Robert Brookings' Institute of Economics in Washington, D.C. "Would you be good enough," he wrote, "to indicate how important the former studies of business cycles proved to be and whether in your judgment a new analysis of the factors in our industrial life, if quickly made and printed, would promise important results?" In reply, Moulton assessed the business cycle study as having been "useful in two respects." It had helped, he said, to bring "the problem sharply to the attention of many people in positions of responsibility" and, beyond this, it had "broadened the conception of the causes responsible for business fluctuations, indicating that many things beside purely financial factors were involved," thus helping to produce policies, "both on the part of the Government and of the larger industries," that were "tending to lessen the fluctuations of business." But about the need for a new study he was not entirely positive. Some, he noted, were convinced that "stabilization and rationalization" had already laid the basis for "permanent prosperity." Besides, there were already at hand a number of useful studies of cyclical behavior and control, studies that he thought went about as far as any "quick general analysis" was likely to go. Perhaps another study modeled on the business cycle investigation could "render a useful service." But in the time projected, it could not provide a truly "critical appraisal" of the problem or "set forth a definitive solution."[20]

Despite Leffingwell's objections and Moulton's less than positive assessment, the Carnegie Corporation finally decided to fund the study. It also decided to make the grant to Hoover's projected committee rather than to the National Bureau, as George May and others who feared "politicization" had urged. Two things, it seems, were responsible for this latter decision. One was Mitchell's restatement of the importance of association with Hoover to the success of the enterprise. "Mitchell," Keppel reported, "says that while he fully appreciates the irritating way in which Hoover brings matters forward," his influence would be of great use "in obtaining without cost much of the material necessary for the fact-finding study."

Second, and probably of greater importance, was a letter of reassurance from Hunt to Keppel. After indicating that Hoover and those around him looked upon the project as "the largest and most important investigation ever undertaken in this country," Hunt went on to add "one frank word about the political situation." The study's timetable had been arranged, he said, so that the Committee on Recent Economic Changes ran "no risk whatever of becoming involved in the political fortunes of any individual." The technical investigation, he noted, would not be completed until after the 1928 elections. And while Hoover and Hunt were "eager to have the results made public early in the Spring of 1929 when the new Administration comes in," the "character of that Administration" would not "affect the plan."[21]

This attempt to discount any political impact was, to say the least, somewhat disingenuous. An election year was approaching; President Coolidge had long since made plain his intention not to stand for re-election; and Hoover was certainly a front-runner for the Republican nomination. Moreover, and for reasons that remain unclear, Hoover would shortly appoint himself chairman of the project's sponsoring committee. Unlike the Committee on Business Cycles and Unemployment, the Committee on Recent Economic Changes would be under the formal direction of a government rather than a business official, and this official would be one who already believed that his activities had made important contributions to the current prosperity. Nor did its early publicity, in which it was portrayed clearly as a "Hoover" project, do much to soothe those who feared they were inadvertently jumping on a Hoover bandwagon.

Nevertheless, Hoover had been successful in securing the kind of funding and organization he wanted. Just as with the business cycle study, the new project was to consist of two parts, the first being the National Bureau-directed technical investigation, and the second the drafting of policy recommendations by a sponsoring committee of business, labor, agricultural, and public representatives. Joining Hoover on the sponsoring committee were Lewis E. Pierson, president of the U.S. Chamber of Commerce; Clarence M. Woolley, chairman of the American Radiator Company; John S. Lawrence, president of the New England Council; Max Mason, president of the University of Chicago; Lewis J. Taber, Master of the National Grange; George McFadden, director of the Penn Mutual Life Insurance Company and a former official of the U.S. Food Administration; Renick W. Dunlap, Assistant Secretary of Agriculture; Adolph C. Miller, a Federal Reserve banker; Julius Klein, director of the Bureau of Foreign and Domestic Commerce; John J. Raskob, a General Motors executive and national Democratic leader; William Green, AFL president; Daniel Willard, president of the Baltimore and Ohio Railroad; Arch Shaw, a Taylorite and business publisher; Walter F. Brown, soon to be Hoover's postmaster general; and Owen D. Young. Hunt was to serve as secretary.[22]

The technical investigation, as envisioned by Mitchell and Gay, was to consist of more than a dozen analytical essays, covering such topics as population, transportation, agriculture, management, corporate organization, money and banking, and price structure. Of these "the sections on Population, Price structure, Profits, Interest and Wages," plus the study's introduction and conclusion, would be worked up by the National Bureau. But the other sections would require outside help. "We hope," they noted in an initial memorandum, "that the Department of Commerce will let us utilize, not only Mr. Hunt as managing editor, but also Dr. Gries as an expert on the construction industry, as well as opening to us the great supply of technical information possessed by its commodity experts and the huge accumulations of quantitative data in its files." In addition, they planned to "ask help from the Bureau of the Census in making fresh computations from its schedules," of the Institute of Economics in dealing with the "problem of Foreign Markets and Loans," and of professors W. J. Cunningham, Melvin Copeland, and Frank W. Taussig in preparing the sections on transportation, marketing, and industry.[23]

Other topics would also have to be assigned to outside experts. Managerial developments, for one, would be so delegated after consulting with "such outstanding authorities in that field as Messrs. A. W. Shaw, H. S. Dennison, Alfred Flynn, and John H. Williams." Similarly, the subject of corporate organization would require expert treatment, perhaps by "Mr. A. A. Berle, Jr." Labor developments would also be dealt with by those with expertise in the field, this after consulting with "Dr. Leo Wolman." And "various authorities" would have to be consulted before disposing of the financial topics. Once into the investigation, Mitchell and Gay concluded, they would "doubtless . . . discover a good many things of which at present none of us has an inkling."[24]

IV

"Those people," wrote Henry Dennison late in 1927, "who, in 1920, were saying that the business cycle was a myth are now beginning to say so again." Dennison knew better, as did Mary Van Kleeck. But while he looked to the development of a better informed and professionalized managerial class to prevent serious slumps, she was now escalating her criticism of the "new managerialism" and beginning to develop an alternative to the Hooverian approach.[25]

The issue now, she continued to insist, was the anomalous phenomenon of unemployment within a general prosperity, a "curious situation" that was unlike anything in recent experience. "It seems to be true," she noted, "that for the country as a whole, production is at a high rate, goods are being sold and people are making money." Yet at the same time, "wage-earners are out of work." And this, so she argued, represented both a problem and an opportunity. It was a problem both to those experiencing it and to those seeking remedies in a nation that wanted to study the causes of prosperity rather than its flaws. But it was also a condition that presented Americans with a new national opportunity, for in the high rates of production and business activity, they had developed "an excellent

142

foundation upon which to build for a new and vigorous attack upon the problem of unemployment."[26]

To Van Kleeck's mind, current unemployment was not "the same old problem." Looking back to "1907, 1914, and 1921," she said, "we can see differences." In 1921, business was in trouble. "Car loadings were falling off; goods were not being transported or sold; bank clearings began to show less activity." Consequently, there was a direct connection between suffering businesses and idle workers. But this connection no longer held for many industries. The business cycle committee, she noted, attributed the unemployment of 1921 "to bad judgment on the part of the collective businessman," who "let his inventories pile up too much; and when the crash came, . . . was forced to the wall." Dealing with unemployment had thus become a problem of improving business judgment and managerial performance. But if "we now have unemployment in a period of prosperity," Van Kleeck argued, "if the businessman's judgment has been good on the whole for himself and for investors," and "if now we have a situation indicating more efficiency in Labor and fine technical equipment in industry as a whole, then we are ready to talk about making employment secure." No longer was it necessary to "concentrate upon the problem of stabilizing business." It was now a "problem of stabilizing employment," which, as she saw it, posed both an opportunity and a challenge for the labor movement.[27]

It also involved the beginnings of an analysis of technological or structural unemployment, which was for Van Kleeck a necessary point of departure for a strategy in which labor would assume a larger role in social management. Where "mechanical equipment and efficiency in production have increased to the point where workers are forced into idleness because they are superfluous," she wrote, "then the problem of unemployment" is no longer the problem of business stabilization but "a problem of human relations." And because the labor movement, "first, last and always is concerned with human relations in industry," it was the labor movement's responsibility "to devise ways for preventing unemployment."[28]

143

Scolding the labor movement for ignoring the difficult issue of irregularity in employment in favor of a more narrow preoccupation with wages, Van Kleeck insisted that continuous full employment was possible. "We in the United States," she said, "have developed industry to a point of technical efficiency where it should be possible to insure the good life for all the people." But to do so, the application of social science would have to go beyond its present function in the Hooverian approach and become a means of providing workers' organizations with the factual data and managerial techniques needed to protect industrial laborers from technological unemployment. In an effectively managed economic system, Van Kleeck felt that "labor's representatives should be in the councils of the business groups . . . , so as to know in advance what the forecast for labor seems to be, just as business forecasts its demand for raw materials and its probable outlook for the year." At the present time, she pointed out, "labor knows the forecast for employment only when wage-earners are laid off."[29]

Specifically, Van Kleeck advocated the creation of joint research committees composed of labor and management representatives and operating as community- or industry-wide agencies. Equipped with staffs of technical experts, she believed such committees could go far toward stabilizing employment as well as business, particularly in the more troubled industries, and could thus avoid the tendency to sacrifice the former goal to the latter. Already, she pointed out, the United Textile Workers of America had approached their industry with just such a proposal and already the assets available for joint research merited "at least a trial." As she saw it, these assets included labor's increasing willingness to cooperate in such ventures; the importance that trade associations attached to industry-wide research; the expansion of the government's statistical capacities, particularly the proliferation of trade and commodity data; and the recent development of "impartial agencies devoted to social research in the public interest." Together, these could be utilized to attack "a problem which

144

affects the whole nation and reaches beyond national boundaries."[30]

But this was early 1928, and by September of the same year Van Kleeck's tone had changed. Labor was not, as she had hoped, moving rapidly to make "full use of the results of social or economic studies." Nor were social scientists "closely enough in contact with labor." Much of the problem, she suggested, could be traced to "labor's fear that the privately supported research institution exists primarily to defend capitalism as it is, and hence cannot be trusted to speak the truth in controversial economic questions."

Thus the vacuum of macroeconomic authority that institutions like the National Bureau had been created to fill was, for Van Kleeck, still in existence. And if it was to be filled, there would have to be new bodies of technocratic competence developed within the labor movement, giving to it a capacity to assess information generated elsewhere and make informed policy decisions. "Labor needs its own research under its own auspices," she concluded, because "the problems of labor today" were "too far-reaching" to be solved without such reinforcement.[31]

V

The Committee on Recent Economic Changes investigation was organized and topics assigned at an initial meeting on February 21, 1928. The investigators met several times between then and the completion of the technical study on October 10, and the staff subsequently held at least six meetings with the sponsoring committee. These produced, by early January 1929, the first draft of the committee's report.[32]

The technical staff eventually chosen closely resembled the one initially envisioned by Mitchell and Gay. They were left to do their work without consultation while the committee suspended meetings for a considerable period in deference to the campaign of 1928. In addition, some thirty scientific, trade, labor, and professional organizations; at least thirty colleges

145

and universities; a total of nine major government agencies; and over a hundred and fifty other individuals helped to provide the data. The chapters based on this information were written by the bureau's staff and eleven outside experts who had been chosen to examine particular topics. Among the latter were Dexter Kimball and Leon P. Alford of the American Engineering Council; Cunningham, Copeland, and Sprague of Harvard; Edwin T. Nourse of the Institute of Economics; and Henry Dennison. The investigation's quality, so Hunt was persuaded, was sufficient to make it "a test of the Hoover method."[33]

On October 10, in the initial meeting held between the research staff and the sponsoring committee, at least one chapter author concluded that the era had witnessed fundamental changes. In "Consumption and the Standard of Living," the first of two chapters written by Leo Wolman of the National Bureau, it was argued that "revolutionary" changes had taken place over the past decade. But this was an unpopular sentiment. Instead, most of the study's authors insisted that the changes under analysis were best understood as evolutionary, and this would become the report's fundamental theme.[34]

When the committee resumed its deliberations shortly after the November elections, concern for what was regarded as an "unsound" trend in the stock market dominated the proceedings. This would continue on into the January meetings. Still, the sentiments generally expressed were ones of cautious optimism. For example, Frederick Mills of the National Bureau staff concluded that the existing stability represented a return to pre-1913 characteristics: "Judging from the earlier experience," he thought, the "tendency to greater stability" would continue. Similarly, Adolph C. Miller was excited by the prospect "that business can be successfully and effectively conducted on a falling price trend." "That in itself," he believed, was "a very important contribution to an understanding of modern economics" and what could be a potential "revolution in economic attitudes."[35]

On January 23, the focus turned to the task of isolating the vital factors responsible for New Era prosperity. "Something had happened," Hunt noted, but what? Arch Shaw, who with Hoover's assumption of pre-presidential duties had become acting chairman, "held it was management which had changed and broadened." But this raised the question, particularly for Lewis Pierson and Adolph Miller, as to why European managerialism had not developed along similar lines. The eventual conclusion was that while both America and Europe had entered the postwar era equipped with potent managerial ideas ("Rathenau and his groups had them"), the Europeans had not had the proper "environment" for implementing and developing them.[36]

Significant changes, the committee agreed, had occurred in management's perception and handling of labor. At the end of the war, Shaw suggested, management had nearly decapitated the labor movement, and "if it had not been for the fear of Bolshevism, it would have been done." But as Wesley Mitchell viewed it, the 1921 depression and the unemployment conference had made the subsequent economic success and industrial peace possible. "I do not believe we could have done as well in 1922 and 1927," said Mitchell, "if we had not had that deflation in 1921." "Business men started back from Washington to liquidate labor," explained Mitchell. But "they did not do that." Instead, they "liquidated their own values."[37]

Worry over rising speculative fevers, and particularly over the Federal Reserve's role in curbing them, also kept surfacing at the January meetings. The Federal Reserve's actions, so Miller argued, had had a "steadying influence on business in recent years." But without proper credit controls, a dangerous situation could get worse. Part of the problem, Lewis Pierson thought, was the "feeling that the millennium has arrived because we have the Federal Reserve System."[38]

VI

Recent Economic Changes in the United States was published in two volumes by McGraw-Hill on May 15, 1929. Its first twenty pages, taken up with the sponsoring committee's report, were followed by nine hundred pages of analysis and explication on thirteen separate topics. These, in turn, were sandwiched between literate essays of introduction and conclusion written by Gay and Mitchell respectively.

Both the technical studies and the committee's report displayed a tempered optimism. "Acceleration rather than structural change," so the committee report began, "is the key to an understanding of our recent economic developments." The more fully one studied the situation, "the more evident it became that the novelty of the period" lay not "in structure but in speed and spread." As Hunt would later note, the committee "could find no evidence of a 'New Era.' "[39]

But if there was "no new principle in installment selling," if cooperative marketing was "no modern discovery," and if "the chain store movement" dated back "at least twenty-five years," nevertheless the "breadth and scale and 'tempo' " of these and similar developments had given them fresh importance. Increasing amounts of power, the spread of mechanization, and a more efficient division of labor, all amounting to "an accumulation of forces which have long been at work," had led to greater productivity and "intense" commercial activity. And while the committee was careful to note the unevenness of the new prosperity, it concluded that "the rising standard of living characteristic of this period" was widespread and had "reached the highest level in our national history."[40]

Unlike *Business Cycles and Unemployment*, the new report was cast mostly in descriptive terms and featured virtually no prescriptive components. On two points, however, it was unmistakably firm. The first, deriving from Dennison's analysis of recent developments in American business management, held that most of the decade's outstanding developments were due to improvements in the training and practice of managers. "Experts and committeemen alike," Hunt pointed out, "agree that the factor which most nearly explains the marked increase in the volume of production and in productivity per man, and the relative stability of business activities from 1922 to the

Spring of 1929, is better management." Gay's introduction also noted that "the problem of correlating abundant resources, expensive labor, and unsurpassed machine equipment" had put "a high premium on management and organizing ability." Scientific management, he observed, was believed by many foreign observers to be "the chief contribution which this country is making to economic welfare." And as management grew more specialized and "far-sighted," it was gradually becoming a "new profession," one whose effect on American industry was already "separating the functions of ownership and management."[41]

The second point, one that appeared repeatedly in the technical studies as well as in the committee's report and seemed at the time to be the most substantive policy conclusion, concerned the need for developing a "technique of balance." Both the technical studies and the committee report had set forth the idea that recent prosperity was the result not only of new stimulants to growth but of the achievement of a rough equilibrium among the nation's economic forces. Put most simply, higher incomes, consumer credit, and mass advertising had helped to spur an expansion of mass demand, which in turn had fostered new investments, greater productivity, and even higher wages. The result had been a balance between productive and consumptive capacities, which had become the basis for stable growth, a steady price level, and higher living standards for more and more people.

Such had been the achievements of the 1920s. The task now, so the committee thought, was to make explicit the factors contributing to macroeconomic balance and fashion them into a conscious technique, one that would amount to nothing less than a mechanism of continuous national management. "As long as the appetite for goods and services is practically insatiable," the report read, "and as long as productivity can be consistently increased," continued prosperity was likely. But securing and maintaining this prosperity would require the nation to "develop a technique of balance," one that would depend on the contributions of economists, statisticians, engineers, and enlightened managers. "To their influence," the committee concluded, "we have come to look in large measure for the maintenance of our economic balance."[42]

Recent Economic Changes was warmly received. "I believe," Hunt wrote in September 1929, "no other diffuse and difficult economic study has ever had such a reception." The first printing, he told George Vincent, president of the Rockefeller Foundation, nearly sold out in advance of publication, and a third was already scheduled. "I hope," so Hunt told Keppel, "that you feel gratified, as do the members of the Committee, at the extraordinary interest in the report."[43]

It is not clear from the evidence that the Hoover publicity apparatus played the large role here that it had with the publication of *Business Cycles and Unemployment*. Nevertheless, the study was "constantly referred to in magazines, newspapers, and public addresses," according to Hunt. "Editorial comment," he indicated, "was overwhelmingly favorable and has been world-wide." P. W. Martin of the Research Division of the International Labor Office thought the study itself to be a valuable step toward construction of a technique of balance. *The Tax Digest* praised the project for developing "an unprecedented array of information." The *Survey Graphic* devoted an entire issue to the question of "Why Prosperity Keeps Up." And Hunt himself contributed to the public comment via speeches and articles throughout 1929. He would continue to promote the study and its generally optimistic conclusions even as the events of late 1929 and 1930 seriously undercut their credibility.[44]

Though real enough, New Era prosperity was never so widespread or balanced as many, including the Committee on Recent Economic Changes, had thought. Nor was the purported equilibrium between production and consumption and the overall soundness of the business structure as real as many assumed. *Recent Economic Changes* would later be faulted, even by its creators, as a hurried and ill-considered job, too much subject to Hoover's deadline pressure. Decades later, however, others would continue to regard it as as "invaluable" source.

And standing somewhere between these views, as 1929 passed into the gathering gloom of 1930, was another group led by Shaw, Hunt, and Mitchell, who looked upon the stock market crash and subsequent contraction not as an invalidation of the study's findings but as evidence of its incompleteness. Throughout 1930, 1931, and 1932 they would work to extend its life and correct its mistakes, still hoping to discover a workable "technique of balance."[45]

CHAPTER 9

After the Crash, 1929–1932

> I tell you, Robineau, in life there are no so-
> lutions. There are only motive forces, and
> our task is to set them acting—then the so-
> lutions follow.
> —Antoine de Saint-Exupery[1]

The collapse of New Era prosperity from 1929 through 1932 shattered the expectations and contradicted the assumptions of Hooverian planning. Not only was the "new capitalism" unable to sustain a stable expansion; it proved incapable, when its business and technical institutions were put to the test, of predicting or mitigating the subsequent deflation.

In Hoover's mind, the setback of 1929 was something that should yield to the same organizational initiatives as had been applied in 1921. Consequently, his actions as president consisted largely of efforts to reproduce earlier successes by invoking a range of presumably proven countercyclical measures. Thus late 1929 saw him winning promises of expanded investment and wage maintenance from business leaders, cooperation from labor, and monetary expansion from the Federal Reserve Board, while from the Congress he obtained a tax cut and a $400 million public works appropriation. These, so he argued at the time, were measures calculated to reduce panic and encourage the compensatory spending needed to reinflate a temporarily disordered economy.[2]

But as activist and up-to-date as these measures were, they were inadequate to the task and would soon be overwhelmed by the most terrible economic contraction in the American experience. The flaws of the New Era system and of the Hoover antidepression program, which were legion, have been analyzed elsewhere and are not our concern here. Instead,

152

this chapter will follow the impact of the economic crisis on the planning activities that were supposed to have insured continued economic growth and permanent prosperity.[3]

II

The story of macroeconomic planning during the Hoover presidency began as an extension and elaboration of the Committee on Recent Economic Changes (REC) study "Toward the Development of a Technique of Balance." By late February 1930, the success and popularity of the initial study was such that its publisher, McGraw-Hill, was readying a fourth printing. A subsidiary study, "Planning and Control of Public Works," had also been underway since the summer of 1929 and was to be published in the spring of 1930. Despite the stock market crash, E. E. Hunt thought the REC findings were holding up well. They had not ignored the threats posed by stock market speculation, and they had brought out the rough balance between production and consumption that had been achieved through sound organization and improving managment—a balance, Hunt believed, that had not been fundamentally altered by the stock market boom and the ensuing crash. "By all the rules of history and principles," he wrote in February 1930, "American industry should have run wild in the traditional way. It didn't. The market did, but business didn't." This, he concluded, was "the first real test of balance."[4]

The second test, already well underway, was the nearly unprecedented intervention by the president "without waiting for major business troubles to develop." Hoover's prompt action in the fall of 1929 had been nothing less than "revolutionary," and while it would be months before the effects of these actions could be measured, the president's "calling into conference" of business, financial, and labor representatives, all "determined to counteract the effects of a dip in the business cycle by the stimulation of private and public construction, by the maintenance of general buying power, and by the preservation of industrial peace," had been "brilliant." Although

the nation was still far from possessing the technique of economic balance envisioned in the REC study, the measures
taken in late 1929 and early 1930 were, as Hunt saw it, a
significant step in that direction. If "we are some day to have
in this country a managed national economy based upon the
full cooperation of industry and Government," he declared,
"the most important move in this direction will be found in
the recent conferences in Washington."[5]

Sharing Hunt's hope for a "managed national economy"
was Mary Van Kleeck. But as we have seen in previous chapters, she had become increasingly critical of the assumptions
and promise of the Hooverian operations. For nearly two years,
she had been pointing to the disparity between the ideal and
reality, arguing that the new prosperity was accompanied by
rising unemployment within sick and supposedly healthy industries alike, a condition that suggested serious structural
flaws and imbalances. And as of early 1930, she saw continuing
disparities and imbalances being obfuscated by "a battle of
statistics." In particular, the overly optimistic assessments and
predictions emanating from the White House did not, in her
view, jibe well with the unemployment figures collected by the
states and by independent researchers.[6]

"Insecurity of employment," Van Kleeck argued, remained
a major flaw in the economy's structure and a primary source
of the erosion of purchasing power. To deal with it and other
problems, far-sighted national planning would be necessary—
and Herbert Hoover, she thought, could rightfully lead the
further development of such planning. His announcement of
the National Business Survey Conference in the fall, "a potential economic planning board," could be a step in this direction, but Van Kleeck was doubtful that such would be the
case or that the measures taken would be adequate to deal
with so severe a national crisis. Recent "statements from the
White House," she wrote in early 1930, "give evidence of a
disappointing opportunism in political leadership, rather than
[the] sober grappling with realities which is characteristic of
engineering."[7]

154

The "battle of statistics" continued and intensified well into the summer of 1930, partly as a result of honest differences over the interpretation of data and the weaknesses of the employment data collection system itself, but also, it seems, as a result of the tendency in the Hoover camp toward optimistic assessments of present conditions and presidential achievements. As part of the 1930 census, the government was now conducting a national survey of unemployment, something that Van Kleeck had urged in order to clear up the statistical confusion. Yet at the same time, Hunt was making statistical estimates that gave Hoover credit for major countercyclical achievements. " A record year in construction of public works and public utilities amounting to more than $7,000,000 now seems probable," he wrote. This was something that would be capable of "providing the income or adding to the income of millions of families," and as a result of the experience and of further study, the government might now move on "to transform the long-range planning of public works from abstract theory into a practical program."[8]

With Hoover's election to the presidency, Arch Shaw had become chairman of the Committee on Recent Economic Changes, and by the spring of 1930 had taken charge of securing monies for an extension of the committee's apparatus and mission, this time to be directed explicitly toward uncovering "a technique of balance." The idea, in essence, was to build on the data already assembled and published in order to provide an updated account of economic behavior since 1928, one that would correct previous interpretive errors and derive a more precise understanding of the sources of macroeconomic stability and instability. The "fundamental question" to be pursued was: "How do changes affecting economic welfare come about, and, particularly, what factors are clearly instrumental in the extremes of change?" Having just "passed through a period when economic equilibrium has been so out of balance through excesses in speculative finance as to retard business activity and increase unemployment," Shaw wrote to F. P. Keppel of the Carnegie Corporation, "continuation of

155

the inquiry" seemed to be "not only essential but peculiarly timely."[9]

NBER board member George O. May, who functioned as an important go-between in the National Bureau's relationship with the Carnegie Corporation, urged the foundation, particularly its most reluctant trustee, Russell M. Leffingwell, to continue its support of the committee and the bureau. "I am more than ever convinced of the value of the Bureau [sic] work," he wrote in February. And in a point he would return to in 1932, May noted how "impressed" he was "with the importance the labor men attached to the Bureau and the faith they had in its ability and willingness to formulate reports that would be fair to all interests." They seemed to feel, he continued, "that it is the one body in the field in which they can trust." As far as May was concerned, this fact alone made the bureau a worthy investment in times of economic trouble.[10]

Neither Keppel nor Leffingwell, however, were much impressed with Shaw's or May's proposals. Keppel, it seems, had come to regard the entire project with distaste, describing Shaw as "a very wooden person," and noting that "it would be difficult to get up a less satisfactory committee" than the one now seeking money. He suspected that the "basic idea" behind continuation of the study was "to maintain the tradition of Hoover prosperity," and he was determined to resist Shaw's efforts "to sting us for a large amount."[11]

More important, perhaps, was the feeling of embarrassment, shared by both Keppel and Leffingwell, at being closely associated with a project whose cautious but generally optimistic conclusions had been badly contradicted by subsequent events. "As you know." Leffingwell would write to Keppel later in 1932, "I consider that the National Bureau disgraced itself and the Carnegie Corporation by its work on Recent Economic Changes." "Presumably under political pressure," in Leffingwell's view, it had "completely disregarded the prospect of disaster which actually occurred after its publication."

Already feeling used by Hoover, the trustees of the Carnegie Corporation decided against further funding of the

Committee on Recent Economic Changes, although small grants would continue to be made to the NBER. With the Rockefellers, however, Shaw and Hunt fared somewhat better, partly because the Harvard economist Edmund E. Day, long associated with efforts to bring social science to bear on policy problems, had now stepped in as director of the Rockefeller Foundation's new division of social science. This had been established in 1929 when the Laura Spelman Rockefeller Memorial was merged with the Foundation and Beardsley Ruml had decided to retire as its director.[12]

In a research proposal drawn up by Mitchell and submitted by Hunt, those associated with the REC apparatus asked Day for a grant of $85,000. "It seems to us," Hunt wrote, "that economic forces may be broadly classified as active and passive"; and there was possibly, he continued, a "zone of tolerance" within which the "active forces" could play safely. Outside this zone, however, such forces endangered economic stability. Hence, any effort to construct "a technique of balance" must first distinguish between "active" and "passive" factors in economic life and then "determine when these forces get beyond the bounds of the zone of tolerance and how their excesses can be moderated."[13]

Some of the phraseology was new, but the method—business cycle analysis—was unchanged. Under the proposal the investigators, to be joined now by John Maurice Clark, an institutionalist and business cycle theorist, would make "a rapid comparative survey" of no more than six months' duration, focusing in particular on fluctuations in profits, prices, interest, and construction activity, and seeking to reconstruct the cyclical record through 1929.[14]

Day was receptive and apparently had little difficulty in winning approval for a $50,000 grant, provided the committee could raise an equivalent amount from other sources. Given Carnegie's unwillingness to contribute, this requirement might have proved troublesome, but by January 1931, as the project began to gear up, Shaw was able to report that individual and corporate contributions had already reached more than half

157

of the required $50,000. In raising the funds, Shaw reported the committee had asked "very wealthy people or corporations to contribute . . . in small amounts in order that we might not interfere in any way with the solicitation of funds for the amelioration of the unemployment situation." He noted also that "so far I have not had a refusal and the money has been contributed by men and institutions like Julius Rosenwald, Eugene Meyer, Lewis Pierson, the Insull Companies, George B. Everitt, John Raskob, the Standard Oil Company of Indiana, and others."[15]

Looking forward to 1931, Shaw was especially appreciative of Day's "sympathy with the philosophy of our undertaking," and by March of that year he was reporting "substantial progress." The study, he said, was proceeding along the well-worn path of collaboration between a sponsoring committee and the National Bureau's technical staff, and was moving swiftly through regular weekly meetings to implement a plan of research designed to uncover and accomplish the following:

1. An explanation of the "recession of 1929–1930."
2. Identification of the factors involved, whether "deep-seated, automatic, [or] artificial."
3. An integration of these findings with those of the initial study "so that we may have as ample a record as possible of a complete, post-war business cycle."
4. A determination of the inadequacies and gaps in the record.
5. A construction of the study in such a way "that it will be a serviceable tool . . . for other investigators," politicians, and business managers.[16]

This last point was apparently what Hoover also had in mind early in 1931 when he approved legislation creating the Federal Employment Stabilization Board (FESB), an agency designed to counter fluctuations in the business cycle through long-range and continuous planning of public works construction. Composed of four cabinet members—the secretaries of

158

commerce, agriculture, treasury, and labor—the board and its technical staff were authorized to develop six-year advance programs for federal construction and guidelines for similar activity on the state level; to organize and maintain up-to-date statistics of business conditions in general and construction levels in particular; and to provide the basis for better managed and more orderly national development. From the FESB's emphasis on this last point would come the New Deal's National Resources Planning Board.[17]

Two other ancillary developments, the deployment of the President's Advisory Committee on Employment Statistics and the internationalization of the REC committee's concerns, should also be noted. The Advisory Committee, appointed in August 1930, was composed of a typically Hooverian mix of public, business, and social science leaders, several of whom had been or were then involved with the National Bureau's work for the unemployment conference and its successor agencies. The mission of the Committee was to develop guidelines for more precise measurement of employment and unemployment, and in February 1931 it submitted recommendations pointing particularly to methods for the improved assessment of technological unemployment.[18]

The internationalization of REC concerns came in September 1930, when the committee was invited to participate in a League of Nations conference on the causes and course of the economic downturn. In March of 1931, Hunt traveled to Geneva for a preliminary conference and was involved both in setting the agenda for a larger conference and in efforts to coordinate the several national investigations then taking place. Nothing much would come from such efforts or from the general conference in July of 1931, but participation by those associated with the REC studies did reflect a greater awareness of the interrelatedness of separate national difficulties, an awareness that Mary Van Kleeck had seized upon, perhaps earlier than most American analysts.[19]

Joining with Mary Fledderus, a sociologist who was also a close friend, Van Kleeck had in 1928 become associate director

159

of the International Industrial Relations Institute (IRI), an organization devoted to the promotion of international economic planning, which by early 1930 was busily organizing a World Social Economic Congress to dramatize planning as a way out of the depression. In April 1930, Van Kleeck had approached Owen Young, Julius Barnes, Paul M. Warburg, and E.R.A. Seligman, asking them to help develop a program for American participation and stressing particularly the need for "internationalizing" the model of the unemployment conference of 1921. The goal, she thought, should be an effort to "apply internationally the method attempted in this country in 1921, when Mr. Hoover said that he was trying to lift the subject of unemployment to a higher plane of industrial statesmanship." There should be machinery, in other words, to push the businessmen of several countries "to use the results of economic research" and "through their influence" to bring about a coordinated international recovery. In Van Kleeck's view, it was especially important that Seligman participate. He was the first editor of the new *International Encyclopedia of the Social Sciences*, and as such could play a role that would enhance "the status of the social sciences in all countries in their bearing upon economic problems."[20]

The international congress, held in Amsterdam in the fall of 1931, brought together representatives from Australia, Canada, China, France, Britain, Germany, the United States, and the Soviet Union. There, and in her subsequent articles for various publications, Van Kleeck insisted that scientific management and social work had already established a fundamental technique of planning. Scientific management, she argued, had demonstrated the efficacy of organizational planning, although by itself it could easily be turned to the antisocial uses of business cartels interested in profit maintenance through reduced production. Thus scientific management must be joined to social work, which was concerned with "raising standards of living in proportion to productive capacity." It was "the contribution of the IRI," she later noted, "that it took the subject of economic planning and showed that it could be

of significance in reducing unemployment and raising standards of living only if the adjective 'social' were added to it."

Social work's long-standing dedication to the "prevention"
of poverty, Van Kleeck thought, had prepared it to embrace
the new "preventative" of "planning." And to this end, she
was now urging the establishment of a "world center for the
study of planning" and the dedication of the social work
profession to the cause of erecting "a planned economy."[21]

III

By July 1931 Shaw was able to report to the Rockefeller
Foundation on the "continued progress" of the REC committee's technical staff, and by August, Wesley Mitchell could de-
clare that "our report on the current depression . . . is rounding into shape better than I had expected." By early 1932 the
technical reports had progressed sufficiently for Shaw to re-
convene the sponsoring committee, but neither he nor the
committee wanted to rush into print until they had traced the
present cycle to its conclusion. Apparently chastened by their
earlier experience with *Recent Economic Changes*, and determined now to track the cycle to its trough, Shaw reported that
it was the sense of the entire committee that "the final and
official report should not be published until such time as the
statistical data for the complete cycle is available."

In the interim Shaw inaugurated an "experiment in bridging
the gap between the work of the technical group and the
practical application of their findings by men of affairs." What
he envisioned was the formation in Chicago of a "cooperating
committee" to "devote an evening . . . to the discussion of each
section of the Bureau's report" and to develop the "salient"
points for the standing committee's consideration. On this "cooperating committee," Shaw noted, would be such men as
Melvin A. Traylor, president of the First National Bank; John
Stuart, president of Quaker Oats; Sewell Avery, Chairman of
U.S. Gypsum; Alexander Legge, president of International

Harvester; George B. Everitt, president of Montgomery Ward; and Victor Olander, a labor official.[22]

Shaw's plans, however, were apparently frustrated by his inability to raise more funds to sustain further investigations. As noted previously, he had relied upon the solicitation of amounts under $2,000 in order to broaden the base of committee support and not interfere with larger relief activities. But by October 1931, as the economic situation grew worse, he wished that he had "asked for larger amounts." The decision against such a policy, he lamented, had not been "the right one."[23]

The more general financial picture of the National Bureau was also becoming increasingly bleak. The Carnegie Corporation had been carrying it on yearly appropriations, but not without the misgivings of some of its trustees, like Leffingwell, who looked upon the bureau's complicity in the Hooverian apparatus as evidence of politicization and illegitimacy. Like Shaw, Gay and Mitchell had to work against the increasingly bad economic climate of late 1931 and early 1932 in their fundraising efforts, and by early 1932 it seemed that only an emergency appropriation could keep the bureau from folding. Shaw and Clarence Woolley were prepared to underwrite personally the REC committee's responsibility to the bureau, but without another grant from one of the foundations, operating expenses could not be met and studies in progress might not be completed.[24]

These financial difficulties had also helped to create a larger crisis of confidence and purpose. Some bureau officials were unhappy with what they regarded as Gay's inattention to the agency's precarious financial position. Others, like Oswald Knauth, expressed an even deeper demoralization. While acknowledging to Harry Laidler, a conservative socialist and now the bureau's president, that the bureau's pre-1929 work had been "worthwhile," Knauth had "come definitely to the conclusion that the Bureau has been drifting and will probably continue to drift." "I feel strongly," he continued, "that the driving impulse of discovering facts in which everyone is interested, has left us." Consequently, he would "recommend at the Annual Meeting that we dissolve at the end of this year if the Carnegie and Rockefeller Corporations will see us through the year."[25]

This was also the proposal that Knauth took to Leffingwell. "It seems," he began, "we have a request before the Carnegie board for $15,000 for this year, in the granting of which you are the final word." He was "disappointed," he said, with the present state of the bureau and hence uncertain about "the advisability of carrying on." But the agency's investigators were "now about to publish several interesting documents," and he was therefore proposing a deal. If Carnegie would stake the bureau to one last appropriation, and thereby help its researchers finish current projects, no further requests would be made, and the bureau would soon close down. "I write," Knauth concluded, "in the hope that you may see your way clear toward granting the $15,000 for this year only, even with the distinct proviso that it will not be renewed."[26]

It is not clear how much Gay, Mitchell, or anyone else knew of this negotiation. Though he shared its contents with Keppel, Leffingwell regarded Knauth's offer as confidential and insisted to Keppel that "it should not be communicated by you to anyone." On March 16, 1932, the Carnegie Board voted a one-year, nonrenewable emergency appropriation of $15,000 to the bureau.[27]

By June, two of the technical studies, Frederick Mills' survey of price movements and Ralph Epstein's study of profits, were nearing completion. Because of the shortage of funding and the difficulty he was having in keeping his consultative machinery in operation, Shaw was ready to have these studies published as the work of the National Bureau, without REC committee oversight or approval. "It seems," he wrote to Edmund Day, "as if the other members of the Committee are constantly being drafted for emergency undertakings growing out of the present acute situation." Both they and the cooperating committee in Chicago remained "keenly interested," but the credit crisis and the new wave of business failures had

163

left these men with other "corporate and public responsibilities." George Everitt of Montgomery Ward, for example, who had assumed the chair of the coordinating committee, "had been entirely immersed" in the affairs of his firm; and when Everitt finally resigned, his replacement seemed equally preoccupied. According to Shaw, he had been drawn into "the affairs of the Insull companies and tells me he will be completely absorbed by them for some weeks yet."[28]

Like almost everyone else, Shaw had not anticipated that the downturn of late 1929–1930 would continue for so long or that the work of his committee would be made so difficult by a cycle that had refused to hit bottom. "Our Committee started in 1930," he told Day, "to continue the record that it had been making of a post-war business cycle, but the cycle, in the most contrary fashion, refuses to complete itself and, therefore, the record itself cannot be completed, although much progress has been made." Still, Shaw felt that the committee must persist in trying "to make a factual record of the movement of economic activities during the long major cycle from 1922 to the close of the period, whenever that may be." The value of this course, he insisted, was high; and he was "more than ever convinced, from our experiences of the last few months, of the value of such an orderly and systematic record. . . . If there had been available similar records of the depressions of the 70's and 90's they would have been of utmost value during our present emergency."

Looking ahead, Shaw also noted that "even after the first upward turn in business activities years may elapse before business reaches what is called normal." A complete and up-to-date record, "issued with reasonable promptness after the change in the trend of business activity," he thought, "should be of help during that period." And just as important, he concluded, "I think I can see in the making a different sort of interest on the part of men of real consequence in the business world toward trying to find out something about how economic forces behave." Once the present emergency passed,

164

Shaw was convinced, more and more businessmen would take an active interest in data-building and interpretation.[29]

IV

The fall of 1932 saw the publication of the first fruits of Shaw's project. Frederick C. Mills' *Economic Tendencies in the United States* was more than the compilation of price movements originally envisioned; now it included a much wider review of economic trends between early 1928 and October 1929. Partly because of its immediate utility and partly because of Shaw's inability to organize his committee for the required oversight and approval function, the volume was not issued under REC committee auspices. Instead it was published by the National Bureau in cooperation with the committee, with Shaw, in the committee's name, providing a brief statement of introduction.[30]

There would soon be other publications under the same auspices. John Maurice Clark's survey of cycles through 1929, originally envisioned as a "rapid" survey needing only six months or so, would be published in early 1934 as *Strategic Factors in Business Cycles*. Also published in 1934 was Ralph Epstein's study of profit structure and movement, *Industrial Profits in the United States*. The surviving evidence, however, suggests that the REC committee had already ceased to function by the spring and summer of 1932, and that these volumes, like the Mills study before them, were published primarily as National Bureau products.[31]

But while the committee dissolved under the weight of the depression, the National Bureau did not. Early in 1933, despite the apparent "deal" of the previous year, it won from the Carnegie Corporation and the Rockefeller Foundation pledges of renewed and continuous support. In the case of the Carnegie Corporation, it would seem that Hoover's banishment from the political scene must have been a helpful if not a decisive factor. In February, Gay reported, George O. May "had talked with Leffingwell who assured him that he

165

would not oppose, in fact is friendly" to the bureau's application for a grant of $50,000 per year for five years, and Day was inclined to grant even more if other foundations, like Carnegie, would help.[32]

Also strengthening the bureau's new applications, it seems, was a scaling down of outside commitments accompanied by an administrative reorganization that allowed Mitchell and Knauth to exert more day-to-day control. Throughout the 1920s, the alliance with Hoover and his planning apparatus had won the bureau financial aid and the respect of important business and labor leaders. But this had come to be a drain as well, notably in the form of overhead and other indirect costs that were never sufficiently funded. In addition, by tying itself so closely to Hoover's program, the bureau had, as we have seen, suffered from the reversal of Hoover's political fortunes and the discrediting of both his ideas and the institutions with which he had been associated.[33]

EPILOGUE

In the 1920s the Hooverian vision of a society managed by enlightened private groups contributed powerfully to the mutual legitimation of technocratic professionals and business planners. And although this techno-corporatism failed to provide for and maintain a balance among Saint-Exupéry's "motive forces," the technocratic constituency upon which it was built did not suffer the repudiation suffered by Hoover and his program. Indeed, by the late 1920s America's social science professions had become an established part of the modern managerial constellation, occupying, to be sure, a difficult and subordinate position, but one in which they would be able to exert a continuing and regular influence on policy formation and implementation.

The National Bureau would continue taking on new research commitments. Its central figure, Wesley Mitchell, would play an important role in New Deal planning activities and would continue to promote and defend data-building as necessary to social science. By the 1940s, he would enjoy a secure reputation as the father of modern business cycle analysis, as a leader in the professionalization of the social sciences, and as the guiding force behind institutions that had helped through data-gathering to enhance the standing and legitimacy of the social sciences.[1]

Another of the era's policy scientists, Mary Van Kleeck, deserves to stand with Mitchell as an architect of social science, and with such women as Mary Parker Follett and Lillian Gilbreth as a founding sister of management science. But she would follow other paths. By 1933 she had begun what would become a series of excursions to the Soviet Union, where she was impressed by the rationality of the five-year plans and the extent of worker participation in their execution. Aghast at the contrast between a working Soviet economy and an idle

167

American one, she would call again and again for the extension of political power to American workers and the use of this power to develop a system of national planning. A severe critic of what she regarded to be a New Deal insufficiently supportive of labor, Van Kleeck would emerge by the mid-1930s as an outspoken leader of the left wing of American social work, urging her colleagues to commit themselves professionally to the cause of planning.[2]

The later influence of social scientists such as these was at least partly the result of the New Era's technocratic bargain between social science and managerial institutions, a bargain institutionalized in the NBER's structure and operations. For a time they had helped to confer legitimacy on efforts to erect planning machinery outside the already constituted political arenas, and in return they had received support for activities that had enhanced their standing as scientists and "disinterested" data builders.

In the hands of socially committed figures like Mitchell and Van Kleeck, such data-building was to serve the twin imperatives of the building of social science and the reconstruction of society. But this intensive empiricism was always open to the charge that it was neither as disinterested nor as socially useful as was claimed. The National Bureau's work, to be sure, had helped to reduce social science's internal legitimation tensions, to promote its prestige and technocratic identity, and by the 1930s to provide an esteemed social science model. But the depression also brought renewed calls for a more usable science and a growing criticism of the bureau's "naive objectivity." Thus Robert Lynd's rhetorical reply to Wesley Mitchell's vision—"Knowledge for What?"—signalled an increasing disillusionment with the idea that intensive data-building unaccompanied by the potent direction of explicitly normative hypotheses was of much use either to society or to social science.[3]

Lynd's criticism, however, contained paradoxical implications. While calling for the propagation and survival of a critical impulse within American social science, he assumed, as had Mitchell and Van Kleeck, that researchers operating within a "going system" could change matters through developing and equipping policy-makers with a science of social reconstruction. As Lynd saw it, for example, "there is no way in which our culture can grow in continual serviceability to its people without a clear and pervasive extension of planning and control." Social science, he concluded, must help "to discover where and how" such planning would "facilitate the human ends of living."

Lynd, Mitchell, and Van Kleeck were people of social democratic or socialist sympathies, but they gave no indication of having understood that the ideas behind social science are not politically neutral, that they are instead a part of a depoliticizing and antidemocratic technology. "Those who pose the problem of ends and propose a humane economy as their goal," suggests Jacques Ellul, "are the very persons who develop techniques further and enhance their specific weights. . . . Technique is the boundary of democracy. What technique wins, democracy loses." Thus while technocratic claims to disinterestedness and independence from business institutions could be analyzed and challenged, the managerial, antidemocratic impulse basic to technocratic action remained. Indeed, it could be seen most starkly in the humane visions of those who would harness this impulse to democratic ends.[4]

Still, data-gathering and the building of social science would continue, and not only in the United States. By the 1930s, efforts to generate national economic data were worldwide, and proceeded, it seems, as part of the modern coalescence of common approaches among public and private managers toward central management and the manipulation of large-scale economic affairs. New Era techno-corporatism was thus an important chapter in the larger development and acceptance of the idea that statistical analysis is the appropriate basis for public policy; that the business cycle can be understood and controlled through such analysis; that public works and improved business management are legitimate countercyclical measures. And perhaps most important, the coincidence of

New Era planning and prosperity encouraged both the modern tendency of the public to accept large-scale public and private management in return for rising levels of income and benefits, and the public's apparent willingness to trade power and control in return for such benefits.[5]

Techno-corporatist ideas and institutions, then, would have an influence well beyond the 1920s. And the vision behind them would not remain long in eclipse, for following the turn toward statism in the 1930s and the era of World War II, corporatist models and rhetoric would surface once again. They would be apparent, for example, in the thinking and influence of the Committee for Economic Development, in the elaboration of postwar philanthropic planning activities (in conjunction with an expanded federal role), and in the resurgence in the 1970s of thinking and proposals looking beyond the welfare state and pluralist conceptions to a "new ideology," a new "social contract," a "new political economy," and a new "industrial connection" between universities and business. In these latter designs, in particular, private power informed and legitimated through social science was again to be used as the instrument through which antistatism could be reconciled with the quest for national managerial capabilities.[6]

Such designs arose within a larger reconstruction debate whose concerns—slowed growth, statist encroachments, and unstable markets—were not dissimilar to those of the period from 1919 to 1922. But the new debate operated in almost total ignorance of the earlier one and its institutional legacy, and thus lay hostage to an inadequate understanding of the modern history of economic crisis and response and of the historical relationship between economic growth and the legitimation of authority. Indeed, nowhere today is there adequate recognition of the techno-corporatist formulations that have been a part of the recent American past.

Instead, today's debate proceeds from a sense of history narrowly focused on ad hoc federal responses to national crisis. It has little or nothing to say about the history of efforts to construct arenas for the public exercise of private managerial authority; about how these efforts were rooted in early twentieth-century developments in philanthropy, economics, social work, and engineering; about how World War I acted to subsidize and encourage such developments; or about how the postwar reconstruction debates generated a technocratic analysis and constituency and potent new institutions for the linkage of such expertise to business management. Nor does it have anything to say about how these developments were tied into a larger apparatus of macroeconomic planning, and how the proximity of this to a brief but substantial prosperity contributed powerfully to the elevation and legitimation of an expanded social authority for social science and managerial institutions, an authority that would succeed in surviving the breakdown of New Era economic growth.[7]

It is clear that the developments of the 1920s constitute a significant, if largely unrecognized, part of the history of modern American planning and authority. And an understanding of them seems particularly important, given today's generally uncritical efforts to recapitulate elements of the New Era designs. For fundamental to those designs was a tendency to depoliticize authority, to remove political issues from political processes, and to encourage the determination of public policy within the administrative precincts of technocratic and managerial elites. This approach, be it in the New Era vision or its modern variants, appears capable of acquiring legitimacy in America only when linked to an economic expansion that can sustain the historic compromise between modern managerial impulses and the democratic ideals of mass opportunity and equity.[8]

ABBREVIATIONS

AEA Papers	American Economic Association Papers
BCU	Committee on Business Cycles and Unemployment
Car. Corp.	Carnegie Corporation of New York
CP	Commerce Papers
CF	The Commonwealth Fund
Dennison Papers	Henry S. Dennison Papers
Gay Papers	Edwin F. Gay Papers
HHP	Herbert Hoover Papers
HHPL	Herbert Hoover Presidential Library
Hunt Papers	Edward Eyre Hunt Papers
Mitchell Papers	Wesley C. Mitchell Papers
NA	National Archives
NBER	National Bureau of Economic Research
PCU	President's Conference on Unemployment
PS	Public Statements
REC	Committee on Recent Economic Changes
RF	Rockefeller Foundation Papers
LSRM	Laura Spelman Rockefeller Memorial
Ruml Papers	Beardsley Ruml Papers
SSRC	Social Science Research Council
MVK Papers	Mary Van Kleeck Papers
ODY	Owen D. Young Papers
ODY 1	Folder 12–23, Box: Hoover Committee on Business Cycles and Unemployment, 1922–1923 (ODY, chairman) Outline, Discussion, and Formulation.

ODY 2   Folder 12–23–1, Box: Hoover Committee on Business Cycles and Unemployment, (1) Printed Copies (2) Subsequent Correspondence, 1921–1931.

ODY 3   Folder 12–23 (January 1) Box: Hoover Committee on Business Cycles and Unemployment, 1922–1923 (ODY, chairman) Publications, Distribution, Reactions to.

ODY 4   Folder 12–23, Miscellaneous Papers, Box: Hoover Committee on Business Cycles and Unemployment, 1922–1923 (ODY, chairman) Outline, Discussion, and Formulation.

ODY 5   Folder 12–23 (May 1) Box: Hoover Committee on Business Cycles and Unemployment, 1922–1923 (ODY, chairman) Publications, Distribution, and Reactions to.

ODY 6   Folder 1–73, Box: Correspondence with H. M. Robinson; Correspondence with Herbert Hoover.

NOTES

INTRODUCTION

1. By "technocratic" I refer to a science-based claim to social authority and policymaking. These professions, especially economics, were among the first of the new social disciplines to cast their claims to authority in terms of their increasing acquisition of techniques of social analysis, understanding, and manipulation that were allegedly analogous to those of natural science. Much of the story to follow is thus necessarily theirs. On the history and dilemmas of such scientism, see Dorothy Ross, "The Development of the Social Sciences," in Alexandra Oleson and John Voss, eds., *The Organization of Knowledge in Modern America, 1860–1920* (Baltimore, 1979), pp. 125–130; Thomas S. Kuhn, *Structure of Scientific Revolutions* (Chicago, 1970); Thomas L. Haskell, *The Emergence of Professional Social Science: The American Social Science Association and the Nineteenth Century Crisis of Authority* (Urbana, 1977), pp. 18–23; Wolf-Dieter Narr, "Reflections on the Form and Content of Social Science: Toward a Consciously Political and Moral Social Science," in Norma Haan et al., *Social Science as Moral Inquiry* (New York, 1983), pp. 275–276; George C. Homans, *The Nature of Social Science* (New York, 1967); Paul Rabinow and William H. Sullivan, "The Interpretive Turn: The Emergence of an Approach," in Rabinow and Sullivan, eds., *Interpretive Social Science* (Berkeley, 1979); and Charles E. Lindblom and David K. Cohen, *Usable Knowledge: Social Science and Social Problem Solving* (New Haven, 1979).

2. The modern definition of the concept of legitimacy stems from the work of Max Weber and Antonio Gramsci. See Wolfgang J. Mommsen, *The Age of Bureaucracy* (New York, 1974), pp. 63–85; Dolf Sternberger, "Legitimacy," in the *International Encyclopedia of the Social Sciences* (New York, 1968), pp. 244–248; and Antonio Gramsci, *Selections From the Prison Notebooks*, eds. and trans. Quinton Hoare and Geoffrey N. Smith (London, 1971). On the legitimation tensions between technocratic elites and modern capitalism, see Alvin Gouldner, *The Dialectic of Ideology and Technology: The Origins, Grammar, and Future of Ideology* (New York,

1976), pp. 231–236; Daniel Bell, *The Cultural Contradictions of Capitalism* (New York, 1976), pp. 11–15, 249–250; Jürgen Habermas, *Legitimation Crisis* (Boston, 1975); and Thomas McCarthy, "The Scientization of Politics," in his *The Critical Theory of Jürgen Habermas* (Cambridge, 1978), pp. 1–16.

CHAPTER 1

1. Robert Wiebe, *The Search for Order, 1877–1920* (New York, 1967); Samuel P. Hays, *Conservation and the Gospel of Efficiency* (New York, 1969) and "The New Organizational Society," in Jerry Israel, ed., *Building the Organizational Society* (New York, 1972); Edwin J. Perkins, ed., *Men and Organizations* (New York, 1977); Graham Adams, *The Age of Industrial Violence, 1900–1915* (New York, 1966); H. M. Gitelman, "Management's Crisis of Confidence and the Origin of The National Industrial Conference Board, 1914–1916," *Business History Review* (Summer 1984); Frederick Jackson Turner, "Pioneer Ideals and the State University," in *The Frontier in American History* (New York, 1920), p. 285; Alan Trachtenberg, *The Incorporation of America: Culture and Society in the Gilded Age* (New York, 1982); R. Jeffrey Lustig, *Corporate Liberalism: The Origins of Modern American Political Theory, 1890–1920* (Berkeley, 1982), pt. 1.

2. Hays, "The New Organizational Society"; Christopher Lasch, *The New Radicalism in America* (New York, 1965), ch. 1; Michael B. Katz, "Origins of the Institutional State," *Marxist Perspectives* (Winter 1978); Jacob Hollander, *The Abolition of Poverty* (Boston, 1914); James B. Gilbert, "Collectivism and Charles Steinmetz," *Business History Review* (Winter 1974) and *Designing the Industrial State* (Chicago, 1972).

3. David Eakins, "The Origins of Corporate Liberal Policy Research, 1916–1922," in Jerry Israel, ed., *Building the Organizational Society*; Charles McCarthy, *The Wisconsin Idea* (New York, 1912); Walter Lippmann, *Drift and Mastery* (New York, 1914); Ronald C. Tobey, *The American Ideology of National Science, 1919–1930* (Pittsburgh, 1971), ch. 1; Martin J. Schiesl, *The Politics of Efficiency* (Berkeley, 1977), pp. 3–4. On both the private and public dimensions of this crisis of authority, see T. Jackson Lears, *No Place of Grace: Antimodernism and the Transformation of American Culture, 1880–1920* (New York, 1981), ch. 1.

4. Eakins, "The Origins," pp. 165–166; Mary Furner, *Advocacy and Objectivity: A Crisis in the Professionalization of American Social Science, 1865–1905* (Lexington, 1975); Hays, "The New Organizational Society," p. 3; Richard T. Ely, *Ground Under Our Feet: An Autobiography* (New York, 1938); Monte Calvert, *The Mechanical Engineer in America, 1830–1910* (Baltimore, 1967), ch. 14; Morris L. Cooke, "The Engineer and the People: A Plan for a Larger Measure of Cooperation Between the Society and the General Public," *Transactions of the American Society of Mechanical Engineers* 30 (1908); Dorothy Ross, "Socialism and American Liberalism: Academic Social Thought in the 1880's," *Perspectives in American History* 2 (1977–1978); Robert L. Church, "Economists as Experts: The making of an Academic Profession in the United States, 1870–1920," in Lawrence Stone, ed., *The University in Society*, vol. 2 (Princeton, 1974); Clark Chambers, *Paul U. Kellogg and The Survey: Voices for Social Welfare and Social Justice* (Minneapolis, 1971), ch. 4; Stephen Skowronek, *Building a New American State: The Expansion of National Administrative Capacities, 1877–1920* (Cambridge, 1982), pp. 42–45.

5. Adams, *Age of Industrial Violence*; Eakins, "The Origins," pp. 165–166; Tobey, *The American Ideology*, p. 12. On organizational and associational movements, see Hays, "The New Organizational Society"; Louis Galambos, "Technology, Political Economy, and Professionalization: Central Themes of the Organizational Synthesis," *Business History Review* (Winter 1983); Ellis W. Hawley, "Herbert Hoover, the Commerce Secretariat, and the Vision of an 'Associative State,' 1921–1928," *Journal of American History* (June 1974); Arthur Eddy, *The New Competition* (New York, 1912); Edward N. Hurley, *The Awakening of Business* (New York, 1917); E. H. Gaunt, *Co-operative Competition* (Providence, 1917). On the concept of cultural lag, see William F. Ogburn, "Cultural Lag as Theory," *Sociology and Social Research* 61 (January–February 1957). On unemployment, see John A. Garraty, *Unemployment in History* (New York, 1978). On pre-World War I data-building, see Gene M. Lyons, *The Uneasy Partnership: Social Science and the Federal Government in the Twentieth Century* (New York, 1969), pp. 22–26; Michael B. Katz, *Poverty and Policy in American History* (New York, 1983), pp. 90–91.

6. Daniel M. Fox, "Introduction" to Simon N. Patten, *The New Basis of Civilization* (Cambridge, 1968); Robert H. Bremner, *Amer-*

ican Philanthropy (Chicago, 1960), ch. 6; Frank J. Bruno, *Trends in Social Work, 1874–1956* (New York, 1964), chs. 13–14; Roy Lubove, *The Professional Altruist* (Cambridge, 1965), chs. 2, 5; James T. Patterson, *America's Struggle Against Poverty, 1900–1980* (Cambridge, 1981); John F. McClymer, *War and Welfare: Social Engineering in America, 1890–1925* (Westport, 1980), pt. 1. Critical assessments of philanthropy's modern function can be found in E. Richard Brown, *Rockefeller Medicine Men: Medicine and Capitalism in America* (Berkeley, 1979); and R. Arnove, ed., *Philanthropy and Cultural Imperialism* (Boston, 1980).

7. Raymond B. Fosdick, *The Story of the Rockefeller Foundation* (New York, 1952), chs. 1–2; Barry Karl, "Philanthropy, Policy Planning, and the Bureaucratization of the Democratic Ideal," *Deedalus* (Fall 1976); Barry Karl and Stanley N. Katz, "The American Private Philanthropic Foundation and the Public Sphere, 1890–1930," *Minerva* (Summer 1981).

8. On managerial developments within large organizations, see Alfred D. Chandler, Jr., *The Visible Hand: The Managerial Revolution in American Business* (Cambridge, 1977); Robert E. Kohler, "A Policy for the Advancement of Science: The Rockefeller Foundation, 1924–1929," *Minerva* (Winter 1978); Daniel M. Fox, *The Discovery of Abundance: Simon N. Patten and the Transformation of Social Theory* (Ithaca, 1967), ch. 6; Edward T. Devine and Mary Van Kleeck, "Positions in Social Work," New York School of Philanthropy, February 1916, Folder 467, Box 25, MVK Papers).

9. Lubove, *The Professional Altruist*; John M. Glenn et al., *Russell Sage Foundation, 1907–1946* (New York, 1947), pp. 5–9; Devine and Van Kleeck, "Positions in Social Work," p. 6; Louise C. Wade, *Graham Taylor, Pioneer for Social Justice, 1851–1938* (Chicago, 1964); Katz, *Poverty and Policy in American History*, pp. 90–92; Allen Davis, *Spearheads for Reform: The Social Settlements and the Progressive Movement* (New York, 1967).

10. Peter Keating, *Into Unknown England, 1866–1913: Selections from the Social Explorers* (Manchester, 1976); Fox, "Introduction"; Patterson, *America's Struggle Against Poverty*, chs. 1–2.

11. Edward T. Devine, "Social Forces," *Charities and the Commons* (March 23, 1907):1071–1072; Peter Keating, *Into Unknown England*; Fox, *The Discovery of Abundance*, ch. 6.

12. Glenn, *Russell Sage Foundation*, pp. 14–15; Chambers, *Paul U. Kellogg and The Survey*, chs. 1–2.

13. Elizabeth Beardsley Butler, *Women and the Trades* (New York, 1909); Crystal Eastman, *Work Accidents and the Law* (New York, 1910); Blanche Wiesen Cook, ed., *Crystal Eastman, On Women and Revolution* (Oxford, 1978), pp. 6–7, 269–270, 360, 366; Chambers, *Paul U. Kellogg and The Survey*, chs. 1–2.

14. Glenn, *Russell Sage Foundation*, pp. 61, 152–170; Eleanor Midman Lewis, "Mary Van Kleeck," *Notable American Women*, vol. 4: *The Modern Period* (Cambridge, 1980), pp. 707–709; Alice Kessler-Harris, *Out to Work: A History of Wage-Earning Women in the United States* (New York, 1982), pp. 114–117.

15. Mary Van Kleeck, "Child Labor in New York City Tenements," *Charities and the Commons* (January 18, 1908); Van Kleeck to Glenn, June 3, 1911, "The Committee on Wonen's Work: Memorandum Regarding Future Plans," Folder 1387, Box 105; "MVK Papers"; Van Kleeck to Mary R. Beard., November 18, 1935, Folder 2, Box 1, MVK Papers; Clarke A. Chambers, *Seedtime of Reform: American Social Service and Social Action, 1918–1933* (Minneapolis, 1963), ch. 4.

16. Mary Van Kleeck, "Working Hours of Women in Factories," *Charities and the Commons* (October 6, 1906); Van Kleeck, "Some Problems in Method of Investigation of Women's Work" (undated manuscript), Folder 1386, Box 105, MVK Papers; Van Kleeck, "Six Lectures: The Problems of Women's Employment in Trades, 1910," Folder 490, Box 28, MVK Papers; Barbara Mayer Wertheimer, *We Were There: The Story of Working Women in America* (New York, 1977), ch. 12; Leslie W. Tentler, *Wage-Earning Women: Industrial Work and Family Life in the United States, 1900–1930* (New York, 1979).

17. Van Kleeck, "Memorandum Regarding Investigation of Industrial Conditions by Russell Sage Foundation," October 26, 1915, Folder 1387, Box 105, MVK Papers; Van Kleeck, "The Committee on Women's Work: Memorandum Regarding Investigation for the Winter of 1911–1912," October 6, 1911, Folder 1387, Box 105, MVK Papers.

18. Van Kleeck, "Working Hours of Women in Factories," People vs. Williams, Court of Appeals, 189 N.Y. 131, 81 N.E. 778 (1907), in Glenn, *Russell Sage Foundation*, p. 154; Louis D. Brandeis, "Coping with Irregular Employment: A Memorandum" (1911), *Journal of the Society for the Advancement of Management* 4 (May 1939).

179

19. Van Kleeck, *Women in the Bookbinding Trade* (New York, 1913); Van Kleeck, "The Committee on Women's Work: Memorandum Regarding Future Policy, March 27, 1913," Folder 1387, Box 105, MVK Papers.

20. Van Kleeck, *Artificial Flower Makers* (New York, 1913); Van Kleeck, *A Seasonal Industry* (New York, 1917).

21. Van Kleeck, *Artificial Flower Makers* and *A Seasonal Industry*; Herman Feldman, *The Regularization of Employment* (New York, 1925), pp. 50–52; Bryce M. Stewart, *Unemployment Benefits in the United States* (New York, 1930), pp. 61–64; Daniel Nelson, *Unemployment Insurance* (Madison, 1969), chs. 1–2.

22. Samuel Haber, *Efficiency and Uplift: Scientific Management in the Progressive Era, 1890–1920* (Chicago, 1964); Daniel Nelson, "Scientific Management, Systematic Management, and Labor, 1880–1915," *Business History Review* (Winter 1974); Frank B. Copley, *Frederick W. Taylor: Father of Scientific Management* (New York, 1923); Frederick W. Taylor, *Scientific Management, Comprising Shop Management, The Principles of Scientific Management and Testimony Before the Special House Committee* (New York, 1947); Harry Braverman, *Labor and Monopoly Capital* (New York, 1974), chs. 4–6; Dan Clawson, *Bureaucracy and the Labor Process: The Transformation of U.S. Industry, 1860–1920* (New York, 1980); Reinhard Bendix, *Work and Authority in Industry: Ideologies of Management in the Course of Industrialization* (New York, 1956); Judith A. Merkle, *Management and Ideology* (Berkeley, 1980).

23. David F. Noble, *America By Design: Science, Technology, and the Rise of Corporate Capitalism* (New York, 1977), pp. 264–265, 275–277; Edwin F. Layton, *The Revolt of the Engineers* (Cleveland, 1971); Milton Nadworny, *Scientific Management and the Unions* (Cambridge, 1959); Henry Eilbert, "The Development of Personnel Management in the U.S.," *Business History Review* 33 (1959).

24. Morris L. Cooke, "Scientific Management as a Solution of the Unemployment Problem," *The Annals of The American Academy* 61 (September 1915) and "Responsibility and Opportunity of the City in the Prevention of Unemployment," *American Labor Legislation Review* 2 (June 1915); Hollis Godfrey, "Attitude of Labor Toward Scientific Management," *The Annals of the American Academy* 44 (November 1912); Harlow Person, "Scientific Management," *Bulletin of the Taylor Society* 2 (October 1916) and "The Manager, the Workman, and the Social Scientist," *Bulletin of the*

NOTES TO CHAPTER 1

Taylor Society 3 (February 1917); Daniel Nelson and Stuart Campbell, "Taylorism Versus Welfare Work in American Industry: H. L. Gantt and the Bancrofts," *Business History Review* 46 (Spring 1972); Magnus W. Alexander, "Hiring and Firing: Its Economic Waste and How to Avoid It," *The Annals of the American Academy* (May 1916); Kim McQuaid, "Henry S. Dennison and the 'Science' of Industrial Reform, 1900–1950," *American Journal of Economics and Sociology* 36 (January 1977).

25. Feldman, *The Regularization of Employment*, ch. 3; Nelson, *Unemployment Insurance*, chs. 1–2; "Proceedings of the Second National Conference on Unemployment (A Practical Program for the Prevention of Unemployment)," *American Labor Legislation Review* 5 (June 1915); Henry S. Dennison, "What the Employment Department Should Be in Industry," *Bureau of Labor Statistics* 227 (October 1917) and "Management," *Recent Economic Changes* (New York, 1929); John R. Commons, "Constructive Investigation and the Wisconsin Industrial Commission," *The Survey* 31 (January 4, 1913); Charles R. Henderson, "Recent Advances in the Struggle Against Unemployment," *American Labor Legislation Review* 2 (February 1912); William M. Leiserson, "The Problem of Unemployment Today," *Political Science Quarterly* 31 (March 1916); James T. Dennison, *Henry S. Dennison: New England Industrialist Who Served America* (New York, 1955); John Kenneth Galbraith, *A Life in Our Times* (Boston, 1981), pp. 61–63.

26. Harlow Person, "Scientific Management and the Reduction of Unemployment," *Bulletin of the Taylor Society* 6 (February 1921); Edward Eyre Hunt, *Scientific Management Since Taylor* (New York, 1924), chs. 1, 3, 7, 17.

27. Person, "Scientific Management."

28. Karl Pribram, *A History of Economic Reasoning* (Baltimore, 1983), pp. 358–362; Joseph Dorfman, *The Economic Mind in American Civilization*, vol. 4 (New York, 1959), ch. 13; Joseph Schumpeter, *History of Economic Analysis* (New York, 1954), p. 954; Karl Worth Bigelow, "Economics," in Harry Elmer Barnes, *The History and Prospects of the Social Sciences* (New York, 1925), pp. 392–394; Thorstein Veblen, *The Theory of Business Enterprise* (New York, 1904); Wesley C. Mitchell, "The Prospects of Economics," in Rexford G. Tugwell, ed., *The Trend of Economics* (New York, 1924); Mitchell, "Human Behavior and Economics," *Quarterly Journal of*

Economics 29 (1914); Mitchell, "The Backward Art of Spending Money," *American Economic Review* 2 (June 1912).

29. Schumpeter, *History of Economic Analysis*; Mitchell, *Lecture Notes on Types of Economic Theory* (New York, 1949), chs. 31–36; Harry Elmer Barnes, "Economic Science and Dynamic History," *Journal of Social Forces* (November 1924); Lucy Sprague Mitchell, *Two Lives: The Story of Wesley Clair Mitchell and Myself* (New York, 1953); Joyce Antler, "Feminism as Life-Process: The Life and Career of Lucy Sprague Mitchell," *Feminist Studies* (Spring 1981).

30. Pribram, *A History of Economic Reasoning*, pp. 360–362; Wesley C. Mitchell, *Business Cycles* (Berkeley, 1913); Garraty, *Unemployment in History*, pp. 142–145; Dorfman, *Economic Mind*, ch. 13; Schumpeter, *History of Economic Analysis*, pp. 1123, 1164.

31. Schumpeter, *History of Economic Analysis*; Garraty, *Unemployment in History*; A. B. Wolfe, "Thoughts on Perusal of Wesley Mitchell's Collected Essays," *Journal of Political Economy* (February 1939); Dorothy Ross, "The Development of the Social Sciences," in Oleson and Voss, eds., *The Organization of Knowledge*.

CHAPTER 2

1. Randolph Bourne, "Twilight of Idols," *The Seven Arts* (June 1917):696.

2. Merle Curti, "The American Scholar in Three Wars," *Journal of the History of Ideas* 3 (June 1942), pp. 241–264; Gil Elliot, *Twentieth Century Book of the Dead* (New York, 1972); Carol Gruber, *Mars and Minerva* (Baton Rouge, 1975), intro.; J. Stanley Lemons, *The Woman Citizen: Social Feminism in the 1920's* (Urbana, 1973), ch. 1.

3. Allyn A. Young, "National Statistics in War and Peace," *Journal of the American Statistical Association* (March 1918):883; Robert Cuff, "American Mobilization for War, 1917–1945: *Political Culture vs. Bureaucratic Administration*," in N. F. Dreisziger, ed., *Mobilization for Total War* (Waterloo, 1981); Ellis W. Hawley, "The Great War and Organizational Innovation: The American Case," unpublished manuscript, 1984; Alan Wolfe, *The Limits of Legitimacy: Political Contradictions of Contemporary Capitalism* (New York, 1977), pp. 108–117.

4. A. W. Coats, "The American Economic Association, 1904–1929," *The American Economic Review* 54 (June 1964):261–265;

Mary Furner, *Advocacy and Objectivity: A Crisis in the Professionalization of American Social Science, 1865–1905* (Lexington, 1975).

5. Robert Cuff, "The Cooperative Impulse and the War: The Origins of the Council of National Defense and Advisory Commission," in Jerry Israel, ed., *Building the Organizational Society* (New York, 1972), pp. 233–246; Cuff, *The War Industries Board* (Baltimore, 1973), ch. 1.

6. Information and Education Service, "Annual Report," Department of Labor (Washington, 1919); David F. Noble, *America By Design: Science, Technology, and the Rise of Corporate Capitalism* (New York, 1977), pp. 293–295, 296–298; Roger Babson, *Actions and Reactions* (New York, 1934).

7. Morrell Heald, *The Social Responsibilities of Business* (Cleveland, 1970), pp. 49–52; Roy Lubove, *The Professional Altruist* (Cambridge, 1965); Clarke A. Chambers, *Seedtime of Reform: American Social Service and Social Action, 1918–1933* (Minneapolis, 1963), ch. 1; Chambers, *Paul U. Kellogg and The Survey: Voices for Social Welfare and Social Justice* (Minneapolis, 1971), ch. 5.

8. Mary Van Kleeck, "For Women in Industry: The Proposed New Division in the Department of Labor," *The Survey* (December 23, 1916):327; Chambers, *Seedtime of Reform*, pp. 8–9; Barbara M. Wertheimer, *We Were There* (New York, 1977), pt. 5; Lemons, *The Woman Citizen*, ch. 1.

9. Morris Cooke to Mary Van Kleeck, July 23, 1917 and Van Kleeck to Cooke, August 7, 1917, Folder 146, Box 10, MVK Papers; Van Kleeck, "Problems of the Possible Employment of Women in the Stores Depots of the United States Army," November 24, 1917, Folder 924, Box 62, MVK Papers; Maurine W. Greenwald, *Women, War, and Work: The Impact of World War I on Women Workers in the United States* (Westport, 1980). See also Valerie Jean Conner, *The National War Labor Board: Stability, Social Justice, and the Voluntary State* (Chapel Hill, 1983).

10. Mary Van Kleeck, "Federal Policies for Women in Industry," *The Annals of the American Academy* (January 1919):3; Van Kleeck, "Women in the Munitions Industry," *Life and Labor* (June 1918), Folder 467, Box 25, MVK Papers.

11. Mary Van Kleeck, "Storage Bulletin Number Nine," November 24, 1917, Folder 923, Box 62, MVK Papers; Van Kleeck, "War Labor Policies Board—Report on Night-Work," September 6, 1918, Folder 1437, Box 112, MVK Papers.

12. Mary Van Kleeck, "Program for Mobilizing Women for Industries During the War," September 28, 1918, Folder 1437, Box 112, MVK Papers; Loren Baritz, *Servants of Power* (Middletown, 1960); Edmund C. Lynch, "Walter Dill Scott: Pioneer Industrial Psychologist," *Business History Review* 42 (Summer 1968). This will be discussed more fully in the next chapter, especially in connection with the career of Beardsley Ruml.

13. Grosvenor Clarkson, *Industrial America in the World War* (Boston, 1923), p. 205; Wesley Mitchell, "Statistics and Government," *Journal of the American Statistical Association* (March 1919):223–236; Young, "National Statistics," pp. 873–885.

14. Glenn, *Russell Sage Foundation*, pp. 246–248; Clarkson, *Industrial America*, p. 201.

15. Clarkson, *Industrial America*, pp. 200–201; Herbert Heaton, *A Scholar in Action: Edwin F. Gay* (Cambridge, 1952), pp. 101–107.

16. Heaton, *A Scholar in Action*, pp. 101–107; Clarkson, *Industrial America*, pp. 200–205; Edward N. Hurley, *The Awakening of Business* (New York, 1917).

17. Edwin F. Gay to Arch Shaw, May 3, 1917, Box 4, #409, Gay Papers; Heaton, *A Scholar in Action*, p. 98; Arch Shaw, *An Approach to Business Problems* (Cambridge, 1916).

18. Heaton, *A Scholar in Action*, pp. 101–107; Mitchell, "Statistics and Government," p. 227; Zenas L. Potter, "The Central Bureau of Planning and Statistics," *Journal of the American Statistical Association* (March 1919); Leo Wolman, "Statistical Work of the War Industries Board," *Journal of the American Statistical Association* (March 1919).

19. Wolman, "Statistical Work"; Mitchell, "Statistics and Government"; Young, "National Statistics," pp. 873–875; Horace Secrist, "Statistical Units as Standards," *Journal of the American Statistical Association* (March 1918).

20. Secrist, "Statistical Units"; Young, "National Statistics," pp. 873–885.

21. A. W. Coats, "The First Two Decades of the American Economic Association," *American Economic Review* (September 1960); Furner, *Advocacy and Objectivity*, pp. 1–81; Joseph Dorfman, *The Economic Mind in American Civilization*, vol. 3 (New York, 1949), pp. 309–342; Richard T. Ely, "Report of the Organization of the AEA," *Publications of the American Econmic Association*, First Series (March 1887), vol. 1, p. 19; Dorothy Ross, "The Liberal Tradition

Revisited and the Republican Tradition Addressed," in John Higham and Paul Conkin, eds., *New Directions in American Intellectual History* (Baltimore, 1977) and "Socialism and American Liberalism: Academic Social Thought in the 1880's," *Perspectives in American History* 2 (1977–1978); Thomas L. Haskell, *The Emergence of Professional Social Science: The American Social Science Association and the Nineteenth-Century Crisis of Authority* (Urbana, 1977), chs. 1–2.

22. Furner, *Advocacy and Objectivity*; Robert L. Church, "Economists as Experts: The Rise of an Academic Profession in the United States, 1820–1920," in L. Stone, ed., *The University in Society*, vol. 2 (Princeton, 1974).

23. Irving Fisher to members of the AEA, March 9, 1918, Irving Fisher—1918, Secretary's File, AEA Papers; John Commons' memo to the Executive Committee, AEA, May 11, 1917, Allyn Young—1917, Secretary's File, AEA Papers; Walton Hamilton to Irving Fisher, April 27, 1918, Irving Fisher—1918, Secretary's File, AEA Papers.

24. Cuff, *The War Industries Board*, chs. 9–10, and "American Mobilization for War, 1917–1945"; Herbert Hoover, "Foreword," to Elisha M. Friedman, ed., *America and the New Era* (New York, 1920); Hoover, "Address Delivered at Banquet of the American Institute of Mining Engineers." August 26, 1920, Public Statements, HHP, HHPL; Robert F. Himmelberg, "Business, Antitrust Policy, and the Industrial Board of the Department of Commerce, 1919," *Business History Review* (Spring 1968); Church, "Economists as Experts."

CHAPTER 3

1. See Robert K. Murray, *Red Scare: A Study in National Hysteria, 1919–1920* (Minneapolis, 1955) and John D. Hicks, *Rehearsal for Disaster: The Boom and Collapse of 1919–1920* (Gainesville, 1961) for examples of the more conventional approach to the reconstruction period. For two recent studies that examine aspects of the larger effort to translate wartime organizations to peacetime routine; see John F. McClymer, *War and Welfare: Social Engineering in America, 1890–1925* (Westport, 1980), and Gary Dean Best, *The Politics of American Individualism: Herbert Hoover in Transition, 1918–1921* (Westport, 1975).

2. Elisha M. Friedman, ed., *American Problems of Reconstruction: A National Symposium on the Economic and Financial Aspects* (New York, 1918); Frederick A. Cleveland and Joseph Schafer, eds., *Democracy in Reconstruction* (Cambridge, 1919). I am indebted to Scott R. Hall for the following citations: Grosvenor Clarkson to Newton Baker, August 20, 1918, and William C. Redfield to Atlee Pomerene, August 26, 1918, both in Commerce Papers, Record Group 40, File 77270, "General Correspondence," N.A. See also, Ordway Tead, "Some Reconstruction Programs," *Political Science Quarterly* (March 1918).

3. Melvin I. Urofsky, *Big Steel and the Wilson Administration* (Columbus, 1979), ch. 8; Ellis W. Hawley, *The Great War and the Search for a Modern Order* (New York, 1979), ch. 3; F. H. Newell, "Reconstruction Agencies," *American Political Science Review* (February 1919).

4. Edwin F. Gay to E. M. Bates, October 11, 1918, Box 1, Gay Papers; Wesley Mitchell, "Statistics and Government," in Joseph Dorfman, ed., *The Backward Art of Spending Money: and other Essays by Wesley C. Mitchell* (New York, 1937), p. 47; Herbert Heaton, *A Scholar in Action: Edwin F. Gay* (Cambridge, 1952), ch. 3.

5. Edmund E. Day to E. F. Gay, November 30, 1918, Box 2, Gay Papers; E. F. Gay, "Report of the Central Bureau of Planning and Statistics, June 1918-June 1919," Box 1, Gay Papers.

6. Memorandum sanctioning Central Bureau of Planning and Statistics as statistical arm of American delegation to the Peace Conference, signed by Woodrow Wilson, Box 1, Gay Papers; Heaton, *A Scholar in Action*, ch. 3.

7. E. F. Gay, "Diary," entries for Friday, December 20, and Friday, December 27, 1918, Box 1, Gay Papers.

8. "Meeting with the President," March 1, 1919, and Gay Diary, "Report of Central Bureau," pp. 16–17, both in Box 1, Gay Papers; "List of Reports Prepared for the President by the Central Bureau of Planning and Statistics," Box 4, Gay Papers. The first Brookings Institution, the Institute for Government Research (1916), took the lead in formulating the notion of a federal budget, which resulted in the legislation of 1921 that created the Bureau of the Budget. See David Eakins, "Policy Planning for the Establishment," in Ronald Radosh and Murray Rothbard, eds., *A New History of Leviathan* (New York, 1972) and Donald T. Critchlow,

"The Brookings Institution: The Early Years, 1916–1952" (Ph.D. dissertation, University of California), Berkeley, 1976.

9. Hawley, *The Great War and the Search for a Modern Order*, pp. 45–48; W. Elliot Brownlee, *Dynamics of Ascent: A History of the American Economy* (New York, 1979), ch. 13; George Soule, *Prosperity Decade: From War to Depression, 1917–1929* (New York, 1947), chs. 4–5.

10. *American Economic Review*, supplement (March 1919); *Journal of the American Statistical Association* 16 (March 1919).

11. Irving Fisher, "Economists in Public Service," *American Economic Review*, supplement (March 1919):5, 11.

12. Wesley Mitchell, "Statistics and Government," *Journal of the American Statistical Association* 16 (March 1919):223–236.

13. Mitchell, "Statistics and Government"; Forest G. Hill, "Wesley Mitchell's Theory of Planning," *Political Science Quarterly* (March 1957).

14. Hill, "Wesley Mitchell's Theory"; David Seckler, *Thorstein Veblen and the Institutionalists* (Boulder, 1975), p. 108.

15. Wesley Mitchell to Lucy Sprague, October 18, 1911, reprinted in Lucy Sprague Mitchell, *Two Lives: The Story of Wesley Clair Mitchell and Myself* (New York, 1953), pp. 187–188, 357–359.

16. Ibid.; Wesley Mitchell, "Quantitative Analysis in Economic Theory," *American Economic Review* 15 (March 1925):7–8.

17. Mitchell, "Statistics and Government," pp. 229–230.

18. Ibid.; Dorothy Ross, "The Development of the Social Sciences," in Alexandra Oleson and John Voss, eds., *The Organization of Knowledge in Modern America 1860–1920* (Baltimore, 1979), pp. 125–130. See also W. C. Mitchell, *The National Bureau's First Quarter Century* (New York, 1945), p. 35.

19. Henry Jones Ford, "Present Tendencies in American Politics," *American Political Science Review* (February 1920):2.

20. Daniel J. Kevles, "Testing the Army's Intelligence: Psychologists and the Military in World War I," *Journal of American History* (December 1968); Edwin G. Boring, ed., *Psychology for the Armed Services* (Washington, 1945); Robert M. Yerkes, *The New World of Science: Its Development During the War* (New York, 1920); Loren Baritz, *Servants of Power* (Middletown, 1960), p. 48; Edmund C. Lynch, "Walter Dill Scott: Pioneer Industrial Psychologist," *Business History Review* 42 (Summer 1968); Gene M. Lyons,

The Uneasy Partnership: Social Science and the Federal Government in the Twentieth Century (New York, 1969), pp. 27–31; Beardsley Ruml, "The Extension of Selective Tests to Industry," *The Annals of the American Academy* (January 1919). In June 1920 the National Research Council and the Engineering Foundation sponsored a Preliminary Conference on Industrial Personnel Problems, which was organized by James Angell of the Carnegie Corporation, to whom Beardsley Ruml had recently become an assistant. See James R. Angell to John R. Commons, May 5, 1920, John R. Commons, 1920, AEA papers.

21. F. Herbert Snow, "The Engineer and the State, *Proceedings of the American Society of Civil Engineers* (January 1919):11–12; Herbert Hoover, "Foreword," in Elisha M. Friedman, ed., *America and the New Era: A Symposium on Social Reconstruction* (New York, 1920), p. xxiv; C. R. Richards quoted in A. A. Potter, "Technical Research," in Friedman, *American Problems of Reconstruction*, p. 100. See also, "Preparing the Profession for a Great Opportunity," *Engineering News Record* 81 (October 10, 1918):651; Edwin F. Layton, *The Revolt of the Engineers* (Cleveland, 1971), pp. 124–127, ch. 8; *Industrial Reconstruction Problems*, Report of Proceedings of the National Conference of the Society of Industrial Engineers, New York City (March 18–21, 1919).

22. The waste survey will be treated in the following chapter. Milton J. Nadworny, *Scientific Management and the Unions, 1900–1932* (Cambridge, 1955), pp. 104–141; Layton, *Revolt of the Engineers*, pp. 193–195; Frank and Lillian Gilbreth, "Scientific Management," in Friedman, *American Problems of Reconstruction*.

23. Arthur Kellogg, "Shall Social Agencies Unite for Reconstruction?" *The Survey* (December 7, 1918):287–317. For articles summarizing the conference, see *The Survey* (December 7, 1918); Clarke A. Chambers, *Paul Kellogg and The Survey: Voices for Social Welfare and Social Justice* (Minneapolis, 1971), pp. 68–71. In April 1919 the Engineering Council, a short-lived effort to unite engineers and organize their talents for war work, advocated a similar cabinet-level department of public works, in this case to be headed by an engineer. See Layton, *Revolt of the Engineers*, pp. 124–127.

24. Mary Van Kleeck, "Women Workers During Reconstruction," *American Labor Legislation Review* (March 1919), 62; Van Kleeck, "Federal Policies for Women in Industry," *The Annals of*

the American Academy (January 1919). See also, Maurine Weiner Greenwald, *Women, War, and Work: The Impact of World War I on Women Workers in the United States* (Westport, 1980); J. A. Fitch, "Gains to be Consolidated in War-Time Industrial Relations," *The Survey* (December 7, 1918); Fitch, "Labor Reconstruction," *The Survey* (December 14, 1918); Van Kleeck, "Women's Invasion of Industry and Changes in Protective Standards," *Proceedings of the American Academy of Political Science* 8 (1918–1920):141–146.

25. Van Kleeck, "Women Workers During Reconstruction," p. 65; Van Kleeck, "Women in Industry," in Friedman, *America and the New Era*, p. 180; Van Kleeck, "Women in Industry After the War," *Vassar Quarterly* (November 1919).

26. Layton, *Revolt of the Engineers*, pp. 124–127, ch. 8; Editorial, *Journal of Electricity* (October 15, 1919); Herbert Hoover, "Inauguration Address"—A.I.M.E., September 16, 1919, Public Statements, HHP, HHPL; Hoover, "Some Notes on Industrial Readjustment," *Saturday Evening Post* (December 27, 1919); "Mr. Hoover's Address Before the Western Society of Engineers at Chicago, February 28, 1920," Public Statements, HHP, HHPL; Robert D. Cuff, "Herbert Hoover, the Ideology of Voluntarism, and War Organization During the Great War," *Journal of American History* (September 1977).

27. Herbert Hoover, *American Individualism* (New York, 1922), pp. 32, 34.

28. "Mr. Hoover's Address Before the San Francisco Commercial Club, October 9, 1919," Public Statements, HHP, HHPL.

29. John M. Glenn et al., *The Russell Sage Foundation, 1907–1946*, vols. 1–2 (New York, 1947), pp. 274–275, 378–385; "Memorandum to John M. Glenn from Division of Industrial Studies, October 25, 1919," unsigned, Folder 418, Box 22, MVK Papers.

30. Van Kleeck, "Memorandum to John M. Glenn."

31. Ibid.

32. Irving Fisher to Allyn Young, November 21, 1918, Irving Fisher—1918, AEA Papers; Mitchell, "Statistics and Government"; Erastus W. Bulkley to Irving Fisher and Allyn Young, case file begins July 15, 1918, Allyn Young—1918, AEA Papers; J. G. Frederick, *Business Research and Statistics* (New York, 1920), p. 295.

33. Fisher, "Economists in Public Service"; Robert Zieger, *Republicans and Labor 1919–1929* (Lexington, 1969), pp. 9–23; Hawley, *The Great War and the Search for a Modern Order*, pp. 45–52.

34. David Michael Grossman, "Professors and Public Service, 1885–1925: A Chapter in the Professionalization of the Social Sciences," Ph.D. dissertation, Washington University, 1973, pp. 294–295; A. W. Coats, "The American Economic Association, 1904–1929," *American Economic Review* 54 (June 1964):261–285.

35. Irving Fisher to Henry B. Gardner, June 4, 1919, Irving Fisher—1919, AEA Papers.

36. Edward D. Jones to Allyn Young, "Proposed Report of the Committee on an Institute for Economic Research," December 9, 1919, Allyn Young—1919, AEA Papers.

37. Ibid.

CHAPTER 4

1. On prewar technocratic reform and the problem of the national income, see chapter 1. See also, E.R.A. Seligman, "Economic and Social Progress," *American Economic Review* (February 1903); S. Slaughter and E. T. Silva, "Looking Backward: How Foundations Formulated Ideology in the Progressive Period," in R. Arnove, ed., *Philanthropy and Cultural Imperialism* (Boston, 1980).

2. Herbert Heaton, *A Scholar in Action: Edwin F. Gay* (Cambridge, 1952), pp. 66–93.

3. Ibid.; Raymond B. Fosdick, *The Story of the Rockefeller Foundation* (New York, 1952), p. 193.

4. N. I. Stone, "The Beginnings of the National Bureau of Economic Research: A Tribute to Its Founder, Malcolm C. Rorty," in Wesley C. Mitchell, ed., *The National Bureau's First Quarter Century* (New York, 1945), pp. 5–10; Heaton, *A Scholar in Action*, pp. 93–95.

5. "The Committee on the Distribution of Income: Its Organization and Purpose," unsigned memo, June 4, 1917, 403-NBER, CF.

6. Ibid.; Barbara Howe, "The Emergence of Scientific Philanthropy, 1900–1920," in Arnove, ed., *Philanthropy and Cultural Imperialism*; "Memorandum to John M. Glenn from Division of Industrial Studies, October 25, 1919," unsigned, Folder 418, Box 22, MVK Papers.

7. M. C. Rorty to Max Farrand, August 9, 1919; N. I. Stone to John Frey, August 19, 1919; John P. Frey to M. C. Rorty, August 22, 1919. All in 403-NBER, CF.

8. Stone to Frey, August 19, 1919; Frey to Rorty, August 22, 1919, CF.

9. M. C. Rorty to Max Farrand, August 9, 1919, 403-NBER, CF; *The Commonwealth Fund: Historical Sketch, 1918–1962* (New York, 1963); Herbert Hoover, *American Epic: V. III* (Chicago, 1961); Edgar Rickard, director of ARA, to Barry Smith, Commonwealth Fund, undated in "The Commonwealth Fund Annual Report, 1921, Extract Copy, Foreign Relief Work," pp. 26–29, Box 13, Commonwealth Fund, Hunt Papers.

10. M. C. Rorty to Samuel C. Fairley, August 14, 1919, 403-NBER, CF.

11. Ibid.

12. "Interview with Mr. Rorty, September 16, 1919," unsigned memo, 403-NBER, CF.

13. M. C. Rorty to T. S. Adams, November 11, 1919; Rorty to Ferrand, November 11, 1919; W. C. Mitchell to Rorty, November 12, 1919; memo #140, "Bureau of Economic Research," December 16, 1920. All in 403-NBER, CF.

14. Henry S. Dennison and Ida Tarbell, "The President's Industrial Conference of October 1919," *Bulletin of the Taylor Society* (April 1920); Ellis W. Hawley, *The Great War and the Search for a Modern Order, 1917–1933* (New York, 1979), pp. 47–50; Henry Dennison to Julius Rosenwald, December 1, 1919, President Wilson's Industrial Conference, Box 2, Dennison Papers; "Report of the Second Industrial Conference," *American Industries* (April 1920): 11–18; Gary Dean Best, "President Wilson's Second Industrial Conference," *Labor History* (Fall 1975).

15. Rorty to Farrand, January 12, 1920; "Minutes of First Annual Meeting, February 2, 1920, National Bureau of Economic Research, Inc." Both in 403a-NBER, CF.

16. Rorty to Farrand, February 10, 1920, 403a-NBER, CF; Lucy Sprague Mitchell, *Two Lives: The Story of Wesley Clair Mitchell and Myself* (New York, 1953), p. 352; Oswald W. Knauth to Allyn Young, February 18, 1920, Allyn-Young-1920, AEA Papers. On the insecurity of the social sciences during this period, see Walter Lippmann, *Public Opinion* (New York, 1922), pp. 233–236; Gene M. Lyons, *The Uneasy Partnership: Social Science and Federal Government in the Twentieth Century* (New York, 1969), pp. 6–8.

17. "The Committee on the Distribution of Income: Its Organization and Purpose," June 4, 1917, 403-NBER, CF.

18. Wesley Mitchell, "Statistics and Government," *Journal of the American Statistical Association* 16 (March 1919); Oswald W. Knauth to Commonwealth Fund, November 18, 1920, 403a-NBER, CF; W. I. King, F. Macaulay, and W. C. Mitchell, *Income in the United States, Its Amount and Distribution, 1909–1919*, vol. 1 (New York, 1921), ch. 4; Henry R. Seager, "Income in the United States," *The Survey* (November 19, 1921).

19. Wesley Mitchell to Max Farrand, March 1, 1920, 403a-NBER, CF; Willford I. King, *The Wealth and Income of the People of the United States* (New York, 1915); Scott Nearing, *Wages in the United States, 1908–1910* (New York, 1911); Jeffrey G. Williamson and Peter H. Lindert, *American Inequality: A Macroeconomic History* (New York, 1980), p. 90.

20. Wesley Mitchell, "Staff Conference, National Bureau of Economic Research," May 17, 1920, handwritten notes, Mitchell Papers.

21. Ibid.; Lucy Sprague Mitchell, *Two Lives*, ch. 20; Arthur F. Burns, *Wesley Clair Mitchell: The Economic Scientist* (New York, 1952), pp. 31–32.

22. "National Bureau of Economic Research: Its Organization and Purposes," undated, 403a-NBER, CF; Oswald Knauth to Commonwealth Fund, November 18, 1920, 403a-NBER, CF.

23. "A Bold Experiment: The Story of the National Bureau of Economic Research," Second Annual Report of the Director of Research, February 6, 1922, quoted in Burns, *Wesley Clair Mitchell*, p. 32; W. C. Mitchell to Lucy Sprague Mitchell, June 11, 1921, quoted in L. S. Mitchell, *Two Lives*, pp. 354–355; King, Macaulay, and Mitchell, *Income in the United States*, vol. 1, p. 5.

24. "Released for Afternoon Papers, of Thursday, October 27, 1921, National Bureau of Economic Research, Inc.," 403a-NBER, CF; "Distribution of Income by States, 1919," unsigned review, *The Survey* (November 1, 1922):203. The study's authority, sustained through subsequent revisions, is reflected in George Soule, *Prosperity Decade: From War to Depression, 1917–1929* (New York, 1947), p. 339; John Maurice Clark, *The Costs of World War to the American People* (New Haven, 1931), p. 8.

25. Jacob Hollander, review of *Income in the United States, Vol. I, Journal of the American Statistical Association* (September 1922):411.

26. Henry Seager, "Income in the United States," *The Survey*

(November 19, 1921):270. See also G. P. Watkins, "Statistics and Its Methods," *American Economic Review* 12 (June 1922):341–343.

27. Burns, *Wesley Clair Mitchell*, pp. 32–33; "A Bold Experiment," quoted in L. S. Mitchell, *Two Lives*, pp. 355–356.

28. "Monthly Newsletter," The National City Bank of New York, February 1922, quoted in David Eakins, "Policy Planning for the Establishment," in Ronald Radosh and Murray Rothbard, eds., *A New History of Leviathan* (New York, 1972), pp. 202–203. This article was probably written by George E. Roberts, director-by-appointment of the American Bankers Association to the National Bureau. See Oswald Knauth to Barry L. Smith of the Commonwealth Fund, August 16, 1921, p. 2, 403a-NBER, CF. See also, Robert Brookings, *Industrial Ownership, Its Economic and Social Significance* (New York, 1925), ch. 4; George Roberts, "Production as a Remedy for Inflation," *Proceedings of the American Academy of Political Science* 9 (1920–1922). J. M. Clark praises the national income study in *The Costs of the World War*, p. 86.

29. Leon P. Alford, "Federated American Engineering Societies: The Birth of a Super-Engineering Organization," *Factory and Industrial Management* (July 1920):53–55; Edwin F. Layton, *The Revolt of the Engineers* (Cleveland, 1971), pp. 179, 189.

30. Layton, *Revolt of the Engineers*, pp. 193–195.

31. Edward Eyre Hunt to Henry S. Pritchett, Carnegie Corporation, December 21, 1921, Unemployment-National Bureau of Economic Research, CP, HHPL; Herbert Hoover, "Address Before American Engineering Council's Executive Board and Convention of Engineers at Syracuse, New York," February 14, 1921, Public Statements, HHPL. On the Hunt-Reed relationship, see Robert A. Rosenstone, *Romantic Revolutionary: A Biography of John Reed* (New York, 1975).

32. Hoover, "Address Before the Federated American Engineering Societies at Washington, D.C.," November 19, 1920, Public Statements, HHPL; Layton, *Revolt of the Engineers*, pp. 189–195; Hawley, *The Great War and the Search for a Modern Order*, pp. 52–55.

33. Hoover, "Address Before the Federated American Engineering Societies at Washington, D.C.," November 19, 1920, Public Statements, HHPL; Layton, *Revolt of the Engineers*, pp. 189–195; Hawley, *The Great War and the Search for a Modern Order*, pp. 52–55.

34. Samuel Gompers to Herbert Hoover, November 30, 1920, folder #1-73, Box: Correspondence with H. M. Robinson-Herbert Hoover, ODY Papers. On John P. Frey, see W. A. Williams, *The Contours of American History* (1966), pp. 431–432.

35. Hunt to Pritchett, December 21, 1921, pp. 2–3, Unemployment-NBER, CP, HHP, HHPL; Layton, *Revolt of the Engineers*, pp. 201–205.

36. Committee on the Elimination of Waste in Industry of the FAES, *Waste in Industry* (New York, 1921).

37. Hunt to Pritchett, December 21, 1921, p. 3, Unemployment-NBER, CP, HHP, HHPL. For public and professional reaction to the waste study, see "What Can Be Done to Eliminate the Wastage of Industry," *Journal of Electricity and Western Industry* (September 15, 1921); L. W. Wallace, "Industrial Waste," *The Annals of the American Academy* (September 1921); Stuart Chase, "Wasting Man Power," *Labor Age* (December 1921); H. S. Person, review of *Waste in Industry*, *Journal of the American Statistical Association* (June 1922):278–280. While most reviewers had praise for the study, despite its hasty nature, Person was ecstatic, calling it "a volume of extraordinary significance."

38. On the bargaining relationships between capitalist and technical elites, see Alvin Gouldner, *The Dialectic of Ideology and Technology: The Origins, Grammar, and Future of Ideology* (New York, 1976) ch. 11. For a brief but important explanation of the "full implications of the First World War," see Christopher Lasch's introduction to Russell Jacoby, *Social Amnesia: A Critique of Conformist Psychology from Adler to Laing* (Boston, 1975), p. xiii. On advanced capitalism's legitimation difficulties, see Alan Wolfe, *The Limits of Legitimacy: Political Contradictions of Contemporary Capitalism* (New York, 1977), intro., ch. 10; Daniel Bell, *The Cultural Contradictions of Capitalism* (New York, 1976), ch. 6; David Held, "Crisis Tendencies, Legitimation, and the State," in John B. Thompson and David Held, eds., *Habermas: Critical Debates* (Cambridge, 1982).

39. Samuel P. Hays suggests that "the political values of an empirical profession can be identified most effectively through its particular categories of empirical description." See Samuel P. Hays, "Political Choice in Regulatory Administration," in Thomas K. McCraw, ed., *Regulation in Perspective* (Boston, 1981), pp. 142–143.

40. On Mitchell's thought, see Chapter 3.

41. Still the most important criticism of social science's abandonment of normative questions is Robert Lynd, *Knowledge for What?: The Place of Social Science in American Culture* (Princeton, 1939). Among the more important recent treatments are Edward A. Purcell, *The Crisis of Democratic Theory: Scientific Naturalism and the Problem of Value* (Lexington, 1973), chs. 2–3; T. S. Simey, *Social Science and Social Purpose* (London, 1968); Trent Schroyer, *The Critique of Domination* (New York, 1973); Paul Blumberg, *Industrial Democracy: The Sociology of Participation* (New York, 1968), introduction; Jacques Ellul, *The Technological Society* (New York, 1964), p. 159. See also, Samuel P. Hays, "Value Premises for Planning and Public Policy: The Historical Context," in Richard N. L. Andrews, ed., *Land in America: Commodity or Natural Resource?* (Lexington, 1979); Mark Smith, " 'Knowledge for What?': Social Science and the Debate Over Its Role in 1930's America," Ph.D. dissertation, University of Texas, Austin, 1980; the essays collected in Norma Haan, Robert N. Bellah, Paul Rabinow, and William M. Sullivan, eds., *Social Science as Moral Inquiry* (New York, 1983); Hans Peter Dreitzel, "Social Science and the Problem of Rationality: Notes on the Sociology of Technocrats," *Politics and Society* (Winter 1972); and Charles E. Lindblom, *Politics and Markets: The World's Political-Economic Systems* (New York, 1977), ch. 25.

CHAPTER 5

1. Evan B. Metcalf, "Economic Stabilization by American Business in the Twentieth Century," Ph. D. dissertation, University of Wisconsin, Madison, 1972, pp. 196–197; George Soule, *Prosperity Decade: From War to Depression, 1917–1929* (New York, 1947), ch. 5; W. Elliot Brownlee, *Dynamics of Ascent: A History of the American Economy* (New York, 1979), p. 380; Wesley C. Mitchell, "Prices and Reconstruction," *American Economic Review* 10, supplement (March 1920); Carolyn Grin, "The Unemployment Conference of 1921: An Experiment in National Cooperative Planning," *Mid-America* (April 1973); Ellis W. Hawley, "Herbert Hoover and Economic Stabilization, 1921–1922," in E. W. Hawley, ed., *Herbert Hoover as Secretary of Commerce, 1921–1928: Studies in New Era Thought and Practice* (Iowa City, 1981); Stanley Lebergott, *Man-*

power in Economic Growth (New York, 1964); request for a grant to finance the Committee on Unemployment and the Business Cycle, Edward E. Hunt, secretary, to H. S. Pritchett, president, Carnegie Corporation of New York, December 21, 1921, President's Conference on Unemployment, 1921–1930, Car. Corp.

2. That historians have largely ignored these efforts at macroeconomic management, including the linkages that developed between the federal executive and such private-sector agencies as the NBER and the Carnegie, Sage, and Rockefeller foundations, can be attributed to the traditional focus of historical writers on public officials and legislative activity. Thus most students of the period have not examined those areas in which private institutions acted in a public capacity. Nor have they appreciated the extent to which these developments furthered the legitimation of authority that was grounded in technocratic social science and corporate management, a legitimation that helped, at a time when the attempted management seemed successful, to validate notions of superior "public men" who had been created through a merger of science and business and were capable of ushering in a "utopia of the productive order." The quoted phrase is Charles Maier's and was used by him to describe similar developments in Europe. Charles S. Maier, "The Two Postwar Eras and the Conditions for Stability in Twentieth-Century Europe," *American Historical Review* (April 1981):333–334. See also, Maier, "Between Taylorism and Technocracy: European Ideologies and the Vision of Industrial Productivity in the 1920s," *Journal of Contemporary History* (January 1970) and *Recasting Bourgeois Europe: Stabilization in France, Germany, and Italy in the Decade after World War I* (Princeton, 1975). Maier's work, particularly the first citation above, is helpful in understanding how macroeconomic performance emerged as a key to managerial legitimation after World War I.

The best accounts of twentieth-century American planning include: Otis Graham, *Toward a Planned Society* (New York, 1976); Marion Clawson, *New Deal Planning* (Baltimore, 1980); and David Wilson, *The National Planning Idea in U.S. Public Policy* (Boulder, 1980). In addition to Hawley, Evan Metcalf is most appreciative of the inadequacies of the above in treating the planning of the 1920s. See Metcalf, "Secretary Hoover and the Emergence of Macroeconomic Management," *Business History Review* (Spring 1975). Also helpful is Barry D. Karl, "Philanthropy, Policy Planning, and the Bureaucratization of the Democratic Ideal," *Daedalus* (Fall 1976).

3. On modern American corporatism, see Ellis W. Hawley, "Techno-Corporatist Formulas in the Liberal State 1920–1960: A Neglected Aspect of America's Search for a New Order," presented at the Harvard Conference on Twentieth Century Capitalism, Cambridge, 1974; "Herbert Hoover and American Corporatism, 1929–1933," in Martin Fausold and George Mazuzan, eds., *The Hoover Presidency: A Reappraisal* (Albany, 1974), pp. 101–119; and "Herbert Hoover, the Commerce Secretariat, and the Vision of an 'Associative State,' " *Journal of American History* (June 1974). See also George C. Lodge, *The New American Ideology* (New York, 1975); Kim McQuaid, "Corporate Liberalism in the American Business Community, 1920–1940," *Business History Review* (Autumn 1978); Robert M. Collins, "The Persistence of Neo-Corporatism in Post-War Business-Government Relations," presented at the annual meeting of the Organization of American Historians, 1981; Hawley, "The New Corporatism and the Liberal Democracies, 1918–1925: The Case of the United States," presented at the annual meeting of the Organization of American Historians, 1977; Howard J. Wiarda, *Corporatism and National Development in Latin America* (Boulder, 1981), chs. 1, 17; Phillipe Schmitter, "Still the Century of Corporatism," *Review of Politics* (January 1974); and Alan Wolfe, *The Limits of Legitimacy: Political Contradictions of Contemporary Capitalism* (New York, 1977), pp. 117–138.

4. On Hoover, European relief, and the foundations, see "The Commonwealth Fund Annual Report, 1921, Extract Copy," The Commonwealth Fund, Box 13, Hunt Papers; Robert D. Cuff, "Herbert Hoover, The Ideology of Voluntarism, and War Organization During the Great War," *Journal of American History* (September 1977); Herbert Hoover to Henry S. Pritchett, November 18, 1921, President's Conference on Unemployment, 1921–1930, Car. Corp. Hoover's letter requested Carnegie Corporation funding of the business cycle committee. Pritchett, however, missed the ideological implications of Carnegie Corporation support. Thus in a letter emphasizing the importance of foundation funding for the appearance of disinterestedness, Hunt clarified Hoover's phrase "the entire community" by changing it to "the business public." Hunt to Pritchett, December 29, 1921, Unemployment-NBER, CP, HHP, HHPL.

5. See Hawley's essay in J. Joseph Huthmacher and Warren Susman, eds., *Herbert Hoover and the Crisis of American Capitalism* (Cambridge, 1973).

6. See Hoover's addresses before the Federated American Engineering Societies, November 19, 1920; the American Institute of Mining and Metallurgical Engineers, February 17, 1920; and the Boston Chamber of Commerce, March 24, 1920, all in Public Statements, HHP. See also, Herbert Hoover, *American Individualism* (Garden City, 1922); and William A. Williams, *The Contours of American History* (Chicago, 1966), pp. 425–438.

7. Hawley, "Herbert Hoover, The Commerce Secretariat, and the Vision of an 'Associative State.'"

8. See Chapter 3 for Mitchell's ideas. See also, Wesley C. Mitchell, "The Crisis of 1920 and the Problem of Controlling Business Cycles," *American Economic Review* 12, supplement (March 1922); *The National Bureau's First Quarter Century*, Twenty-fifth Annual Report, NBER, New York (May 1945), p. 9; Oswald Knauth to Barry Smith, August 11, 1921, 403a-NBER, CF.

9. See Chapter 1 for the origins of the Russell Sage Foundation. Also see the forthcoming history of the foundation by David Hammack; Raymond B. Fosdick, *The Story of the Rockefeller Foundation* (New York, 1952), pp. 193–198; Herbert Heaton, *A Scholar in Action: Edwin F. Gay* (Cambridge, 1952); Karl, "Philanthropy, Policy Planning, and the Bureaucratization of the Democratic Ideal."

10. Alva Johnston, "Beardsley Ruml: A Profile," *The New Yorker* (February 10, 17, 24, 1945).

11. Hawley, "Herbert Hoover and Economic Stabilization, 1921–1922."

12. Metcalf, "Secretary Hoover."

13. Hoover, "What Government Can Do," *Nation's Business* (June 1921); Hoover to William Rossiter, April 14, 1921, Commerce, Bureau of Census, Advisory Committee; Hoover to National Research Council, July 9, 1921, CP, HHP, HHPL; Joint Committee of the American Statistical Association and American Economic Association, "Final Report," *Journal of the American Statistical Association* (March 1923). The Advisory Committee on the Census was organized late in 1918 by Commerce Secretary William Redfield. See Irving Fisher to Allyn Young, November 21, 1918, Allyn Young 1918, Secretary's File, AEA Papers.

14. Grin, "The Unemployment Conference"; John A Garraty, *Unemployment in History: Economic Thought and Pubic Policy* (New

York, 1978), ch. 8; J. B. Andrews to E. E. Hunt, July 26, 1922, Unemployment Business Cycles Report, Greenwich Meeting Correspondence, CP, HHP, HHPL.

15. Hoover to James Brookmire, February 9, 1925, Unemployment-Business Cycles; Hoover to Edwin F. Gay, August 29, 1921, Unemployment-Gay, Edwin F., 1921–22, CP, HHP.

16. Ross Thomas Runfola, "Herbert C. Hoover as Secretary of Commerce, 1921–1923: Domestic Economic Planning in the Harding Years," Ph. D. dissertation, State University of New York at Buffalo, 1973, ch. 3; "President's Conference on Unemployment—General Recommendations for an Emergency Program," Unemployment Recommendations for an Emergency Program 1921; "Report of the Economic Advisory Committee to the Unemployment Conference," September 26, 1921, Unemployment Conference: Plans and Programs 1921-Sepember; Hunt to Joseph Defrees, November 5, 1921, Unemployment 1921, November-December; Hoover to Arthur T. Hadley, September 8, 1921, Unemployment, Advisory Committee Organization, CP, HHP; Hoover's farewell address to the conference, October 13, 1921, Public Statements, HHP.

17. "Report of the Economic Advisory Committee to the Unemployment Conference"; Hunt to Defrees, November 5, 1921; Hunt to Edgar Rickard, October 20, 1921, Unemployment 1921, September-October, CP, HHP; Mitchell, "The Crisis of 1920"; E. Stewart Freeman, "The American Economic Association Meeting, Tuesday, December 27, 1921, Topic—Business Cycles," memorandum apparently written for Henry S. Dennison, Carton 2, Dennison Papers; Arthur F. Burns, *Wesley Clair Mitchell: The Economic Scientist* (New York, 1952), pp. 21-26.

18. Metcalf, "Secretary Hoover"; Grin, "The Unemployment Conference"; Hunt to Beardsley Ruml, December 12, 1923, President's Conference on Unemployment, 1923–1927, Box 86, LSRM. The three indicative studies that followed and built on the foundation laid by the business cycle committee were: "Seasonal Operations in the Construction Industries, 1923–24"; "Recent Economic Changes, 1928–29"; and "Planning and Control of Public Works, 1930." See memo by Arch W. Shaw, June 17, 1931, Commerce Papers, RG 40, General Correspondence, 85414, NA.

19. Edgar Rickard to R. A. Franks, Carnegie Corporation, October 14, 1921, President's Conference on Unemployment, 1921–30, Car. Corp. "Memo in Support of an Application for a Grant

of $50,000 for an Investigation of Unemployment and the Business Cycle," undated, Unemployment, Business Cycles, undated, CP, HHP.

20. Hoover to Rickard, November 14, 1921; Hoover to H. S. Pritchett, November 18, 1921, President's Conference on Unemployment, 1921–30, Car. Corp; Hoover to Rickard, November 18, 1921, Unemployment, 1921, November-December, CP, HHP.

21. Hunt to Pritchett, December 21, 1921, Unemployment-NBER, CP, HHP, HHPL. On Owen Young, see Josephine Young Case and Everett Needham Case, *Owen D. Young and American Enterprise* (Boston, 1982); Ida Tarbell, *Owen D. Young: A New Type of Industrial Leader* (New York, 1932); Kim McQuaid, "Owen D. Young, Gerard Swope, and the 'New Capitalism' of the General Electric Company, 1920–1933," *American Journal of Economics and Sociology* (July 1977). Young had supported the Hoover-for-president boom in California in 1920 and thought highly of Hoover's "sound philosophy and good sense." See Owen D. Young to Ralph Arnold, February 25, 1920, and Young to Hoover, December 29, 1922, Folder 1–73, Correspondence with H. M. Robinson and H. Hoover, ODY 6.

22. Hoover to Gay, August 29, 1921; Hoover to W. C. Mitchell, July 29, 1921, Mitchell Papers.

23. Mitchell to Hunt, October 20, 1921, Unemployment-Business Cycles, 1921; Mitchell to Hoover, October 24, 1921, Unemployment-National Bureau of Economic Research, CP, HHP.

24. Mitchell to Royal Meeker, March 2, 1922, Mitchell Papers; Oswald Knauth to Barry Smith, August 11, 1921, 403a-NBER, CF; Mitchell to Hoover, October 24, 1921, CP, HHP.

25. Mitchell to Hoover, October 24, 1921, CP, HHP; J.R.A. (James R. Angell), "National Bureau of Economic Research," December 15, 1920, 4031-NBER, CF; Gay to Hoover, October 22, 1921, Unemployment-National Bureau of Economic Research, CP, HHP.

26. Hoover to Pritchett, November 18, 1921; Rickard to Smith, October 14, 1921; Rickard to Christian Herter, November 16, 1921; and Rickard to O. D. Young, November 21, 1921, Unemployment, 1921, November-December, CP, HHP; Abraham Flexner, *Henry S. Pritchett: A Biography* (New York, 1943), pp. 139–140. The Commonwealth Fund's board eventually turned down

Hoover's request; B. Smith to Rickard, December 8, 1921, Unemployment, 1921, November-December, CP, HHP.

27. Hoover to Pritchett, November 18, 1921; Pritchett to Hoover, November 23, 1921, President's Conference on Unemployment, 1921–30, Car. Corp., Hoover to Rickard, November 18, 1921, Unemployment, 1921 November-December, CP, HHP, HHPL. On Carnegie Corporation financial problems in the early 1920s, see Waldemar Nielsen, *The Big Foundations* (New York, 1972), p. 36.

28. Hunt to Pritchett, December 21, 1921, cover letter and proposal, President's Conference on Unemployment, 1921–30, Car. Corp.

29. See Chapter 4 for a treatment of Rorty. See also, Pritchett to Hunt, December 24, 1921; Hunt to Pritchett, December 29, 1921; Hunt to Pritchett, January 25, 1922, President's Conference on Unemployment, 1921–30, Car. Corp.

30. On the NBER-business cycle committee negotiations see the correspondence in Unemployment, Business Cycles, 1922, CP, HHP, See also, "Unemployment and Business Cycles: Tentative Outline of Investigations and Report," February 20, 1922, Unemployment, 1922, January-March, CP, HHP.

31. Letter of invitation to the business cycle committee meeting, February 20, 1922, from E. E. Hunt, February 13, 1922, Unemployment, Business Cycles, 1922, January-March; Hunt to Young, February 13, 1922, Unemployment, Business Cycles, 1922; "Meeting of Economists with Members of the Committee on the Business Cycle, December 28, 1922 . . . ," p. 1, Unemployment, Business Cycles: Report-Chicago Minutes and Notes, CP, HHP.

32. Press release, Department of Commerce, November 22, 1921, Unemployment, 1922, January-March, CP, HHP; Robert Littell, "The Unemployed and a Weatherman," *The New Republic* (March 1, 1922):22; Irving Bernstein, *The Lean Years* (Boston, 1960), p. 270; Robert Zieger, *Republicans and Labor, 1919–1929* (Lexington, 1969), pp. 217, 257.

33. "Please Answer These Questions for Hoover," March 25, 1922, Unemployment, 1922, January-March, CP, HHP; Hunt to Pritchett, April 10, 1922; "Unemployment and Business Cycles: Condensed Summary of Tentative Outline and Time Schedule, Revised Edition, April 1, 1922," President's Conference on Unemployment, 1921–30, Car. Corp.

34. Hunt to Pritchett, April 10, 1922, Car. Corp.; W. C. Mitchell, "Meeting of Trade Associations, Department of Commerce, 2:30 PM, April 13, 1922," handwritten notes, Mitchell Papers. "Business Cycle Meeting," April 13, 1922, Unemployment, Business Cycles, 1922, CP, HHP.

35. President's Conference on Unemployment, Committee on Business Cycles and Unemployment, *Business Cycles and Unemployment* (New York, 1923); Hunt to Pritchett, June 10, 1922, and June 23, 1922, President's Conference on Unemployment, 1921–30, Car. Corp.; Mitchell to Hunt, July 24, 1922, Unemployment-Business Cycles Report—Greenwich Meeting Correspondence, CP, HHP. On Hoover's public relations apparatus, see Craig Lloyd, *Aggressive Introvert: A Study of Herbert Hoover and Public Relations Management, 1912–1932* (Columbus, 1972).

36. Stuart Rice to Hunt, July 27, 1922; Otto Mallery, "Suggestions to the Business Cycle Committee," July 26, 1922; J. B. Andrews to Hunt, July 26, 1922; Unemployment-Business Cycles Report—Greenwich Meeting Correspondence, CP, HHP; Mary Van Kleeck, "Unemployment Ended?" *The Survey* (June 1922); William Chenery, "Unemployment in Washington," *The Survey* (October 8, 1921).

CHAPTER 6

1. It is not certain that Young made these statements at the August meetings, but it seems likely. See the undated memo, "Three Divisions: Stabilization—Legislative Proposals—Statistics," in Folder 12–23, Misc. Papers, ODY 4, "Summary of Action Taken at Meeting of Business Cycle Committee, August 7, 8, 9, 1922," and Hunt to Young, August 22, 1922, Folder 12–23, ODY 1; Memorandum, Hunt to Hoover, August 18, 1922, Unemployment 1922, April-November, CP, HHP. On the referendum, see "Miss Reynolds' Notes, Chicago Meeting," pp. 18–19, Unemployment, Business Cycles: Report—Chicago Minutes and Notes, CP, HHP.

2. Mary Van Kleeck, "Unemployment Ended?" *The Survey* (June 15, 1922); J. B. Andrews to Hunt, July 26, 1922; Wesley Mitchell to Hunt, July 24, 1922, Unemployment—Business Cycles Report—Greenwich Meeting Correspondence; "Miss Reynolds' Notes," Mary Van Kleeck's statement, p. 14, CP, HHP. Hoover proposed a program of nonstatist unemployment insurance un-

der the auspices of the insurance industry and leading employers. See "Address of Secretary Hoover—Metropolitan Insurance Managers Banquet, January 27, 1923," Unemployment, 1923–25, CP, HHP. I have yet to discover Hunt's draft, but we do have a memorandum critical of it that reveals much. See "Memorandum on Present Recommendations," unsigned and undated, but most likely the work of Wallace B. Donham, Dean of Harvard Business School, ODY 4.

3. "Miss Reynolds' Notes," CP, HHP; Daniel Nelson, *Unemployment Insurance* (Madison, 1969), p. 39.

4. "Memorandum on Present Recommendations," ODY 4; Stuart Crocker to Wallace Donham, October 6, 1922, Folder 12–23–1, ODY 2.

5. Crocker to Hunt, September 12, 1922, ODY 1; "Memorandum on Present Recommendations," ODY 4; Crocker to Donham, October 6, 1922, ODY 2.

6. Compare Donham's objections in the memorandum cited above with Wesley Mitchell's draft recommendations in "Unemployment—Business Cycles Report—Chicago Meeting Drafts," CP, HHP.

7. "Memorandum on Present Recommendations," ODY 4. See also, Donham to Crocker, January 22, 1923, ODY 3.

8. "Miss Reynolds' Notes," pp. 2–3, CP, HHP; Mitchell to Hunt, October 13, 1922, ODY 1.

9. "Miss Reynolds' Notes," pp. 11–14, 25, CP, HHP.

10. Crocker to Donham, October 6, 1922; Crocker to Donham, October 14, 1922; Crocker to Donald K. David, November 20, 1922, ODY 2. See also the Crocker-Van Kleeck memorandum, "Harvard Bureau of Economic Research," November 10, 1922, ODY 4.

11. "Rough Draft—Confidential and Tentative Only. Please Return to Edward Eyre Hunt," copy no. 7, undated; L. P. Alford to Hunt, October 25, 1922; Hunt to O. D. Young, October 26, 1922, ODY 2; John Commons to Hunt, October 19, 1922, ODY 1.

12. Hunt to Young, October 18, 1922, ODY 1; Gay to Hunt, October 23, 1922; Donham to Crocker, October 27–28, 1922, ODY 2.

13. Young to Hunt, November 8, 1922; Hunt to Young, November 9, 1922, ODY 1. On the American Federation of Labor's conception of its role in the impending referendum see the at-

tached memo by Florence C. Thorne in Hunt to Young, November 15, 1922, ODY 1. Crocker to Van Kleeck, November 24, 1922, ODY 2.

14. Van Kleeck, "Harvard Bureau of Economic Research," November 10, 1922, ODY 4.

15. Hunt to Crocker, December 5, 1922, ODY 1.

16. Among those present at the meeting were Richard T. Ely, John R. Commons, J. M. Clark, Irving Fisher, and Allyn Young. "Meeting of Economists with Members of the Committee on the Business Cycle, December 28, 1922, to discuss the tentative draft of the Committee's report," pp. 1–2, Unemployment, Business Cycles: Report—Chicago Minutes and Notes, CP, HHP.

17. "Meeting of Economists," pp. 2–5, CP, HHP.

18. Ibid., pp. 5–6.

19. Ibid., pp. 6–10.

20. Ibid., pp. 10–11; W. C. Mitchell, "The Crisis of 1920 and the Problem of Controlling Business Cycles," *American Economic Review* 12, supplement (March 1922).

21. "Meeting of Economists," pp. 13–17, CP, HHP. See also, Moulton to Mitchell, January 2, 1923, ODY 3.

22. "Meeting of Economists," pp. 26–27.

23. Crocker to Young, December 29, 1922, ODY 1.

24. "Meeting of Economists," pp. 27–28, CP, HHP.

25. "Committee on the Business Cycle, Notes of Discussion at the meeting of the Committee in the office of the General Electric Company," January 27, 1923, 20, ODY 2.

26. Press Release, April 2, 1923, Unemployment, 1923–25, CP, HHP.

27. *The New Republic* (April 11, 1923):173. *The American Labor Legislation Review* was similarly critical. See Frederick W. MacKenzie, "Stabilizing Employment: Official Findings," *American Labor Legislation Review* 13 (June 1923):148. On the same theme, see the letter from Darwin J. Meserole, President, National Unemployment League, to Crocker, May 25, 1923, ODY 5.

28. W. C. Clark, review of *Business Cycles and Unemployment, The Journal of the American Statistical Association* (December 1923):1053–1056; Willard E. Hotchkiss, review of *Business Cycles and Unemployment, Bulletin of the Taylor Society* 9 (April 1924):86–89; John Commons, review of *Business Cycles and Unemployment, American Review*, quoted in Hotchkiss.

29. Arch Shaw to Young, May 11, 1923; W. B. Remington to Young, October 6, 1923, ODY 5; R. Forbes to Young, April 24, 1923, ODY 2. Further examples of the generally favorable reaction of the business press include: "Urge Business Cycle Control," *Iron Age* (April 5, 1923); "Experts Suggest Ways to Remove Kinks From the Business Cycle," *Lumber* (April 6, 1923); and "The Business Cycle," *The Credit Monthly* (June 1923). See also the many clippings in the folders entitled "Unemployment—Business Cycles—Clippings and Unemployment and Business Cycle Publicity," 1923, CP, HHP.

30. Hunt to President and Trustees of Carnegie Corporation, May 1, 1923, President's Conference on Unemployment, 1921–30, Car. Corp.; Hunt, "The Long Look Ahead," *The Survey* (June 1, 1923).

31. Young to Elihu Root, September 17, 1923, President's Conference on Unemployment, 1921–30, Car. Corp.

32. Hoover to Frederick Keppel, October 26, 1923, U.S. Department of Commerce, Committee on Business Cycles and Unemployment, Box 37, Hunt Papers.

33. George Soule, *Prosperity Decade: From War to Depression, 1917–1929* (New York, 1947), pp. 114–115; W. Elliot Brownlee, *Dynamics of Ascent: A History of the American Economy* (New York, 1979), ch. 14.

CHAPTER 7

1. For contemporary perceptions of the success of these subsidiary investigations, see E. E. Hunt to Beardsley Ruml, February 24, 1925, President's Conference on Unemployment, 1923–1927, Box 86, LSRM. On seasonal industries, particularly construction, see Henry S. Pritchett to Herbert Hoover, May 22, 1923, President's Conference on Recent Economic Changes, Carnegie Corporation, 1921–30, Box 38, Hunt Papers; Hunt to Hoover, "Seasonal and Intermittent Studies," November 14, 1921, Unemployment, Business Cycles, 1922, and Hoover to Ernest Trigg, May 28, 1923, Seasonal Industries Investigation, CP, HHP; and U.S. Department of Commerce, Elimination of Waste Series, *Seasonal Operation in the Construction Industries* (Washington, 1924). On coal, see Ellis W. Hawley, "Secretary Hoover and the Bituminous Coal Problem," *Business History Review* (Autumn 1968).

On a similar but aborted investigation into bases for resolving industrial disputes, see Herbert Hoover to Arthur Woods, September 26, 1924; E. E. Hunt to Hoover, February 14, 1925; Hunt to Hoover, May 14, 1926, all in Rockefeller Foundation, CP, HHP.

2. On the older deductive paradigms and the rise of new syntheses in the 1920s, see Edward A. Purcell, Jr., *The Crisis of Democratic Theory: Scientific Naturalism and the Problem of Value* (Lexington, 1973), chs. 1–2; Louis Wirth, "The Social Sciences," in Merle Curti, ed., *American Scholarship in the Twentieth Century* (Cambridge, 1953); Thomas L. Haskell, *The Emergence of Professional Social Science: The American Social Science Association and the Nineteenth-Century Crisis of Authority* (Urbana, 1977), chs. 1, 2, 11; Dorothy Ross, "The Development of the Social Sciences," in Alexandra Oleson and John Voss, eds., *The Organization of Knowledge in Modern America, 1860–1920* (Baltimore, 1979).

3. Wesley C. Mitchell, "Quantitative Analysis in Economic Theory," *American Economic Review* 15 (March 1925), reprinted in Joseph Dorfman, ed., *The Backward Art of Spending Money: And Other Essays by Wesley C. Mitchell* (New York, 1937) pp. 22–23; W. C. Mitchell, "The Prospects of Economics," in Rexford G. Tugwell, ed., *The Trend of Economics* (New York, 1924), pp. 28–29; Warren Persons, "Economics and Statistics," in William F. Ogburn et al., eds., *The Social Sciences and Their Interrelations* (Cambridge, 1927), p. 162. Persons was careful to attribute most of the growth to the war.

4. Mitchell, "Quantitative Analysis," p. 30; Mitchell, "The Prospects," p. 25.

5. Tugwell, *The Trend of Economics*, pp. x, xi. An important criticism of the institutionalist renaissance is found in David Seckler, *Thorstein Veblen and the Institutionalists: A Study in the Social Philosophy of Economics* (Boulder, 1975).

6. Ogburn et al., *The Social Sciences*, preface, ch. 1; Barbara Laslett, "Science and Social Action: The Dilemma of William Fielding Ogburn," unpublished manuscript, Univeristy of Minnesota, 1984; Purcell, *The Crisis*, ch. 2; Gene Lyons, *The Uneasy Partnership: Social Science and the Federal Government in the Twentieth Century* (New York, 1969), pp. 42–44; Albert J. Reiss, Jr., "Sociology: The Field," in David L. Sills, ed., *International Encyclopedia of the Social Sciences* (New York, 1968), pp. 10–11. Anthropology was least affected by the new empiricism. See Christopher Lasch, *Haven in a Heartless World: The Family Besieged* (New York, 1979),

ch. 4; and Eric R. Wolf, *Europe and the People Without History* (Berkeley, 1982), pp. 13–19.

7. Mitchell, "Quantitative Analysis," p. 27.

8. On the importance of the concept of "interdependence" to the development of modern social science, see the dissimilar interpretations of Thomas L. Haskell, *The Emergence of Professional Social Science*, ch. 2, and Christopher Lasch, *Haven in a Heartless World*, introduction. Whether or not the idea of "interdependence" has advanced social understanding or mystified modern social relations (or both), it was reinforced by Hooverian technocorporatism.

9. Charles Merriam, "Political Research," *American Political Science Review* 16 (1922):315; Social Science Research Council, "History and Purposes of the Social Science Research Council," in *Fifth Annual Report, 1928–1929* (New York, 1930); Lyons, *The Uneasy Partnership*, pp. 42–43; Wirth, "The Social Sciences"; p. 78; Raymond B. Fosdick, *The Story of the Rockefeller Foundation* (New York, 1952), ch. 16; Barry Karl, "Presidential Planning and Social Research: Mr. Hoover's Experts," in Donald Fleming and Bernard Bailyn, eds., *Perspectives in American History* (Cambridge, 1969); Forrest G. Hill, "Wesley Mitchell's Theory of Planning," *Political Science Quarterly* (March 1957); Albert Somit and Joseph Tanenhaus, *The Development of Political Science* (Boston, 1967), pp. 110–117; Barry Karl, *Charles E. Merriam and the Study of Politics* (Chicago, 1974).

10. Wirth, "The Social Sciences," pp. 77–82.

11. Ibid.

12. Fosdick, *The Story*, pp. 92–202; Purcell, *The Crisis*, p. 28; Lyons, *The Uneasy Partnership*, p. 44; Barry Karl "Philanthropy, Policy Planning, and the Bureaucratization of the Democratic Ideal," *Daedalus* (Fall 1976).

13. Abraham Flexner to J. R. Angell, November 28, 1921, Beardsley Ruml Papers; Alva Johnston, "Beardsley Ruml: A Profile," *The New Yorker* (February 10, 1945), p. 28; Harold D. Lasswell, *A Pre-View of Policy Sciences* (New York, 1971), preface; Robert E. Kohler, "A Policy for the Advancement of Science: The Rockefeller Foundation, 1924–1929," *Minerva* (Winter 1978):482, 488.

14. "Memorial Policy in Social Sciences: Extracts From Various Memoranda and Dockets," pp. 1–4, Folder 8, Box 1, Ruml Papers.

15. Ibid., pp. 3–4; on Mary Van Kleeck, Wesley Mitchell, and

E. E. Hunt, see Chapters 5 and 6; Fosdick, *The Story*, pp. 26, 195–200.

16. "Memorial Policy," Ruml Papers, pp. 2–6; Fosdick, *The Story*, pp. 26, 195–200; Johnston, "Beardsley Ruml." Twelve principles designed to maintain such insulation were adopted by the memorial's trustees in November 1924.

17. "Memorial Policy," pp. 18–23; "The Laura Spelman Rockefeller Memorial, Report for 1923" (New York, 1924), p. 15, Rockefeller Foundation, CP, HHP; Wesley Mitchell to Raymond Fosdick, January 18, 1927, Mitchell Papers.

18. Evan B. Metcalf, "Economic Stabilization by American Business in the Twentieth Century," Ph. D. dissertation, University of Wisconsin, Madison, 1972, ch. 7. Expressions of managerial ideology include Henry Dennison, "Business Management as a Profession," address to the Bureau of Personnel Administration, New York, October 1, 1925, Dennison Papers; Ida M. Tarbell, *Owen D. Young: A New Type of Industrial Leader* (New York, 1932); Ernest G. Draper, "The Manager and His Incipient Art," *Survey Graphic* (June 1929), and Sam Lewisohn, *The New Leadership in Industry*, (New York, 1926). Interpretations of this ideology are included in John D. Hicks, *Republican Ascendancy* (New York, 1960); Ellis W. Hawley, *The Great War and the Search for a Modern Order 1917–1933* (New York, 1979); Stuart Ewen, *Captains of Consciousness* (New York, 1976); Morrel Heald, *The Social Responsibilities of Business* (Cleveland, 1970); and Stuart O. Brandes, *American Welfare Capitalism* (Chicago, 1970).

19. The process of mutual legitimation between technical and depoliticized public authority is treated in Jürgen Habermas, *Legitimation Crisis* (Boston, 1975), pp. 33–37; Alvin Gouldner, *The Dialectic of Ideology and Technology: The Origins, Grammar, and Future of Ideology* (New York, 1976), pp. 267–270; and Thomas McCarthy, "The Scientization of Politics," in his *The Critical Theory of Jürgen Habermas* (Cambridge, 1978), pp. 1–16.

20. Joseph H. Barber, "Are Statistics Stabilizing Business?" *The Management Review* (August 1926); Henry S. Dennison, "Unemployment Relief—A Burden or an Investment?" *System* (June 1926); Johnson Heywood, "How the Dennison Manufacturing Company Meets the Slumps," *Advertising and Selling Fortnightly* (March 1925); Henry Dennison, "To Cut the Waste of Unemployment," *Nation's Business* (October 1924); Gerard Swope, "The Engineer's Place in

Society," *The Survey* (March 1, 1924); William S. Green, "Labor's Ideal Concerning Management," *Bulletin of the Taylor Society* (December 1925); Henry Dennison, "Stabilizing Employment in a Diversified Seasonal Industry," *The Annals* (September 1922); Ernest Draper, "It Can't Be Done in Our Business," *American Management Review* (September 1924). See also the entire issue of the *American Labor Legislation Review* for March 1923 and June 1924, and of *The Survey* for April 1, 1929, as well as Ernest G. Draper, "The Manager and His Incipient Art"; Rudolph Binder, *Business and the Professions* (New York, 1922); and Edward A. Filene, *The Way Out* (New York, 1925).

21. Metcalf, "Economic Stabilization," pp. 239, 269–271, 275; William C. Proctor, "An Idea That Added Thousands of Profits in 24 Months," *System* (May 1925).

22. Metcalf, "Economic Stabilization," p. 277, ch. 8.

23. Mary Van Kleeck and Graham R. Taylor, "The Professional Organization of Social Work," *The Annals of the American Academy* 101 (May 1922):164.

24. Sam A. Lewisohn. *The New Leadership in Industry* (New York, 1926), pp. 100–101; Owen D. Young, Address to Annual Meeting of the National Electric Light Association, May 1926, quoted in Mary Van Kleeck, "The Interview as a Method of Research," *Bulletin of the Taylor Society* (December 1926):269–270; S. A. Courtis quoted in same; E. A. Filene, *The Way Out* (New York, 1925); Gerard Swope, "The Engineer's Place in Society."

25. Dennison, "Business Management as a Profession," Dennison Papers.

26. Ibid., pp. 2–4.

27. Mary Van Kleeck, "Modern Industry and Society," *American Federationist* (June 1926):700, 702, 703. See also, Van Kleeck, "Justice and the Invididual," *Workers' Education* (August 1926); "Employment Statistics and Trade Unions," *American Federationist* (April 1927).

CHAPTER 8

1. Hoover to Frederick P. Keppel, October 26, 1927, PCU, Car. Corp.; P. W. Martin, "The Technique of Balance: Its Place in American Prosperity," President's Conference on Unemployment, REC, Memoranda, Notes, Box 39, Hunt Papers; "World-

Wide Business Conditions Pictured," *News-Bulletin of the National Bureau of Economic Research*, May 20, 1927, Unemployment, Business Cycles, 1922, CP, HHPL. Good analyses of the New Era economic vision at high tide include Joseph S. Davis, *The World Between the Wars, 1929–39* (Baltimore, 1975), ch. 6; and Joseph Dorfman, *The Economic Mind in American Civilization*, vols, 4–5 (New York, 1959), ch. 3, p. 21.

2. Hunt, "Draft," October 26, 1929, REC, General, Box 39, Hunt Papers; Hunt to Joseph Willits, October 26, 1924, Correspondence, Memos, Clippings, Etc., Hunt Collection, HHPL.

3. Hoover to Keppel, October 26, 1927, PCU, Car. Corp.; Hunt, "Draft," October 26, 1929; "Draft," September 26, 1928, REC, Memoranda, Notes, Box 39, Hunt Papers.

4. On the European economic surveys see Hunt, "Self-Conscious Business," *The Forum* (August 1929); Hoover to Keppel, October 26, 1927; Hunt, untitled, unsigned draft, June 21, 1934, REC, Memoranda, Notes, Box 39, Hunt Papers.

5. Wesley C. Mitchell to Henry Dennison, May 26, 1927, Mitchell Papers; Hunt, "Draft," September 26, 1928, REC, Hunt Papers.

6. George Soule, *Prosperity Decade: From War to Depression, 1917–1929* (New York, 1947), ch. 13; "World-Wide Business Conditions Pictured," May 20, 1927, CP, HHPL; Mitchell to Dennison, May 26, 1927, Mitchell Papers; Ellis W. Hawley, *The Great War and the Search for a Modern Order, 1917–1933* (New York, 1979), pp. 97–99, 173–174.

7. Hunt, "Business Cycles and Unemployment," October 1, 1927, 5, President's Conference on Unemployment, BCU, Box 37, Hunt Papers.

8. Hunt to Willits, October 26, 1924, Hunt Collection, HHPL.

9. Hunt, "Planning," address before the North Carolina Conference for Social Service, February 10, 1927, Correspondence, Speech Material, Hunt Collection, HHPL; "National Planning Board," July 2, 1926, National Planning, Notes, etc., Box 19, Hunt Papers.

10. Mary Van Kleeck, "Barometers of Unemployment," March 1, 1927, Folder 470, Box 5, MVK Papers.

11. Ibid.

12. Mary Van Kleeck, "What Will You Do Next?" *American Federationist* (September 1927):1091–1092.

13. Ibid., pp. 1092–1094. On the need to arm labor with technical expertise, see Geoffrey Brown, "Workers' Participation in Management," *Bulletin of the Taylor Society* (February 1929).

14. Hunt, "Draft," September 26, 1928, REC, Hunt Papers. George O. May to Frederick Keppel, December 2, 1927, and E. F. Gay and W. C. Mitchell to Hunt, October 24, 1927, both PCU, Car. Corp.

15. Gay and Mitchell to Hunt, October 24, 1927, PCU, Car. Corp.

16. Ibid.

17. Gay to Keppel, October 17, 1927, NBER, 1924–1929, Car. Corp.; George O. May to Keppel, December 2, 1927, PCU, Car. Corp.

18. Hoover to Keppel, October 26, 1927, PCU, Car. Corp.; Hoover to Col. Arthur Woods, December 23, 1927, President's Conference on Unemployment, 1923–1927, Box 86, LSRM.

19. Hoover to Keppel, October 26, 1927, PCU, Car. Corp.; Hoover to Woods, December 23, 1927, LSRM; Russell M. Leffingwell to Frederick P. Keppel, October 21, 1927, PCU, Car. Corp.

20. Keppel to Harold G. Moulton, November 18, 1927, PCU, Car. Corp.; Moulton to Keppel, November 22, 1927, PCU, Car. Corp.

21. "Memorandum of Interview: George O. May" November 22, 1927, and "Memorandum of Interview: FPK and Wesley Mitchell," November 29, 1927, both PCU, Car. Corp.; "Draft of letter to Dr. Keppel," December 12, 1927, REC, Correspondence, general, Box 38, Hunt Papers.

22. On the Carnegie Corporation's irritation with Hoover's handling of the early publicity for the Committee on Recent Economic Changes, see the correspondence and internal memos of February 18–28, 1928, among Keppel, Leffingwell, Hunt, and others in PCU, Car. Corp. On the composition of the sponsoring committee, see Hoover to Keppel, December 3, 1927, PCU, Car. Corp.; Committee on Recent Economic Changes of the President's Conference on Unemployment, *Recent Economic Changes in the United States*, 2 vols. (New York, 1929), p. xxii; Hoover to Julius Klein, February 13, 1928, REC, Correspondence, General, Box 38, Hunt Papers.

23. Gay and Mitchell to Hunt, October 24, 1927, PCU, Car. Corp.

24. Ibid.; National Bureau of Economic Research, "Survey of Recent Economic Changes," Press Release, April 23, 1928, PCU, Car. Corp.

25. "I have my own doubts whether . . . there is any business cycle at all," wrote Percival White in "Business Cycles—Wheels of Chance?" *Nation's Business* (March 1928):78; Henry Dennison, "Insuring Tomorrow's Business Today," *Chicago Commerce* (December 10, 1927):9.

26. Van Kleeck, "Unemployment in Passaic," *American Federationist* (May 1928):597–602.

27. Ibid.

28. Ibid. Little treatment was given to technological unemployment in the 1920s. *Recent Economic Changes* would make note of it as an emerging issue, but most analysts thought technical improvements did not reduce absolutely the number of jobs. See John A. Garraty, *Unemployment in History: Economic Thought and Public Policy* (New York, 1978), p. 1952; Isador Lubin, *The Absorption of the Unemployed by American Industry* (New York, 1929).

29. Van Kleeck, "Unemployment in Passaic," pp. 600–602.

30. Van Kleeck, "Recent Gains in Industrial Relations," *The World Tomorrow* (May 1928), Folder 470, Box 25, MVK Papers.

31. Van Kleeck, "Labor and Institutions for Social Research" *Journal of Electrical Workers and Operators* (September 1928), Folder 470, Box 25, MVK Papers; Milton J. Nadworny, *Scientific Management and the Unions, 1900–1932* (Cambridge, 1955), ch. 8.

32. "Origin of Recent Economic Changes," undated summary, REC, General, Box 38, Hunt Papers; "Recent Economic Changes," July 4, 1934, unsigned notes, REC, Notes, Box 39, Hunt Papers; Hunt to Keppel, October 16, 1928, and Hunt to Keppel, December 15, 1928, PCU, Car. Corp.

33. National Bureau, "Survey of Recent Economic Changes," PCU, Car. Corp.; Committee on Recent Economic Changes of the President's Conference on Unemployment, *Recent Economic Changes in the United States* (New York, 1929), acknowledgments, editor's note, p. xxxiii, contents page; "Recent Economic Changes," July 4, 1934, REC, Hunt Papers.

34. National Bureau, "Survey of Recent Economic Changes" PCU, Car. Corp.; *"Recent Economic Changes,"* REC, Hunt Papers.

35. Untitled, unsigned notes, June 20, 1934, REC, Notes, Box 39, Hunt Papers.

36. Ibid.

37. Ibid.

38. Ibid.

39. Committee on Recent Economic Changes, *Recent Economic Changes*, p. ix; Hunt, "Economic Changes in 1929," *Mechanical Engineering* (February 1930):1.

40. Committee on Recent Economic Changes, *Recent Economic Changes*, pp. ix, x.

41. Dennison, "Management," and Gay, "Introduction," both in *Recent Economic Changes*, pp. 495–546; Hunt, "The Influence of Scientific Management in American Industry," 1929, Drafts, Notes, Box 58, Hunt Papers.

42. Committee on Recent Economic Changes, *Recent Economic Changes*, pp. xix–xxiii; Hunt, "Economic Changes in 1929"; "A Technique of Balance," unsigned memo, 1929, National Planning, Notes, Drafts, Box 19, Hunt Papers.

43. Hunt to George E. Vincent, September 5, 1929, President's Conference on Unemployment, 1928–1930, Box 86, LSRM; Hunt to Keppel, February 25, 1930, PCU, Car. Corp. Hunt would shortly write a book-length summary of *Recent Economic Changes* designed to make the study more accessible to a wider readership. It would be published in 1930 as *An Audit of America: A Summary of Recent Economic Changes in the United States*.

44. Hunt to Keppel, October 18, 1929, PCU, Car. Corp.; Hunt to Edmund E. Day, April 22, 1930, President's Conference on Unemployment, 1930–31, Box 387, RF; P. W. Martin, "The Technique of Balance"; *The Tax Digest* (January 1930):33; "Why Prosperity Keeps Up," *The Survey Graphic* 15 (June 1929); Hunt, "Recent Economic Changes in the United States," May 31, 1929, and "Our Changing America," both in Drafts, Notes, Box 58, Hunt Papers. See also the review by Charles O. Hardy in the *Journal of Political Economy* (April 1930):213–227. A more critical review, published before the crisis of late 1929, can be found in the *Commercial and Financial Chronicle* (May 18, 1929):32–46. Another review similarly critical of the study's tendency to downplay the significance of dangerous trends in the stock market and in industrial over-capacity is that of J. Jewkes in the *Economic Journal* (December 1930):650–667.

45. According to Herbert Heaton, Gay was especially unhappy with the hurriedness of the study. See Heaton, *A Scholar in Action: Edwin F. Gay* (Cambridge, 1952), pp. 202–203. William E. Leuchtenburg cites *Recent Economic Changes* as "an invaluable compendium," in *The Perils of Prosperity, 1914–1932* (Chicago, 1958), p. 293.

CHAPTER 9

1. Antoine de Saint-Exupéry, *Night Flight* (New York, 1932), p. 110, quoted in Arch Shaw to E. E. Day, September 10, 1932, PCU, RF.

2. Ellis W. Hawley, *The Great War and the Search for a Modern Order, 1917–1933* (New York, 1979), pp. 180–185; Hawley essay in J. Joseph Huthmacher and Warren Susman, eds., *Herbert Hoover and the Crisis of American Capitalism* (Cambridge, 1973).

3. Hawley, *The Great War*, chs. 10–12; Albert U. Romasco, *The Poverty of Abundance* (Oxford, 1965); Broadus Mitchell, *Depression Decade* (New York, 1947); Herbert Stein, *The Fiscal Revolution in America* (Chicago, 1969), ch. 2.

4. A parallel Committee on Recent Social Trends, organized in the fall of 1929, included several of the same members, was organized along the same lines, and was similarly dedicated to data-building and interpretation. E. E. Hunt to F. P. Keppel, February 25, 1930, NBER, 1924–29, Car. Corp.; G. R. Stahl to Hunt, October 3 (1929), NBER, Inc., Correspondence, 1928–31, Box 18, Hunt Papers; Committee on Recent Economic Changes, *Planning and Control of Public Works* (New York, 1930); Hunt, "Economic Changes in 1929," *Mechanical Engineering* (February 1930):1–2.

5. Hunt, "Economic Changes in 1929," p. 2.

6. Mary Van Kleeck, "Employment or Unemployment? That is the Question," *American Labor Legislation Review* (March 1930):1, and "America's Unemployment Puzzle," typescript, March 17, 1930, both in Folder 471, Box 25, MVK Papers.

7. Van Kleeck, "Employment or Unemployment?" and "America's Unemployment Puzzle":5, 11, MVK Papers.

8. Van Kleeck, "Employment or Unemployment?" MVK Papers; Van Kleeck and Ada M. Matthews, "Shall We Count the Unemployed?" *Survey Graphic* (April 1, 1929); Hunt, "President

Hoover and Unemployment," 1930, Correspondence, Speeches, Articles, Hunt Papers, HHPL.

9. "Next Steps in the Work of the Committee on Recent Economic Changes," undated, and Arch Shaw to F. P. Keppel, April 10, 1930, both in NBER, 1924–29, Car. Corp.

10. George O. May to "Russell," February 14, 1930, NBER, 1030–35, Car. Corp.

11. Memorandum of Interview between RML and FPK (Leffingwell and Keppel), April 10, 1930, and Memorandum of Interview between FPK and D. F. Houston, April 14, 1930, both NBER, 1930–35, Car. Corp.

12. Leffingwell to Keppel, March 14, 1932; Leffingwell to Keppel, April 28, 1930; Keppel to Shaw, October 16, 1930; Keppel to Gay, February 21, 1930; Keppel to May, February 20, 1930, all in NBER, 1930–35, Car. Corp.; Raymond Fosdick, *The Story of the Rockefeller Foundation* (New York, 1952), p. 199; Hunt to Day, April 22, 1930, and "Next Steps in the Work of the Committee on Recent Economic Changes of the President's Conference on Unemployment," undated, both in PCU, 1930–31, Box 387, RF.

13. Hunt to Day, April 22, 1930, PCU, RF.

14. "Next Steps," PCU, RF.

15. Untitled memorandum of grant, Rockefeller Foundation to Committee on Recent Economic Changes, May 8, 1930, and Shaw to Day, January 7, 1931, both in PCU, 1930–31, Box 387, RF.

16. Shaw to Day, January 7, 1931, PCU, RF; "Progress of Committee on Recent Economic Changes," March 12, 1931, PCU, 1930–31, Box 387, RF.

17. FESB legislation was largely the work of Senator Robert F. Wagner. Hoover vetoed another Wagner initiative designed to establish a federally financed system of state employment services. See Romasco, *The Poverty of Abundance,* p. 215; Hawley, *The Great War,* pp. 194–195; Jordan A. Schwarz, *Interregnum of Despair: Hoover, Congress, and the Depression* (Urbana, 1970); Hunt, "Excerpts from book manuscript, *Nation Planning,* to be coauthored with Charles Eliot," May-June 1930, pp. 13–14, National Planning, Notes Drafts, Box 19, Hunt Papers. See also the entire folder of Federal Employment Stabilization Board Correspondence, 1931–33, Box 136, Presidential Papers HHP. On the National Resources

Planning Board, see Marion Clawson, *New Deal Planning* (Baltimore, 1980); Otis Graham, *Toward a Planned Society* (New York, 1976); and Patrick D. Reagan, "Architects of Modern American National Planning," Ph.D. dissertation, The Ohio State University, 1982, chs. 6–7.

18. Joseph S. Willits to Herbert Hoover, February 9, 1931, Unemployment-Advisory Committee on Employment Statistics, Presidential Papers, HHP.

19. Arch W. Shaw, untitled memorandum prepared for Committee on Recent Economic Changes, June 17, 1931, Commerce Papers, Record Group 40, General Correspondence, 85414, N.A. See also press clippings on Hunt and the Geneva Conference in Correspondence, Speeches, Lists, Hunt Papers, HHPL.

20. Van Kleeck, "Memorandum of Interview with E.R.A. Seligman," April 17, 1930, Folder 430, Box 22, MVK Papers.

21. Van Kleeck, "Planning and the World Paradox," *Survey Graphic* (November 1, 1931); Van Kleeck to Mary R. Beard, November 18, 1935, p. 3, Folder 2, Box 1, MVK Papers; Van Kleeck to Raymond Fosdick, October 29, 1931, Folder 184, Box 12, MVK Papers; Van Kleeck, "Social Planning and Social Work," draft of article for *Survey Graphic*, January 12, 1932, Folder 471, Box 25, MVK Papers. H. S. Person of the Taylor Society also attended the World Congress and joined in Van Kleeck's assessment. See Van Kleeck, "Planning and the World Paradox," and H. S. Person, "Planning: A Technique as Well as an Attitude," abstract, December 6, 1934, Folder 1333, Box 99, MVK Papers.

22. Shaw to Day, July 1, 1931, PCU, 1930–31, Box 387, RF; Mitchell to Hunt, August 15, 1931, and Mitchell, W. C., 1931–33, Box 5, Hunt Papers; Shaw to John S. Lawrence, January 27, 1932, PCU, 1930–31, Box 387, RF.

23. Shaw to Day, October 1, 1931, PCU, 1930–31, Box 387, RF.

24. Ibid.; Leffingwell to Keppel, March 14, 1932, NBER, Car. Corp.

25. Knauth to Laidler, March 12, 1932, NBER, 1930–35, Car. Corp.; Herbert Heaton, *A Scholar in Action: Edwin F. Gay* (Cambridge, 1952), p. 202.

26. Knauth to Leffingwell, March 12, 1932, NBER, 1930–35, Car. Corp.

27. Pierce Williams to Keppel, March 12, 1932; Keppel to Pierce

Williams, March 16, 1932; and Leffingwell to Keppel, March 14, 1932, all in NBER, 1930–35, Car. Corp.

28. Shaw to Day, June 23, 1932, PCU, 1932–35, Box 387, RF.

29. Ibid.; Shaw to Day, February 5, 1932, and Shaw to Day, July 21, 1932, PCU, 1932–35, Box 387, RF.

30. Frederick C. Mills, *Economic Tendencies in the United States: Aspects of Pre-War and Post-War Changes*, with an introduction by the Committee on Recent Economic Changes (New York: National Bureau of Economic Research, 1932).

31. John Maurice Clark, *Strategic Factors in Business Cycles* (New York: National Bureau of Economic Research, 1934); Ralph C. Epstein, *Industrial Profits in the United States* (New York: National Bureau of Economic Research, 1934).

32. Gay to Keppel, February 21, 1933, and Keppel to Mitchell, March 27, 30, 1933, in NBER, 1930–35, Car. Corp. The National Bureau won a succession of $5,000 annual grants from the Carnegie Corporation and larger but unspecified amounts from the Rockefeller Foundation.

33. "FPK and Wesley Mitchell," memorandum of conversation, February 28, 1933, NBER, 1930–35, Car. Corp.

EPILOGUE

1. "Progress Report to the Trustees of the Carnegie Corporation," NBER, June 1, 1934, 1930–35, Car. Corp. See the commemorative essays in Arthur Burns, *Wesley C. Mitchell: The Economic Scientist* (New York, 1952). On Mitchell and New Deal planning, see Patrick D. Reagan, "Architects of Modern American National Planning," Ph.D. dissertation, The Ohio State University, Columbus, 1982.

2. Van Kleeck, "A Planned Economy as a National Objective for Social Work," *The Compass* (May 1933), "Scientific Management in the Second Five Year Plan," *Soviet Russia Today* (June 1933), and "Dictatorship and Democracy," *Soviet Russia Today* (November 1933); Clarke A. Chambers, *Seedtime of Reform* (Minneapolis, 1963), p. 243, and *Paul U. Kellogg and the Survey* (Minneapolis, 1971), pp. 159–160; Mary Van Kleeck, *Creative America* (New York, 1936); Lillian M. Gilbreth, *The Psychology of Management* (New York, 1914); W. R. Spriegel and Clark E. Myers, eds., *The Writings of the Gilbreths* (Homewood, 1953); Mary Parker Fol-

lett, *Creative Experience* (London, 1924), and *Freedom and Co-ordination* (London, 1949); Ruth Oldenziel, "Mary Van Kleeck: A Career of Idealism," unpublished manuscript in author's possession.

3. Edward A. Purcell, Jr., *The Crisis of Democratic Theory: Scientific Naturalism and the Problem of Value* (Lexington, 1973), pt. 3; Robert S. Lynd, *Knowledge For What?: The Place of Social Science in American Culture* (Princeton, 1939), ch. 4.

4. Lynd, *Knowledge for What?*, p. 209; Jacques Ellul, *The Technological Society* (New York, 1964), pp. 159, 209; R. Jeffrey Lustig, *Corporate Liberalism: The Origins of Modern American Political Theory, 1880–1920* (Berkeley, 1982), pp. 183–192; Charles E. Lindblom and David K. Cohen, *Usable Knowledge: Social Science and Social Problem Solving* (New Haven, 1979).

5. On the internationalization of data-building, see Paul Studenski, *The Income of Nations, Theory, Measurement, and Analysis: Past and Present* (New York, 1958).

6. E. W. Hawley, "Techno-Corporatist Formulas in the Liberal State, 1920–1960: A Neglected Aspect of America's Search for a New Order," Harvard Conference on Twentieth Century Capitalism, Cambridge, 1974; Robert M. Collins, *The Business Response to Keynes, 1929–1964* (New York, 1981); Herbert Stein, *The Fiscal Revolution in America* (Chicago, 1969), ch. 9; Alfred C. Neal, *Business Power and Public Policy* (New York, 1981), chs. 2, 8; George C. Lodge, *The New American Ideology* (New York, 1975); "The Reindustrialization of America," *Business Week* (June 30, 1980); Bruce L. R. Smith, ed., *The New Political Economy: The Public Use of the Private Sector* (New York, 1975); David F. Noble and Nancy Pfund, "Business Goes Back to College," *The Nation* (September 20, 1980); David Dickson, "Technocrats vs. Democracy," *democracy* (January 1981); Jeffrey D. Straussman, *The Limits of Technocratic Politics* (New Brunswick, 1978), ch. 7; Waldemar Nielsen, *The Big Foundations* (New York, 1972); Gene M. Lyons, *The Uneasy Partnership: Social Science and the Federal Government in the Twentieth Century* (New York, 1969); Alan Wolfe, *The Limits of Legitimacy: Political Contradictions of Contemporary Capitalism* (New York, 1977), pp. 337–347.

7. Jacob K. Javits, "The Need for National Planning," *Wall Street Journal* (July 8, 1975); Herbert Stein and Wassily Leontief, *The Economic System in an Age of Discontinuity* (New York, 1976); Walter

Goldstein, ed., *Planning, Politics, and the Public Interest* (New York, 1978); Herbert Stein, *Economic Planning and the Improvement of Economic Policy* (Washington, 1975); A. L. Chickering, ed., *The Politics of Planning* (San Francisco, 1976); Robert Heilbroner, *Beyond Boom and Crash* (New York, 1978); Gar Alperovitz, "A Political Program for the Last Quarter," *In These Times* (August 30, 1978); Irving S. Shapiro, *America's Third Revolution: Public Interest and the Private Role* (New York, 1984); Lester Thurow, *The Zero-Sum Society: Distribution and the Possibilities for Economic Change* (New York, 1980); Alan Wolfe, *America's Impasse: The Rise and Fall of the Politics of Growth* (New York, 1981), ch. 9; Chalmers Johnson, *MITI and the Japanese Miracle: The Growth of Industrial Policy, 1925–1975* (Stanford, 1982), ch. 9; Samuel Bowles, David M. Gordon, and Thomas Weisskopf, *Beyond the Waste Land: A Democratic Alternative to Economic Decline* (New York, 1983); Felix G. Rohatyn, "New York and the Nation," *New York Review of Books* (January, 1982); Martin Carnoy et al., *A New Social Contract: The Economy and Government After Reagan* (New York 1983).

8. Suggestive analyses of the contemporary dilemma include: Arthur S. Miller, *Democratic Dictatorship: The Emergent Constitution of Control* (Westport, 1981); Richard Rubenstein, *The Cunning of History: The Holocaust and the American Future* (New York, 1975); Kevin P. Phillips, *Post-Conservative America: People, Politics, and Ideology in a Time of Crisis* (New York, 1982); Charles E. Lindblom, *Politics and Markets: The World's Political-Economic Systems* (New York, 1977); Alan Wolfe, *Limits of Legitimacy: Political Contradictions of Contemporary Capitalism* (New York, 1977); Christopher Lasch, "Politics and Social Theory: A Reply to the Critics," *Salmagundi* (Spring 1979); David Dickson and David Noble, "By Force of Reason: The Politics of Science and Technology Policy," in Thomas Ferguson and Joel Rogers, eds., *The Hidden Election* (New York, 1981), pp. 260–312; Jacques Ellul, *The Technological Society* (New York, 1964). See also, Max Horkheimer, "The End of Reason," in A. Arato and E. Gebhardt, eds., *The Essential Frankfurt School Reader* (New York, 1978); Theodor W. Adorno, "Cultural Criticism and Society," in Paul Conerton, ed., *Critical Sociology* (New York, 1976); Paul Blumberg, *Inequality in an Age of Decline* (New York, 1980); and Paul Johnson, *Modern Times: The World from the Twenties to the Eighties* (New York, 1983).

BIBLIOGRAPHY

PRIMARY SOURCES
Manuscript Collections

American Economic Association Papers. Deering Library, Northwestern University, Evanston, Illinois.

Carnegie Corporation of New York. New York, New York.

Commerce Department Papers. National Archives, Washington, D.C.

The Commonwealth Fund. New York, New York.

Henry S. Dennison Papers. Baker Library, Harvard Business School, Cambridge, Massachusetts.

Edwin F. Gay Papers. Hoover Institution, Stanford, California.

Herbert Hoover Papers, Herbert Hoover Presidential Library, West Branch, Iowa.

Edward Eyre Hunt Papers. Hoover Institution, Stanford, California.

Wesley C. Mitchell Papers. Columbia University, New York, New York.

Rockefeller Foundation Papers. Rockefeller Archive Center, Tarrytown, New York.

Laura Spelman Rockefeller Memorial Papers. Rockefeller Archive Center, Tarrytown, New York.

Beardsley Ruml Papers. Regenstein Library, University of Chicago, Chicago, Illinois.

Mary Van Kleeck Papers. The Sophia Smith Collection, Women's History Archive, Smith College, Northampton, Massachusetts.

Owen D. Young Papers. Van Hornesville, New York.

SECONDARY SOURCES
Books

Adams, Graham, *The Age of Industrial Violence, 1900–1915*. New York: Columbia University Press, 1966.

Arnove, R., ed. *Philanthropy and Cultural Imperialism*. Boston: G. K. Hall, 1980.

Babson, Roger. *Actions and Reactions*. New York: Harper and Brothers, 1934.

Baritz, Loren. *Servants of Power*. Middletown: Wesleyan University Press, 1960.

Bell, Daniel. *The Cultural Contradictions of Capitalism*. New York: Basic Books, 1976.

Bendix, Reinhard. *Work and Authority in Industry: Ideologies of Management in the Course of Industrialization*. New York: Wiley, 1956.

Bernstein, Irving. *The Lean Years*. Boston: Houghton Mifflin, 1960.

Best, Gary Dean. *The Politics of American Individualism: Herbert Hoover in Transition, 1918–1921*. Westport: Greenwood Press, 1975.

Binder, Rudolph. *Business and the Professions*. New York: Prentice-Hall, 1922.

Blackburn, Robin. *Ideology in Social Science*. London: Fontana, 1972.

Blumberg, Paul. *Industrial Democracy: The Sociology of Participation*. New York: Schocken Books, 1968.

———. *Inequality in an Age of Decline*. New York: Oxford University Press, 1980.

Boring, Edwin G., ed. *Psychology for the Armed Services*. Washington, D.C.: Government Printing Office, 1945.

Bowles, Samuel; Gordon, David M.; and Weisskopf, Thomas. *Beyond the Waste Land: A Democratic Alternative to Economic Decline*. New York: Anchor Press, 1983.

Brandes, Stuart O. *American Welfare Capitalism*. Chicago: University of Chicago Press, 1970.

Braverman, Harry. *Labor and Monopoly Capital*. New York: Monthly Review Press, 1974.

Bremner, Robert H. *American Philanthropy*. Chicago: Univeristy of Chicago Press, 1960.

Brookings, Robert. *Industrial Ownership: Its Economic and Social Significance*. 1925. New York: Books for Libraries Press, 1972.

Brown, E. Richard. *Rockefeller Medicine Men: Medicine and Capitalism in America*. Berkeley: University of California Press, 1979.

Brownlee, W. Elliot. *Dynamics of Ascent: A History of the American Economy*. New York: Knopf, 1979.

Bruno, Frank. *Trends in Social Work, 1874–1956*. New York: Columbia University Press, 1964.

Burns, Arthur F. *Wesley Clair Mitchell: The Economic Scientist*. New York: National Bureau of Economic Research, 1952.

Butler, Elizabeth Beardsley. *Women and the Trades.* New York: Charities Publications Committee, 1909.

Calvert, Monte. *The Mechanical Engineer in America, 1830–1910.* Baltimore: Johns Hopkins University Press, 1967.

Carnoy, Martin et al. *A New Social Contract: The Economy and Government After Reagan.* New York: Harper and Row, 1983.

Case, Josephine Young, and Everett Needham. *Owen D. Young and American Enterprise.* Boston: David Godine, 1982.

Chambers, Clark A. *Seedtime of Reform: American Social Science and Social Action, 1918–33.* Minneapolis: University of Minnesota Press, 1963.

————. *Paul U. Kellogg and The Survey: Voices for Social Welfare and Social Justice.* Minneapolis: University of Minnesota Press, 1971.

Chandler, Alfred D., Jr. *The Visible Hand: The Managerial Revolution in American Business.* Cambridge: Belknap Press, 1977.

Chase, Stuart. *The Tragedy of Waste.* New York: Macmillan, 1926.

Chickering, A. L., ed. *The Politics of Planning.* San Francisco: Institute for Contemporary Studies, 1976.

Clark, John Maurice. *The Costs of the World War to the American People.* New Haven: Yale University Press, 1931.

————. *Strategic Factors in Business Cycles.* New York: National Bureau of Economic Research, 1934.

Clarkson, Grosvenor. *Industrial America in the World War.* Boston: Houghton Mifflin, 1923.

Clawson, Dan. *Bureaucracy and the Labor Process: The Transformation of U.S. Industry, 1860–1920.* New York: Monthly Review Press, 1980.

Clawson, Marion. *New Deal Planning.* Baltimore: Johns Hopkins University Press, 1980.

Cleveland, Frederick A., and Schafer, Joseph, eds. *Democracy in Reconstruction.* Boston: Houghton Mifflin, 1919.

Collins, Robert M. *The Business Response to Keynes, 1929–1964.* New York: Columbia University Press, 1981.

Committee on Business Cycles and Unemployment of the President's Conference on Unemployment. *Business Cycles and Unemployment.* New York: National Bureau of Economic Research, 1923.

Committee on the Elimination of Waste in Industry of the Federated American Engineering Societies. *Waste in Industry.* New York: McGraw-Hill, 1921.

Committee on Recent Economic Changes of the President's Conference on Unemployment. *Recent Economic Change in the U.S.* 2 vols. New York: National Bureau of Economic Research, 1929.
————. *Planning and Control of Public Works.* New York: National Bureau of Economic Research, 1930.

The Commonwealth Fund: Historical Sketch, 1918–1962. New York: Harkness House, 1963.

Conner, Valerie Jean. *The National War Labor Board: Stability, Social Justice, and the Voluntary State.* Chapel Hill: University of North Carolina Press, 1983.

Cook, Blanche Wiesen, ed. *Crystal Eastman: On Women and Revolution.* Oxford: Oxford University Press, 1978.

Copley, Frank B. *Frederick W. Taylor: Father of Scientific Management.* New York: A. M. Kelley, 1923.

Cuff, Robert. *The War Industries Board.* Baltimore: Johns Hopkins University Press, 1973.

Davis, Allen. *Spearheads for Reform: The Social Settlements and the Progressive Movements.* New York: Oxford University Press, 1967.

Davis, Joseph S. *The World Between the Wars, 1929–39.* Baltimore: Johns Hopkins University Press, 1975.

Dennison, James T. *Henry S. Dennison: New England Industrialist Who Served America.* New York: The Newcomen Society, 1955.

Dorfman, Joseph, ed. *The Backward Art of Spending Money: And Other Essays by Wesley C. Mitchell.* New York: McGraw-Hill, 1937.
————. *The Economic Mind in American Civilization.* Vol. 3. New York: The Viking Press, 1949.
————. *The Economic Mind in American Civilization.* Vols. 4 and 5. New York: The Viking Press, 1959.

Eastman, Crystal. *Work Accidents and the Law.* 1910. New York: Arno Press, 1970.

Eddy, Arthur. *The New Competition.* Chicago: McClurg, 1912.

Edie, Lionel D., ed. *The Stabilization of Business.* New York: Macmillan, 1923.

Elliot, Gil. *Twentieth Century Book of the Dead.* New York: Scribner's, 1972.

Ellul, Jacques. *The Technological Society.* New York: Knopf, 1964.

Ely, Richard T. *Ground Under Our Feet: An Autobiography.* New York: Macmillan, 1938.

Epstein, Ralph C. *Industrial Profits in the United States.* New York: National Bureau of Economic Research, 1934.

Ewen, Stuart. *Captains of Consciousness*. New York: McGraw-Hill, 1976.

Feldman, Herman. *The Regularization of Employment*. New York: Harper, 1925.

Filene, E. A. *The Way Out: A Forecast of Coming Changes in American Business and Industry*. New York: Doubleday, Page, 1925.

Flexner, Abraham. *Henry S. Pritchett: A Biography*. New York: Columbia University Press, 1943.

Follett, Mary Parker. *Creative Experience*. London: Longmans, Green, 1924.

————. *Freedom and Co-Ordination*. London: Management Publications Trust, 1949.

Fosdick, Raymond B. *The Story of the Rockefeller Foundation*. New York: Harper, 1952.

Fox, Daniel M. *The Discovery of Abundance: Simon N. Patten and the Transformation of Social Theory*. Ithaca: Cornell University Press, 1967.

————, ed. *The New Basis of Civilization*, Simon N. Patten. Cambridge: Harvard University Press, 1968.

Frederick, J. G. *Business Research and Statistics*. New York: D. Appleton, 1920.

Friedman, Elisha M., ed. *American Problems of Reconstruction: A National Symposium on the Economic and Financial Aspects*. New York: E. P. Dutton, 1918.

————. *America and the New Era: A Symposium on Reconstruction*. New York: E. P. Dutton, 1920.

Furner, Mary. *Advocacy and Objectivity: A Crisis in the Professionalization of American Social Science, 1865–1905*. Lexington: University of Kentucky Press, 1975.

Galbraith, John Kenneth. *A Life in Our Times*. Boston: Houghton Mifflin, 1981.

Garraty, John A. *Unemployment in History: Economic Thought and Public Policy*. New York: Harper & Row, 1978.

Gaunt, E. H. *Co-operative Competition*. Providence: Stevens Press, 1917.

Gilbert, James B. *Designing the Industrial State*. Chicago: University of Chicago Press, 1972.

Gilbreth, Lillian M. *The Psychology of Management*. New York: Sturgis and Walton, 1914.

Glenn, John M. et al. *Russell Sage Foundation, 1907–1946.* New York: Russell Sage Foundation, 1947.

Goldstein, Walter, ed. *Planning, Politics, and the Public Interest.* New York: Columbia University Press, 1978.

Goodwyn, Lawrence. *The Populist Moment.* New York: Oxford University Press, 1978.

Gouldner, Alvin. *The Dialectic of Ideology and Technology: The Origins, Grammar, and Future of Ideology.* New York: Seabury Press, 1976.

Graham, Otis. *Toward a Planned Society.* New York: Oxford University Press, 1976.

Gramsci, Antonio. *Selections from the Prison Notebooks.* Translated and edited by Quinton Hoare and Geoffrey N. Smith. London: Lawrence and Wishart, 1971.

Greenwald, Maurine Weiner. *Women, War, and Work: The Impact of World War I on Women Workers in the United States.* Westport: Greenwood Press, 1980.

Gruber, Carol. *Mars and Minerva.* Baton Rouge: Louisana State University Press, 1975.

Haan, Norma; Bellah, Robert N.; Rabinow, Paul; and Sullivan, William M., eds. *Social Science as Moral Inquiry.* New York: Columbia University Press, 1983.

Haber, Samuel. *Efficiency and Uplift: Scientific Management in the Progressive Era, 1880–1920.* Chicago: University of Chicago Press, 1964.

Habermas, Jürgen. *Legitimation Crisis.* Boston: Beacon Press, 1975.

Haskell, Thomas L. *The Emergence of Professional Social Science: The American Social Science Association and the Nineteenth-Century Crisis of Authority.* Urbana: University of Illinois Press, 1977.

Hawley, Ellis W. *The Great War and the Search for a Modern Order, 1917–1933.* New York: St. Martin's Press, 1979.

———, ed. *Herbert Hoover as Secretary of Commerce, 1921–1928: Studies in the New Era Thought and Practice.* Iowa City: University of Iowa Press, 1981.

Hays, Samuel P. *Conservation and the Gospel of Efficiency.* New York: Atheneum, 1969.

Heald, Morrell. *The Social Responsibilities of Business.* Cleveland: Case Western Reserve University Press, 1970.

Heaton, Herbert. *A Scholar in Action: Edwin F. Gay.* Cambridge: Harvard University Press, 1952.

Heilbroner, Robert. *Beyond Boom and Crash.* New York: Norton, 1978.

225

Hicks, John D. *Republican Ascendancy*. New York: Harper, 1960.
———. *Rehearsal for Disaster: The Boom and Collapse of 1919–1920*. Gainesville: University of Florida Press, 1961.

Higham, John, and Conkin, Paul, eds. *New Directions in American Intellectual History*. Baltimore: Johns Hopkins University Press, 1977.

Hollander, Jacob. *The Abolition of Poverty*. Boston: Houghton Mifflin, 1914.

Homans, George C. *The Nature of Social Science*. New York: Harcourt, Brace & World, 1967.

Hoover, Herbert. *American Individualism*. New York: Doubleday, 1922.
———. *American Epic: V. III*. Chicago: H. Regnery, 1961.

Hunt, E. B. *An Audit of America: A Summary of Recent Economic Changes in the U.S.* New York: McGraw-Hill, 1930.

Hunt, Edward E. *Scientific Management Since Taylor*. New York: McGraw-Hill, 1924.

Hurley, Edward N. *The Awakening of Business*. New York: Doubleday, Page, 1917.

Huthmacher, J. Joseph, and Susman, Warren, eds. *Herbert Hoover and the Crisis of American Capitalism*. Cambridge: Schenkman, 1973.

Industrial Reconstruction Problems. Report of the Proceedings of the National Conference of the Society of Industrial Engineers. New York: March 18–21, 1919.

Jacoby, Russell. *Social Amnesia: A Critique of Conformist Psychology from Adler to Laing*. Boston: Beacon Press, 1975.

Johnson, Chalmers. *MITI and the Japanese Miracle: The Growth of Industrial Policy, 1925–1975*. Stanford: Stanford University Press, 1982.

Johnson, Paul. *Modern Times: The World from the Twenties to the Eighties*. New York: Harper and Row, 1983.

Karl, Barry D. *Charles E. Merriam and the Study of Politics*. Chicago: University of Chicago Press, 1974.

Katz, Michael B. *Poverty and Policy in American History*. New York: Academic Press, 1983.

Keating, Peter. *Into Unknown England, 1866–1913: Selections from the Social Explorers*. Manchester: Fontana, 1976.

Kessler-Harris, Alice. *Out to Work: A History of Wage-Earning Women in the United States*. New York: Oxford University Press, 1982.

BIBLIOGRAPHY

King, Willford I. *The Wealth and Income of the People of the United States*. New York: Macmillan, 1915.

King, Willford I.; Macaulay, F.; and Mitchell, Wesley C. *Income in the United States, Its Amount and Distribution, 1909–1919*. 2 vols. New York: National Bureau of Economic Research, 1921, 1922.

Knauth, Oswald W. *Distribution of Income by States in 1919*. New York: Harcourt, Brace, 1922.

Kuhn, Thomas S. *Structure of Scientific Revolutions*. 2nd ed. Chicago: University of Chicago Press, 1970.

Lasch, Christopher. *The New Radicalism in America*. New York: Knopf, 1965.

———. *Haven in a Heartless World: The Family Besieged*. New York: Basic Books, 1979.

Lasswell, Harold D. *A Pre-View of Policy Sciences*. New York: American Elsevier, 1971.

Layton, Edwin F. *The Revolt of the Engineers*. Cleveland: Case Western Reserve University Press, 1971.

Lears, T. Jackson. *No Place of Grace: Antimodernism and the Transformation of American Culture, 1880–1920*. New York: Pantheon, 1981.

Lebergott, Stanley. *Manpower in Economic Growth*. New York: McGraw-Hill, 1964.

Lemons, J. Stanley. *The Woman Citizen: Social Feminism in the 1920's*. Urbana: University of Illinois Press, 1973.

Leuchtenburg, William E. *The Perils of Prosperity, 1914–32*. Chicago: University of Chicago Press, 1958.

Lewisohn, Sam; Draper, Ernest; et al. *Can Business Prevent Unemployment?* New York: Knopf, 1925.

Lewisohn, Sam A. *The New Leadership in Industry*. New York: E. P. Dutton, 1926.

Lindblom, Charles E. *Politics and Markets: The World's Political-Economic Systems*. New York: Basic Books, 1977.

Lindblom, Charles E., and Cohen, David K. *Usable Knowlege: Social Science and Social Problem Solving*. New Haven: Yale University Press, 1979.

Lippmann, Walter. *Drift and Mastery*. New York: Mitchell Kennerly, 1914.

———. *Public Opinion*. New York: Macmillan, 1922.

Lloyd, Craig. *Aggressive Introvert: Herbert Hoover and Public Rela-*

227

tions Management, 1912–1932. Columbus: Ohio State University Press, 1972.

Lodge, George C. *The New American Ideology*. New York: Knopf, 1975.

Lubin, Isador. *The Absorption of the Unemployed by American Industry*. Washington: The Brookings Institution, 1929.

Lubove, Roy. *The Professional Altruist*. Cambridge: Harvard University Press, 1965.

Lustig, R. Jeffrey. *Corporate Liberalism: The Origins of Modern American Political Theory, 1880–1920*. Berkeley: University of California Press, 1982.

Lynd, Robert S. *Knowledge for What? The Place of Social Science in American Culture*. Princeton: Princeton University Press, 1939.

Lyons, Gene M. *The Uneasy Partnership: Social Science and the Federal Government in the Twentieth Century*. New York: Russell Sage Foundation, 1969.

Maier, Charles S. *Recasting Bourgeois Europe: Stabilization in France, Germany, and Italy in the Decade After World War I*. Princeton: Princeton University Press, 1975.

McCarthy, Charles. *The Wisconsin Idea*. New York: Macmillan, 1912.

McCarthy, Thomas. *The Critical Theory of Jürgen Habermas*. Cambridge: MIT Press, 1978.

McClymer, John F. *War and Welfare: Social Engineering in America, 1890–1925*. Westport: Greenwood Press, 1980.

Merkle, Judith A. *Management and Ideology: The Legacy of the International Scientific Management Movement*. Berkeley: Univ. of California Press, 1980.

Miller, Arthur S. *The Modern Corporate State*. Westport: Greenwood Press, 1976.

———. *Democratic Dictatorship: The Emergent Constitution of Control*. Westport: Greenwood Press, 1981.

Mills, Frederick C. *Economic Tendencies in the United States: Aspects of Pre-War and Post-War Changes*. New York: National Bureau of Economic Research, 1932.

Mitchell, Broadus. *Depression Decade*. New York: Holt, Rinehart & Winston, 1947.

Mitchell, Lucy Sprague. *Two Lives: The Story of Wesley Clair Mitchell and Myself*. New York: Simon & Schuster, 1953.

Mitchell, Wesley C. *Business Cycles*. Berkeley: University of California Press, 1913.

228

————, ed. *The National Bureau's First Quarter Century*. New York: National Bureau of Economic Research, 1945.

————. *Lecture Notes on Types of Economic Theory*. New York: A. M. Kelly, 1949.

Mommsen, Wolfgang J. *The Age of Bureaucracy*. New York: Harper, 1974.

Murray, Robert K. *Red Scare: A Study in National Hysteria, 1919–1920*. Minneapolis: University of Minnesota Press, 1955.

Nadworny, Milton J. *Scientific Management and the Unions, 1900–1932*. Cambridge: Harvard University Press, 1955.

Neal, Alfred C. *Business Power and Public Policy*. New York: Praeger, 1981.

Nearing, Scott. *Wages in the United States, 1908–1910*. New York: Macmillan, 1911.

Nelson, Daniel. *Unemployment Insurance*. Madison: University of Wisconsin Press, 1969.

Nielsen, Waldemar. *The Big Foundations*. New York: Columbia University Press, 1972.

Noble, David F. *America by Design: Science, Technology, and the Rise of Corporate Capitalism*. New York: Knopf, 1977.

Patterson, James T. *America's Struggle Against Poverty, 1900–1980*. Cambridge: Harvard University Press, 1981.

Perkins, Edwin J., ed. *Men and Organizations*. New York: Putnam, 1977.

Phillips, Kevin P. *Post-Conservative America: People, Politics, and Ideology in a Time of Crisis*. New York: Random House, 1982.

Pribram, Karl. *A History of Economic Reasoning*. Baltimore: Johns Hopkins University Press, 1983.

Purcell, Edward A., Jr. *The Crisis of the Democratic Theory: Scientific Naturalism and the Problem of Value*. Lexington: University of Kentucky Press, 1973.

Reich, Robert. *The Next American Frontier*. New York: Times Books, 1983.

Romasco, Albert U. *The Poverty of Abundance*. Oxford: Oxford University Press, 1965.

Rosenstone, Robert A. *Romantic Revolutionary: A Biography of John Reed*. New York: Knopf, 1975.

Rubenstein, Richard. *The Cunning of History: The Holocaust and the American Future*. New York: Harper, 1975.

Saint-Exupéry, Antoine de. *Night Flight*. New York: Century, 1932.

229

Schiesl, Martin J. *The Politics of Efficiency*. Berkeley: University of California Press, 1977.

Schroyer, Trent. *The Critique of Domination*. New York: George Braziller, 1973.

Schumpeter, Joseph. *History of Economic Analysis*. New York: Oxford University Press, 1954.

Schwarz, Jordan A. *Interregnum of Despair: Hoover, Congress, and the Depression*. Urbana: University of Illinois Press, 1970.

Seckler, David. *Thorstein Veblen and the Institutionalists. A Study in the Social Philosophy of Economics*. Boulder: Colorado Associated University Press, 1975.

Shapiro, Irving S. *America's Third Revolution: Public Interest and the Private Role*. New York: Harper & Row, 1984.

Shaw, Arch. *An Approach to Business Problems*. Cambridge: Harvard University Press, 1916.

Simey, T. S. *Social Science and Social Purpose*. London: Constable, 1968.

Skowronek, Stephen. *Building a New American State: The Expansion of National Administrative Capacities, 1877–1920*. Cambridge: Cambridge University Press, 1982.

Smith, Bruce L. R., ed. *The New Political Economy: The Public Use of the Private Sector*. New York: Wiley, 1975.

Somit, Albert, and Tanenhaus, Joseph. *The Development of Political Science*. Boston: Allyn and Bacon, 1967.

Soule, George. *Prosperity Decade: From War to Depression, 1917–1929*. New York: Holt, Rinehart, & Winston, 1947.

Spriegel, W. R., and Myers, Clark E., eds. *The Writings of the Gilbreths*. Homewood: W. D. Irwin, 1953.

Stein, Herbert. *The Fiscal Revolution in America*. Chicago: University of Chicago Press, 1969.

————. *Economic Planning and the Improvement of Economic Policy*. Washington: American Enterprise Institute, 1975.

Stein, Herbert, and Leontieff, Wassily. *The Economic System in an Age of Discontinuity*. New York: New York University Press, 1976.

Stewart, Bryce M. *Unemployment Benefits in the United States*. New York: Industrial Relations Counselors, 1930.

Straussman, Jeffrey D. *The Limits of Technocratic Politics*. New Brunswick: Transaction Books, 1978.

Studenski, Paul. *The Income of Nations, Theory, Measurement, and*

Analysis: Past and Present. New York: New York University Press, 1958.

Tarbell, Ida. *Owen D. Young: A New Type of Industrial Leader.* New York: Macmillan, 1932.

Taylor, Frederick W. *Scientific Management, Comprising Shop Management, The Principles of Scientific Management and Testimony Before the Special House Committee.* New York: Harper, 1947.

Tentler, Leslie W. *Wage-Earning Women: Industrial Work and Family Life in the United States, 1900–1930.* New York: Oxford University Press, 1979.

Thurow, Lester. *The Zero-Sum Society: Distribution and the Possibilities for Economic Change.* New York: Basic Books, 1980.

Tobey, Ronald C. *The American Ideology of Natural Science, 1919–1930.* Pittsburgh: University of Pittsburgh Press, 1971.

Trachtenberg, Alan. *The Incorporation of America: Culture and Society in the Gilded Age.* New York: Hill and Wang, 1982.

Tugwell, Rexford G., ed. *The Trend of Economics.* New York: Knopf, 1924.

Urofsky, Melvin I. *Big Steel and the Wilson Administration.* Columbus: Ohio State University Press, 1979.

Van Kleeck, Mary. *Artificial Flower Makers.* New York: Survey Associates, 1913.

———. *Women in the Bookbinding Trade.* New York: Russell Sage Foundation, 1913.

———. *A Seasonal Industry.* New York: Russell Sage Foundation, 1917.

———. *Creative America.* New York: Covici-Friede, 1936.

Veblen, Thorstein. *The Theory of Business Enterprise.* New York: Scribner's, 1904.

Wade, Louise C. *Graham Taylor, Pioneer for Social Justice, 1851–1938.* Chicago: University of Chicago Press, 1964.

Wertheimer, Barbara M. *We Were There: The Story of Working Women in America.* New York: Pantheon, 1977.

Wiarda, Howard J. *Corporatism and National Development in Latin America.* Boulder: Westview Press, 1981.

Wiebe, Robert. *The Search for Order, 1877–1920.* New York: Hill and Wang, 1967.

Williams, W. A. *The Contours of American History.* Chicago: Quadrangle Books, 1966.

Williamson, Jeffrey G., and Lindert, Peter H. *American Inequality:*

A Macroeconomic History. New York: Academic Press, 1980.

Wilson, David. *The National Planning Idea in U.S. Public Policy.* Boulder: Westview Press, 1980.

Wolf, Eric R. *Europe and the People Without History.* Berkeley: University of California Press, 1982.

Wolfe, Alan. *America's Impasse: The Rise and Fall of the Politics of Growth.* New York: Pantheon, 1981.

————. *The Limits of Legitimacy: Political Contradictions of Contemporary Capitalism.* New York: Free Press, 1977.

Yerkes, Robert M. *The New World of Science: Its Development During the War.* 1920. New York: Books for Libraries Press, 1969.

Zieger, Robert. *Republicans and Labor, 1919–1929.* Lexington: University of Kentucky Press, 1969.

Articles

Adorno, Theodor W. "Cultural Criticism and Society." In *Critical Sociology,* edited by Paul Conerton. New York: n.p., 1976.

Alexander, Magnus W. "Hiring and Firing: Its Economic Waste and How to Avoid It." *The Annals of the American Academy* (May 1916).

Alford, L. P. "Federated American Engineering Societies: The Birth of a Super-Engineering Organization." *Factory and Industrial Management* (July 1920).

Alperovitz, Gar. "A Political Program for the Last Quarter." *In These Times* (August 30, 1978).

Antler, Joyce. "Feminism as Life-Process: The Life and Career of Lucy Sprague Mitchell." *Feminist Studies* (Spring 1981).

Barber, Joseph. "Are Statistics Stabilizing Business?" *The Management Review* (August 1926).

Barnes, Harry Elmer. "Economic Science and Dynamic History." *Journal of Social Forces* (November 1924).

Best, Gary Dean. "President Wilson's Second Industrial Conference." *Labor History* (Fall 1975).

Bigelow, Karl W. "Economics." In *The History and Prospects of the Social Sciences,* edited by Harry Elmer Barnes. New York: Knopf, 1925.

Bourne, Randolph. "Twilight of Idols." *The Seven Arts* (June 1917).

Brandeis, Louis D. "Coping with Irregular Employment: A Memorandum (1911)." *Journal of the Society for the Advancement of Management* (May 1939).

Brown, Geoffrey. "Workers' Participation in Management." *Bulletin of the Taylor Society* (February 1929).

Campbell, Stuart. "Taylorism Versus Welfare Work in American Industry: H. L. Grant and the Bancrofts." *Business History Review* (Spring 1972).

Chase, Stuart. "Wasting Man Power." *Labor Age* (December 1921).

Chenery, William. "Unemployment in Washington." *The Survey* (October 8, 1921).

Church, Robert L. "Economists as Experts: The Making of an Academic Profession in the United States, 1870–1920." In *The University in Society*, vol. 2, edited by Lawrence Stone. Princeton: Princeton University Press, 1974.

Coats, A. W. "The First Two Decades of the American Economic Association." *American Economic Review* (September 1960).

———. "The American Economic Association, 1904–1929." *American Economic Review* (June 1964).

Collins, Robert M. "Positive Business Responses to the New Deal: The Roots of the Committee for Economic Development, 1933–1942." *Business History Review* (Autumn 1978).

Commons, John R. "Constructive Investigation and the Wisconsin Industrial Commission." *The Survey* (January 4, 1913).

Cooke, Morris L. "The Engineer and the People: A Plan for a Larger Measure of Cooperation Between the Society and the General Public." *Transactions of the American Society of Mechanical Engineers* 30 (1908).

———. "Responsibility and Opportunity of the City in the Prevention of Unemployment." *American Labor Legislation Review* 2 (June 1915).

———. "Scientific Management as a Solution of the Unemployment Problem." *The Annals of the American Academy* (September 1915).

Cuff, Robert D. "The Cooperative Impulse and the War: The Origins of the Council of National Defense and Advisory Commission." In *Building the Organizational Society*, edited by Jerry Israel. New York: n.p., 1972.

———. "Herbert Hoover, the Ideology of Voluntarism, and War Organization During the Great War." *Journal of American History* (September 1977).

———. "American Mobilization for War, 1917–1945: Political Culture vs. Bureaucratic Administration." In *Mobilization for*

Total War, edited by N. F. Dreisziger. Waterloo, Ontario: Wilfrid Laurier University Press, 1981.

Curti, Merle. "The American Scholar in Three Wars." *Journal of the History of Ideas* (June 1942).

Dennison, Henry S. "What the Employment Department Should Be in Industry." *Bureau of Labor Statistics* (October 1917).

———. "Stabilizing Employment in a Diversified Seasonal Industry." *The Annals of the American Academy* (September 1922).

———. "To Cut the Waste of Unemployment." *Nation's Business* (October 1924).

———. "Unemployment Relief—A Burden or an Investment?" *System* (June 1926).

———. "Insuring Tomorrow's Business Today." *Chicago Commerce* (December 10, 1927).

———. "Management." In *Recent Economic Changes in the United States*. New York: National Bureau of Economic Research, 1929.

Dennison, Henry S., and Tarbell, Ida. "The President's Industrial Conference of October 1919." *Bulletin of the Taylor Society* (April 1920).

Devine, Edward T. "Social Forces." *Charities and the Commons* (March 23, 1907).

Dickson, David. "Technocrats vs. Democracy." *democracy* (January 1981).

Dickson, David, and Noble, David. "By Force of Reason: The Politics of Science and Technology Policy." In *The Hidden Election*, edited by Thomas Ferguson and Joel Rogers. New York: Pantheon, 1981.

Draper, Ernest. "It Can't Be Done in Our Business." *American Management Review* (September 1924).

———. "The Manager and His Incipient Art." *Survey Graphic* (June 1929).

Dreitzel, Hans Peter. "Social Science and the Problem of Rationality: Notes on the Sociology of Technocrats." *Politics and Society* (Winter 1972).

Eakins, David. "The Origins of Corporate Liberal Policy Research, 1916–1922." In *Building the Organizational Society*, edited by Jerry Israel. New York: Free Press, 1972.

———. "Policy Planning for the Establishment." In *A New History of Leviathan*, edited by Ronald Radosh and Murray Rothbard, New York: E. P. Dutton, 1972.

Eilbert, Henry. "The Development of Personnel Management in the United States." *Business History Review* 33 (1959).

Ely, Richard T. "Report of the Organization of the AEA." *Publications of the American Economic Association*, first series, vol. 1, (March 1887).

Fisher, Irving. "Economists in Public Service." *American Economic Review*, supplement (March 1919).

Fitch, J. A. "Gains to be Consolidated in War-Time Industrial Relations." *The Survey* (December 7, 1918).

―――. "Labor Reconstruction." *The Survey* (December 14, 1918).

Ford, Henry Jones. "Present Tendencies in American Politics." *American Political Science Review* (February 1920).

Galambos, Louis. "Technology, Political Economy, and Professionalization: Central Themes of the Organizational Synthesis." *Business History Review* (Winter 1983).

Gilbert, James B. "Collectivism and Charles Steinmetz." *Business History Review* (Winter 1974).

Gitelman, H. M. "Management's Crisis of Confidence and the Origin of the National Industrial Conference Board, 1914–1916." *Business History Review* (Summer 1984).

Godfrey, Hollis. "Attitude of Labor Toward Scientific Management." *The Annals of the American Academy* (November 1912).

Green, William S. "Labor's Ideal Concerning Management." *Bulletin of the Taylor Society* (December 1925).

Grin, Carolyn. "The Unemployment Conference of 1921: An Experiment in National Cooperative Planning." *Mid-America* (April 1973).

Hawley, Ellis W. "Herbert Hoover and American Corporatism, 1929–1933." In *The Hoover Presidency: A Reappraisal*, edited by Martin Fausold and George Mazuzan. Albany: State University of New York Press, 1974.

―――. "Herbert Hoover, the Commerce Secretariat, and the Vision of an 'Associative State,' 1921–1929." *Journal of American History* (June 1974).

―――. "Herbert Hoover and Economic Stabilization, 1921–1922." In *Herbert Hoover as Secretary of Commerce 1921–28: Studies in New Era Thought and Practice*, edited by Ellis W. Hawley. Iowa City: University of Iowa Press, 1981.

―――. "Secretary Hoover and the Bituminous Coal Problem." *Business History Review* (Autumn 1981).

Hays, Samuel P. "The New Organizational Society." In *Building the Organizational Society*, edited by Jerry Israel. New York: Free Press, 1972.

————. "Value Premises for Planning and Public Policy: The Historical Context." In *Land in America: Commodity or Natural Resource?* edited by Richard N. L. Andrews. Lexington: Lexington Books, 1979.

————. "Political Choice in Regulatory Administration." In *Regulation in Perspective*, edited by Thomas K. McCraw. Cambridge: Harvard University Press, 1981.

Held, David. "Crisis Tendencies, Legitimation, and the State." In *Habermas: Critical Debates*, edited by John B. Thompson and David Held. Cambridge: MIT Press, 1982.

Hendersen, Charles R. "Recent Advances in the Struggle Against Unemployment." *American Labor Legislation Review* (February 1912).

Heywood, Johnson. "How the Dennison Manufacturing Company Meets the Slumps." *Advertising and Selling Fortnightly* (March 1925).

Hill, Forrest G. "Wesley Mitchell's Theory of Planning." *Political Science Quarterly* (March 1957).

Himmelberg, Robert F. "Business, Antitrust Policy, and the Industrial Board of the Department of Commerce, 1919." *Business History Review* (Spring 1968).

Hoover, Herbert. "Some Notes on Industrial Readjustment." *Saturday Evening Post* (December 27, 1919).

Hoover, Herbert. "What Government Can Do." *Nation's Business* (June 1921).

Horkheimer, Max. "The End of Reason." In *The Essential Frankfurt School Reader*, edited by A. Arato and E. Gebhardt. New York: n.p., 1978.

Howe, Barbara. "The Emergence of Scientific Philanthropy, 1900–1920." In *Philanthropy and Cultural Imperialism*, edited by R. Arnove. Boston: G. K. Hall, 1980.

Hunt, E. E. "The Long Look Ahead." *The Survey* (June 1, 1923).

————. "Self-Conscious Business." *The Forum* (August 1929).

————. "Economic Changes in 1929." *Mechanical Engineering* (February 1930).

"Information and Education Service." Annual Report, Department of Labor. Washington: Department of Labor, 1919.

236

Javits, Jacob K. "The Need for National Planning." *Wall Street Journal* (July 8, 1975).

Johnston, Alva. "Beardsley Ruml: A Profile." *The New Yorker* (February 10, 17, 24, 1945).

Karl, Barry D. "Presidential Planning and Social Research: Mr. Hoover's Experts." In *Perspectives in American History*, edited by Donald Fleming and Bernard Bailyn. Cambridge: Harvard University Press, 1969.

————. "Philanthropy, Policy Planning, and the Bureaucratization of the Democratic Ideal." *Daedalus* (Fall 1976).

Karl, Barry D., and Katz, Stanley N. "The American Private Philanthropic Foundation and the Public Sphere, 1890–1930." *Minerva* (Summer 1981).

Katz, Michael B. "Origins of the Institutional State." *Marxist Perspectives* (Winter 1978).

Kellogg, Arthur. "Shall Social Agencies Unite for Reconstruction?" *The Survey* (December 7, 1918).

Kevles, Daniel J. "Testing the Army's Intelligence: Psychologists and the Military in World War I." *Journal of American History* (December 1968).

Kohler, Robert E. "A Policy for the Advancement of Science: The Rockefeller Foundation, 1924–1929." *Minerva* (Winter 1978).

Lasch, Christopher. "Politics and Social Theory: A Reply to the Critics." *Salmagundi* (Spring 1979).

Leiserson, William M. "The Problem of Unemployment Today," *Political Science Quarterly* (March 1916).

Lewis, Eleanor Midman. "Mary Van Kleeck." In *Notable American Women*, vol. 4: The Modern Period. Cambridge: Harvard University Press, 1980.

Littell, R. "The Unemployed and a Weatherman." *The New Republic* (March 1, 1922).

Lynch, Edmund C. "Walter Dill Scott: Pioneer Industrial Psychologist." *Business History Review* (Summer 1968).

MacKenzie, Frederick W. "Stabilizing Employment: Official Findings." *American Labor Legislation Review* (June 1923).

McQuaid, Kim. "Henry S. Dennison and the 'Science' of Industrial Reform, 1900–1950." *American Journal of Economics and Sociology* (January 1977).

————. "Corporate Liberalism in the American Business Community, 1920–1940." *Business History Review* (Autumn 1978).

McQuaid, Kim. "Owen D. Young, Gerard Swope, and the 'New Capitalism' of the General Electric Company, 1920–1933." *American Journal of Economics and Sociology* (July 1979).

Maier, Charles S. "Between Taylorism and Technocracy: European Ideologies and the Vision of Industrial Productivity in the 1920's." *Journal of Contemporary History* (January 1970).

———. "The Two Postwar Eras and the Conditions for Stability in Twentieth Century Europe." *American Historical Review* (April 1981).

Merriam, Charles. "Political Research." *American Political Science Review* 16 (1922).

Metcalf, Evan. "Secretary Hoover and the Emergence of Macroeconomic Management." *Business History Review* (Spring 1975).

Mitchell, Wesley C. "The Backward Art of Spending Money." *American Economic Review* (June 1912).

———. "Human Behavior and Economics." *Quarterly Journal of Economics* 29 (1914).

———. "Statistics and Government." *Journal of the American Statistical Association* (March 1919).

———. "Prices and Reconstruction." *American Economic Review*, supplement (March 1920).

———. "The Crisis of 1920 and the Problem of Controlling Business Cycles." *American Economic Review*, supplement (March 1922).

———. "The Prospects of Economics." In *The Trend of Economics*, edited by Rexford G. Tugwell. New York: Knopf, 1924.

———. "Quantitative Analysis in Economic Theory." *American Economic Review* (March 1925).

Narr, Wolf-Dieter. "Reflections on the Form and Content of Social Science: Toward a Consciously Political and Moral Social Science." In *Social Science as Moral Inquiry*, edited by Norma Haan et al. New York: Columbia University Press, 1983.

Nelson, Daniel. "Scientific Management, Systematic Management, and Labor, 1880–1915." *Business History Review* (Winter 1974).

Nelson, Daniel, and Campbell, Stuart. "Taylorism Versus Welfare Work in American Industry: H. L. Gantt and the Bancrofts." *Business History Review* 46 (Spring 1972).

Newell, F. H. "Reconstruction Agencies." *American Political Science Review* (February 1919).

Noble, David, and Pfund, Nancy. "Business Goes Back to College." *The Nation* (September 20, 1980).

Ogburn, William F. "Cultural Lag as Theory." *Sociology and Social Research* (January–February 1957).

Person, Harlow. "Scientific Management." *Bulletin of the Taylor Society* (October 1916).

———. "The Manager, the Workman, and the Social Scientist." *Bulletin of the Taylor Society* (February 1917).

———. "Scientific Management and the Reduction of Unemployment." *Bulletin of the Taylor Society* (February 1921).

Persons, Warren. "Economics and Statistics." In *The Social Sciences and Their Interrelations*, edited by W. F. Ogburn et al. Cambridge: Harvard University Press, 1927.

Potter, Zenas L. "The Central Bureau of Planning and Statistics." *Journal of the American Statistical Association* (March 1919).

"Proceedings of the Second National Conference on Unemployment (A Practical Program for the Prevention of Unemployment)." *American Labor Legislation Review* 5 (June 1915).

Proctor, William C. "An Idea that Added Thousands of Profits in 24 Months." *System* (May 1925).

Rabinow, Paul, and Sullivan, William H. "The Interpretive Turn: The Emergence of an Approach." In *Interpretive Social Science*, edited by Paul Rabinow and William Sullivan. Berkeley: University of California Press, 1979.

Reiss, Albert J., Jr. "Sociology: The Field." In *International Encyclopedia of the Social Sciences*, edited by David L. Sills. New York: Macmillan, 1968.

"Report of the Second Industrial Conference." *American Industries* (April 1920).

Roberts, George. "Production as a Remedy for Inflation." *Proceedings of the American Academy of Political Science* 9 (1920–1922).

Rohatyn, Felix G. "New York and the Nation." *New York Review of Books* (January 21, 1982).

Ross, Dorothy. "The Liberal Tradition Revisited and the Republican Tradition Addressed." In *New Directions in American Intellectual History*, edited by John Higham and Paul Conkin. Baltimore: Johns Hopkins University Press, 1977.

———. "Socialism and American Liberalism: Academic Social Thought in the 1880's." *Perspectives in American History* 2 (1977–1978).

———. "The Development of the Social Sciences." In *The Organization of Knowledge in Modern America, 1860–1920*, edited by

Alexandra Oleson and John Voss. Baltimore: Johns Hopkins University Press, 1979.

Ruml, Beardsley. "The Extension of Selective Tests to Industry." *The Annals of the American Academy* (January 1919).

Schmitter, Phillipe. "Still the Century of Corporatism." *Review of Politics* (January 1974).

Seager, Henry R. "Income in the United States." *The Survey* (November 19, 1921).

Secrist, Horace. "Statistical Units as Standards." *Journal of the American Statistical Association* (March 1918).

Seligman, E.R.A. "Economic and Social Progress." *American Economic Review* (February 1903).

Slaughter, S., and Silva, E. T. "Looking Backward: How Foundations Formulated Ideology in the Progressive Period." In *Philanthropy and Cultural Imperialism*, edited by R. Arnove. Boston: G. K. Hall, 1980.

Snow, F. Herbert. "The Engineer and the State." *Proceedings of the American Society of Civil Engineers* (January 1919).

Social Science Research Council. "History and Purposes of the Social Science Research Council." In *Fifth Annual Report, 1928–1929*. New York: Social Science Research Council, 1930.

Sternberger, Dolf. "Legitimacy." In *International Encyclopedia of the Social Sciences*, edited by David L. Sills. New York: Macmillan, 1968.

Swope, Gerard. "The Engineer's Place in Society." *The Survey* (March 1, 1924).

Tead, Ordway. "Some Reconstruction Programs." *Political Science Quarterly* (March 1918).

Turner, Frederick J. "Pioneer Ideals and the State University." In his *The Frontier in American History*. New York: H. Holt, 1920.

Van Kleeck, Mary. "Working Hours of Women in Factories." *Charities and the Commons* (October 16, 1906).

———. "Child Labor in New York City Tenements." *Charities and the Commons* (January 18, 1908).

———. "For Women in Industry: The Proposed New Division in the Department of Labor." *The Survey* (December 23, 1916).

———. "Women in the Munitions Industry." *Life and Labor* (June 1918).

———. "Federal Policies for Women in Industry." *The Annals of the American Academy* (January 1919).

———. "Women Workers During Reconstruction." *American Labor Legislation Review* (March 1919).

———. "Women in Industry After the War." *Vassar Quarterly* (November 1919).

———. "Women's Invasion of Industry and Changes in Protective Standards." *Proceedings of the American Academy of Political Science* 8 (1918–1920).

———. "Unemployment Ended?" *The Survey* (June 15, 1922).

———. "Modern Industry and Society." *American Federationist* (June 1926).

———. "Justice and the Individual." *Worker's Education* (August 1926).

———. "The Interview as a Method of Research." *Bulletin of the Taylor Society* (December 1926).

———. "Employment Statistics and Trade Unions." *American Federationist* (April 1927).

———. "What Will You Do Next?" *American Federationist* (September 1927).

———. "Recent Gains in Industrial Relations." *The World Tomorrow* (May 1928).

———. "Unemployment in Passaic." *American Federationist* (May 1928).

———. "Labor and Institutions of Social Research." *Journal of Electrical Workers and Operators* (September 1928)

———. "Employment or Unemployment? That is the Question." *American Labor Legislation Review* (March 1930).

———. "Planning and the World Paradox." *Survey Graphic* (November 1, 1931).

———. "A Planned Economy as a National Objective for Social Work." *The Compass* (May 1933).

———. "Scientific Management in the Second Five Year Plan." *Soviet Russia Today* (June 1933).

———. "Dictatorship and Democracy." *Soviet Russia Today* (November 1933).

Van Kleeck, Mary, and Matthews, Ada. "Shall We Count the Unemployed?" *Survey Graphic* (April 1, 1929).

Van Kleeck, Mary, and Taylor, Graham. "The Professional Organization of Social Work." *The Annals of the American Academy* (May 1922).

BIBLIOGRAPHY

Wallace, L. W. "Industrial Waste." *The Annals of the American Academy* (September 1921).

Watkins, G. P. "Statistics and Its Methods." *American Economic Review* (June 1922).

White, Percival. "Business Cycles—Wheels of Chance?" *Nation's Business* (March 1928).

Wirth, Louis. "The Social Sciences." In *American Scholarship in the Twentieth Century*, edited by Merle Curti. Cambridge: Harvard University Press, 1953.

Wolfe, A. B. "Thoughts on Perusal of Wesley Mitchell's Collected Essays." *Journal of Political Economy* (February 1939).

Wolman, Leo. "Statistical Work of the War Industries Board." *Journal of the American Statistical Association* (March 1919).

Young, Allyn A. "National Statistics in War and Peace." *Journal of the American Statistical Association* (March 1918).

Unpublished Materials

Collins, Robert M. "The Persistence of Neo-Corporatism in Post-War Business-Government Relations." Paper presented at the annual meeting of the Organization of American Historians, 1981.

Critchlow, Donald T. "The Brookings Institution: The Early History, 1916–1952." Ph.D. dissertation, University of California, Berkeley, 1976.

Grossman, David Michael. "Professors and Public Service, 1885–1925: A Chapter in the Professionalization of the Social Sciences." Ph.D. dissertation, Washington University, St. Louis, 1973.

Hawley, Ellis W. "Techno-Corporatist Formulas in the Liberal State, 1920–1960: A Neglected Aspect of America's Search for a New Order." Harvard Conference on Twentieth-Century Capitalism, Cambridge, 1974.

———. "The New Corporatism and the Liberal Democracies, 1918–1925: The Case of the United States." University of Iowa, 1977.

———. "The Great War and Organizational Innovation: The American Case." Unpublished manuscript, University of Iowa, 1984.

Laslett, Barbara. "Science and Social Action: The Dilemma of

William Fielding Ogburn." Unpublished manuscript, University of Minnestoa, 1984.

Metcalf, Evan B. "Economic Stabilization by American Business in the Twentieth Century." Ph.D. dissertation, University of Wisconsin, Madison, 1972.

Oldenziel, Ruth. "Mary Van Kleeck: A Career of Idealism." Unpublished manuscript in author's possession.

Reagan, Patrick D. "Architects of Modern American National Planning." Ph.D. dissertation, The Ohio State University, Columbus, 1982.

Runfola, Ross Thomas. "Herbert C. Hoover as Secretary of Commerce, 1921–1923: Domestic Economic Planning in the Harding Years." Ph.D. dissertation, State University of New York, Buffalo, 1973.

Smith, Mark. " 'Knowledge for What?': Social Science and the Debate Over Its Role in 1930's America." Ph.D. dissertation, University of Texas, Austin, 1980.

INDEX

Library of Congress Cataloging in Publication Data

Alchon, Guy, 1951-
    The invisible hand of planning.

    Bibliography: p.
    Includes index.
    1. Planning—United States—History—20th century.
    2. Social sciences—United States—History—20th century.
    3. Corporate planning—United States—History—20th
        century.   4. United States—Economic policy—To 1933.
    I. Title.
HD87.5.A4   1985   361.6'0973   84-42873
ISBN 0-691-04723-5 (alk. paper)